EDITOR'S NOTE

In the early '80s, David Lynch, flush from the success of *The Elephant Man* (1980), was invited to visit Skywalker Ranch by George Lucas, who was considering Lynch as a potential director for the planned final entry in his *Star Wars* trilogy. We can't say with any certainty what it was about Lynch that made Lucas think *this* was the man to steer his sprawling space opera home, but the tantalizing prospect of what Tatooine and Endor might have looked like through Lynch's eyes is enough to send the imagination reeling.

The only remnant from the unlikely meeting? Lynch's very amusing account (which one can watch on YouTube), in which he describes being presented with several Wookiees before an increasingly debilitating headache and tinnitus hum in his ear caused him to flee the Ranch, and untold millions. But while Lynch and Lucas may seem at a glance to occupy opposite poles of American film culture, they are not without affinities. One of these is their audacious and enormously influential experiments in film audio: Lynch and sound designer Alan Splet, finding prefab library FX falling short, created the anxiety-gnawed industrial soundscapes that distinguish *Eraserhead* (1977) almost totally from scratch… at very nearly the same time that Lucas's team at Skywalker Sound, led by Ben Burtt, were creating their own new, otherworldly aural vocabulary.

This strange synchronicity, discussed in our interview between Burtt and Lynch collaborator Dean Hurley, is one of a host of odd-couple connections that run through this, the second issue of *The Metrograph*. In Khon Kaen, in northeast Thailand, a young Apichatpong Weerasethakul got the urge to make movies from hearing Burtt's work. Our cover artist, the British painter Louise Giovanelli, finds in *Buffalo '66* (1998), the debut feature by Vincent Gallo, inspiration in the vulnerability and intimacy of its heroine, played by Christina Ricci. A ticket from a Cannes Film Festival premiere screening of Gallo's second feature, personally sent by him to the elder underground icon Paul Morrissey, is uncovered, decades later, in Morrissey's New York apartment—republished here as part of the archival dossier that sits as this issue's centerpiece—hinting at a possible mutual admiration. Figures as disparate as Max Schreck's Count Orlok, John Wayne, Mbissine Thérèse Diop, and Gustave Flaubert recur throughout, surfacing in the most unexpected places, as does Lynch himself, whose loss continues to be felt by the international film community. If anything, we hope that this issue of *The Metrograph* speaks to the idea that cinema is a house with many rooms and many, many, many entrances. Come on in.

Contents

Create or Perish: Khady Sylla 24

1

CRIES & WHISPERS 04

2

ESSAYS & INTERVIEWS 16

3

DEPARTMENT HEADS 114

Ominous Whoosh 144

Elaine May Speaks 104

4

MARTINI SHOTS 150

1

CRIES & WHISPERS

Contents

METROGRAPH A TO Z

G

Metrograph A–Z
G Is for Gallo

Paintings and words by
Louise Giovanelli

About A to Z
Kicking off the next installment of our alphabetical tribute to all we love about movies and moviegoing, with personal contributions from some of our favorite artists.

If I'm being honest, I'm actually quite a bad film watcher. I just can't follow a plot. I'm not wired that way. Instead, I'm looking at formal aspects: color, lighting, psychological tone, and mood, which are precisely the elements you have to think about when you're making a painting. I guess I'm trying to say that painting and cinema share the same aim, which is fundamentally to keep the viewer's eye within the picture plane. Whether on a cinema screen or a canvas, you're organizing space, shape, light, tone, and color to create a visually arresting and alluring image. The Venn diagram where the two overlap—painterly films and cinematic paintings—is art at its most interesting.

I became interested in cinema between 14 and 17, when I discovered the internet. I'd torrent loads of movies onto my laptop and give it a thousand viruses. So I first saw *Buffalo '66* (1998) and *The Brown Bunny* (2003), two films directed by and starring Vincent Gallo, probably at too young an age. But his performances had an immediate effect: I needed to watch everything I could.

In *Buffalo '66*, his portrayal of Billy is so multilayered. The character doesn't fit into conventional movie tropes, and I think that really frustrates some people. There's a subtlety to the character that people can miss—the tender parts, the roots of his vulnerabilities. There's a moment in the car when he threatens Christina Ricci's character, Layla, saying, "If you make me look bad, I will never ever talk to you again, ever. But if you do a good job, well, then you can be my best friend." That's such a bizarre line. It really stuck with me.

Of the two, *The Brown Bunny* is obviously the more intense film, raw and dark and bleak. I didn't know a film could be like that, that it could offer no redemption. Gallo also subverts the formal qualities of a road movie. His character is going to find his girlfriend and, as a viewer, we're getting the idea of a journey, and there's something sublime about that—but throughout there's dirt on the windscreen, so we're constantly brought back to the grit obscuring the road. We're unable to see into the distance. Gallo also uses extreme close-ups: in both films, the camera is often really tight on his face, which creates a feeling of claustrophobia and anxiety. He's not allowing us to place characters in context. That's what I do, and have done for a long time in my paintings, that intense cropping and zooming in. It creates an unnerving sensation. Maybe I learned it from watching these films so early on.

One of the most striking elements of *Buffalo '66* is the visual style: the washed-out coloration and the slow pace, which create a dream-like dimension. The scene on which I based the image of my painting is one of the best examples. It's a shot of Ricci's face as Gallo is talking, where she is making these subtle eye movements. There's a lightness to Layla, especially in relation to Billy, who presents as this dark, troubled figure. We see her blue eye shadow, the red sheen on her lips. Ricci is so iconic in this movie. To be honest, I sort of just wanted to capture how great she looks. To portray her as the muse that I believe she becomes.

I took so many screenshots of this scene. From moment to moment, different sections of her face or hair take on incredible color. As a result, the painting has two distinct surfaces. The right-hand side is more matte, because it's on a particular gesso ground [primer]; I've treated her hair differently on the left-hand side. There's a distinct sensation, or rhythm, which I hope is discernible if people see the painting in person. I tried to fuse them together to create one complete, perfect Layla.

Prope, 2025. Louise Giovanelli takes inspiration from an intimate scene in Vincent Gallo's *The Brown Bunny* (2003).

FRAMED!

Black Girl

The story behind the still.

Written by
Nicolas Rapold

1

Mbissine Thérèse Diop stars as Diouana, the spiraling protagonist of Ousmane Sembène's *Black Girl* (in French: *La Noire de...*). Hired from a village outside of Dakar, Senegal, to mind an unnamed family's kids on holiday in Antibes on the French Riviera, Diouana is exploited as a live-in maid and cook. She wears a flat wig covering up her braids, part of the uniform that her strident boss (Anne-Marie Jelinek) insists on completing with an apron. Here, moments after a portly white guest has kissed her at her boss's lunch party, Diouana shows her disgust and dejection. Behind her are cheap bottles, remnants of other people's pleasures.

2

According to Diop, the plan was to shoot in both France and Senegal, but they never made it to France. Stand-in locations were found in Dakar, including the harbor; the apartment pictured; and the street where Diouana is plucked out of the "maid market" and hired.

3

Diop was not originally an actress. The 16-year-old seamstress was studying fashion at the School of the Arts in Dakar. But she was a regular at a ciné-club in Dakar (where she and friends had spotted Sembène), and watched French releases, American classics, and documentaries about history and politics. At 13, she'd written a letter to the performer Josephine Baker, who sent back a signed photo and an invitation to France, warning her that film was a tough business.

4

Diop's performance as Diouana is gutting. She begins to wear this polka-dot summer dress every day—perhaps in protest, but also a sign of depression. (The angle of the shot obscures her sunny flower earrings.) You wouldn't know that Diop had just started acting, or that Robert Fontaine, who plays the ineffectual husband, was Diop's acting professor and mentor. Diop also made all of her own costumes—except this dress.

5

Offscreen left from the kitchenette is the living room, where an African mask that Diouana gave to her boss hangs. (It evokes both Frantz Fanon's critique of colonial identity and becomes a contested symbol of her homeland.) Sembène, who adapted the film from his short story "The Promised Land"—published in his collection *Tribal Scars*—was inspired by a 1958 news item in *Nice-Matin* about Diouana Gomis, a 31-year-old woman from Boutoupa in Ziguinchor, the same region where he was born. In a poem appended to the short story, Sembène refers to Diouana as "Effigie de Notre Mère l'Afrique." Intriguingly, some of Sembène's film team had previously worked on news crews.

6

Sembène, who studied filmmaking in Moscow, regarded himself as a modern-day griot. He makes a cameo in the film as a schoolmaster, chomping on his signature pipe. He'd make other such appearances, but don't compare him to Hitchcock: "It is not Hitchcock's way; it is Sembène's way," he said.

7

The muted grays of the black-and-white photography suit Diouana's flattened mood. Sembène wrote color scenes as well—rosy visions of the Riviera—but these were cut to shorten his debut feature for French regulations, down from the hour and a half of his original screenplay. In a flashback, Diouana shares a few happy moments with a lover in Dakar, a poster visible on his wall of Congolese revolutionary Patrice Lumumba, who was killed in January 1961—not even a full year after several African countries, including Senegal, gained their independence. (In Sembène's work, the walls speak: a poster of *Black Girl* appears in his 1975 film *Xala*.)

8

While *Black Girl* won plaudits, including the Prix Jean Vigo, Diop later revealed that some back home had given her trouble (particularly for her scene in a bathtub). "It was as if I'd thrown a bomb," she told the critic Fatou Kiné Sène. The actress eventually settled in Paris, and can be seen in Johanna Makabi's 2021 portrait film *Notre mémoire*, properly framed as a doyenne of cinema (and happily employed weaving tapestry).

Notes

Director	Country	Cinematographer	Featured actor	Costume designer	Year
Ousmane Sembène	Senegal	Christian Lacoste	M'Bissine T. Diop	M'Bissine T. Diop	1966

CINEMAP: BELGRADE

A tour of cinephile-sacred landmarks in Serbia's capital city.

Cartography by Greg de Cuir Jr.

Illustration by Lucinda Rogers

1.
4 Terazije Street
On this city square, in 1896, at cafe Zlatni krst (Golden Cross), the Lumière Cinématographe was introduced to the Belgrade public and the first film projections were shown.

2.
Zemun Gymnasium, 1 Gradski Park, Zemun
The second-oldest preparatory school in Belgrade was founded in 1858, when the province of Vojvodina in Serbia was part of the Austro-Hungarian Empire. Early film artists Slavko Vorkapić and Boško Tokin became best friends while in attendance together during World War I.

3.
Topčider
The first Serbian avant-garde film, *God Be with Us*, was shot in 1923 in this neighborhood by Tokin and Dragan Aleksić. This mythical film was not completed and is considered lost.

4.
Filmske novosti (Film Newsreels), 41 Vojvode Mišića Boulevard
Founded in 1944, this was the national production center for film newsreels during the time of Yugoslavia. The archives contain countless significant documentary images of the 20th century.

5.
11 Kosovska Street
In 1952, the Yugoslav Kinoteka opened its museum and cinema hall at this address. It quickly became a revered space that nurtured multiple generations of cinephiles and welcomed many legendary figures, among them Alfred Hitchcock and the founder of the Cinémathèque Française, Henri Langlois.

6.
Filmski grad
The city's equivalent of Cinecittà or a Hollywood backlot, and the headquarters of Avala Film, the first studio set up in postwar Yugoslavia. Many international productions were shot here during the golden age of Yugoslavia, and some of the greatest international stars and directors graced the sets.

7.
Hotel Moskva, Balkanska 1
American director Nicholas Ray most likely stayed here during his ill-fated time in Belgrade preparing *The Doctor and the Devils* for Avala Film.

8.
King Aleksandar Boulevard
This thoroughfare was known as Revolution Boulevard in socialist Yugoslavia. In 1964, artist Tomislav Gotovac shot his proto-structuralist film *Straight Line* from the front of a tram progressing in a straight line down the boulevard.

9.
Albania Palace, 2 Prince Mihailo Street
When Albania Palace was built in 1939, it was one of the first skyscrapers in Southeast Europe. In 1964, on the top of the Palace building, Gotovac shot another daring proto-structuralist film, *Circle*, composed of a continuously revolving view of the Belgrade skyline.

10.
43 Novopazarska Street
Aleksandar Petrović, the well-respected director known for his sweeping emotional dramas and elegant style, lived at this address. A memorial to Petrović marks the building.

11.
Charlie Chaplin Street
This is the rare street in Belgrade named after an Englishman, and an icon from film history. Legendary Yugoslav-Serbian filmmaker Dušan Makavejev, known for the subversive humor and frank sexuality of his work, lived here for most of his adult life.

12.
Hotel Yugoslavia, 3 Nikola Tesla Boulevard, Zemun
Opened in 1969 as one of the standout luxury hotels in Europe, it accommodated numerous foreign dignitaries and international travelers during their visits to Yugoslavia. Jovan Jovanović shot the climax to his Black Wave classic *Young and Healthy as a Rose* here in 1971, in which the rebellious youths engage in all-out war with the police. This landmark is currently being demolished to make way for new commercial properties.

13.
Belgrade Youth Center, 22 Makedonska Street
Used by many film festivals, the screening hall in this cultural center is the site of some of the greatest film projections in the city over the decades. Actress Eva Ras passes by this center and a marquee bearing her name in a sly, self-reflexive scene in Makavejev's *Love Affair, or The Case of the Missing Switchboard Operator* (1967).

14.
Student Park
A central site of the epochal June 1968 student demonstrations. The radical filmmaker Želimir Žilnik shot his short documentary *June Turmoil* (1969) here, amid the revolutionary actions that shaped an international generation.

15.
Gospodar Jevremova Street
Vukica Đilas lived on this street with her partner, the writer Branko Vučićević. Đilas shot experimental 8mm "home movies" in the 1970s as diaries of her life with Vučićević and the avant-garde communities they were a part of.

16.
Sremska Street
In a scene from the notorious 1971 Black Wave film *Plastic Jesus* by Lazar Stojanović, lead actor Gotovac ran naked down this street. It was his longest recorded piece as a performance artist up to that point.

17.
Students City Cultural Center, 179 Zoran Djindjić Boulevard
This cultural center is the longtime home of Academic Film Center (the successor to Academic Film Club), which organizes Alternative Film Video, one of the oldest festivals of experimental film in Europe, established in 1982.

18.
5 Zadarska Street
The location of the Topalović family house in the 1982 cult film *The Marathon Family* directed by Slobodan Šijan.

19.
20 Boulevard of the Arts
In 1974 the Faculty of Dramatic Arts opened its new campus at this address. This national film school was one of the first to be established in postwar Europe. Significant figures taught and educated here include Petrović, Vorkapić, Vlada Petrić, and Živojin Pavlović.

20.
39 Majke Jevrosime Street
A memorial marker on this building is dedicated to the writer-director Zivojin Pavlović, who lived here. Pavlović made some of the more celebrated films of the Black Wave, characterized by his sardonic and "brutal poetic" touch.

21.
6 Braće Jugovića Street
Professor Vlada Petrić lived at this address during his retirement years. He was a pioneering film theorist, a film and television director, the Henry Luce Chair of Cinema at Harvard University, and a co-founder and the founding curator of the Harvard Film Archive.

22.
Belgrade Cultural Center, 6 Kolarčeva Street
Another screening hall used by many film festivals in the city, this center has hosted some of the greatest film events over the decades. When Joshua Oppenheimer showed *The Act of Killing* (2012) here, his former Harvard professor, Makavejev, joined him for a memorable post-screening discussion.

23.
Main Railway Station
The city's principal station for more than a century, it was recently closed and turned into a museum. In 1995, Žilnik shot his Berlinale Teddy Award–winning film *Marble Ass*, about trans sex workers, in the rough surrounding streets.

24.
Saint Aleksandar Nevsky Church, 63b Cara Dušana Street
The grande dame of Yugoslav-Serbian cinema, actress Milena Dravić was born across the street from this church. Her screen career stretched from the 1950s to the 2000s, and she acted in many notable films, such as the war epic *Battle of Neretva* (1969), alongside Orson Welles and Yul Brynner, and Makavejev's masterpiece, *WR: Mysteries of the Organism* (1971).

25.
Akira Kurosawa Street, Altina
This is the other street in the city named after a major figure in international cinema.

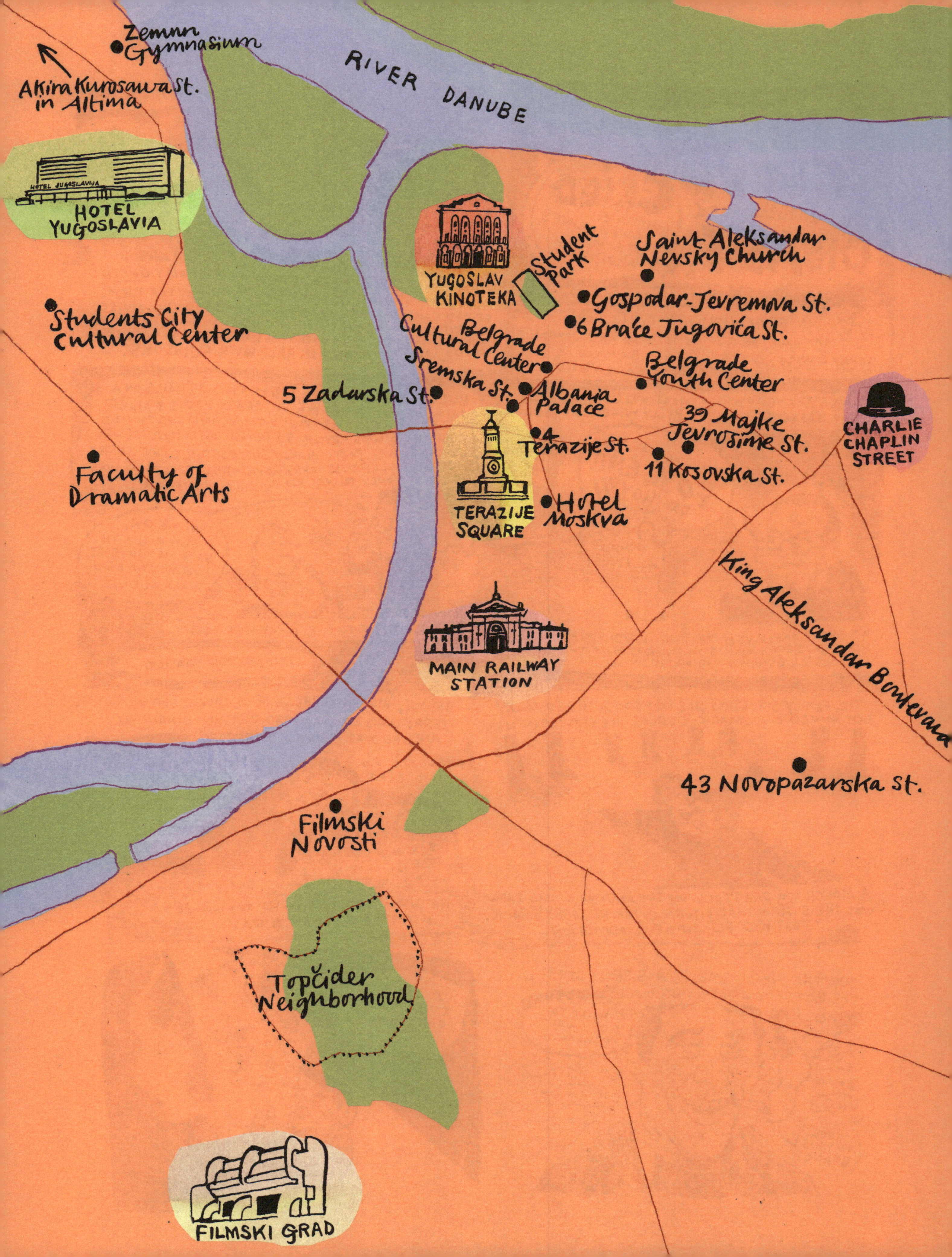
Zemun Gymnasium
Akira Kurosawa St. in Altima
RIVER DANUBE
HOTEL JUGOSLAVIJA
HOTEL YUGOSLAVIA
YUGOSLAV KINOTEKA
Student Park
Saint Aleksandar Nevsky Church
Gospodar-Jevremova St.
6 Braće Jugovića St.
Students City Cultural Center
Belgrade Cultural Center
Sremska St.
Albania Palace
Belgrade Youth Center
5 Zadarska St.
39 Majke Jevrosime St.
CHARLIE CHAPLIN STREET
4 Terazije St.
11 Kosovska St.
Faculty of Dramatic Arts
Hotel Moskva
TERAZIJE SQUARE
King Aleksandar Boulevard
MAIN RAILWAY STATION
43 Novopazarska St.
Filmski Novosti
Topčider Neighborhood
FILMSKI GRAD

THE DAY THE CLOWN CRIED
the unauthorized DISASTER
WRITTEN BY OWEN KLINE & STEPHEN KRONINGER
DRAWN BY OWEN KLINE
INTERVIEWER: WHY IS IT...THAT SO MANY OF THE TOP COMEDIANS ARE JEWISH?
JERRY LEWIS: WELL.... WE GET BACK TO LAUGHTER AND TEARS AGAIN...
JERRY LEWIS WAS 19 WHEN HE MET 27-YEAR-OLD DEAN MARTIN...
HA HA
AND BY AGE 25, ALONG WITH DEAN, HE BASICALLY OWNED PARAMOUNT STUDIOS, HE MADE SO MUCH MONEY FOR THEM. HE HAD CARTE BLANCHE TO DO WHATEVER THE HELL HE WANTED. EVERYONE LOVED "THAT KID"... JERRY HAD SO MUCH POWER THAT HE WOULD GO UP TO EXECUTIVES, GRAB THEM BY THE LAPEL, AND CUT THEIR TIES IN HALF WITH SCISSORS.
WHILE TRYING TO WRITE, MARTIN & LEWIS WOULD PLAY BASKETBALL UNDER BILLY WILDER'S WINDOW.
OHHHHHHH FOYGEN!! DAH-HOYY!!!
CLICK-CLACK-CLICK
WILDER COMPLAINED TO THE STUDIO HEADS WHO TOLD HIM: "IF JERRY WANTS TO BURN DOWN THE STUDIO, WE'LL GIVE HIM THE MATCH."
BUT BY THE MID-60'S, "THAT KID" WAS NAILS ON A CHALKBOARD TO THE PUBLIC. JERRY HAD A FAILED TALK SHOW, A FAILED VARIETY SHOW, AND THE MOVIES IN WHICH HE WAS TRYING TO TRANSITION INTO A MATURE ACTOR WEREN'T PARTICULARLY SUCCESSFUL. THE JERRY LEWIS MUSCULAR DYSTROPHY ASSOCIATION TELETHON WAS ONE OF THE ONLY THINGS KEEPING HIM IN THE PUBLIC EYE.
♪ WALK ON, WALK ON, WITH HOPE IN YUH HEART, AND YOU'LL NEVAH WALK ALONE...
JERRY'S KIDS
NEEDLESS TO SAY, JERRY WAS DESPERATE.
CHANGE THE STATION.
THE FAMILY SITUATION WAS NOT GOOD. HIS SON GARY GOT HOOKED ON SMACK DURING HIS SERVICE IN 'NAM.
A MARCH '65 PRATFALL ON THE ANDY WILLIAMS SHOW WAS THE STRAW THAT (LITERALLY) BROKE JERRY'S BACK. "THAT KID" FELL INTO PILL ADDICTION.
BY '71, HIS ENTREPRENEURIAL MOVIE CHAIN PROJECT, JERRY LEWIS CINEMAS, HAD CRASHED FINANCIALLY, AND HE WAS MAJORLY DEPRESSED.
THE FRENCH LOVE ME...
JERRY LEWIS CINEMA
HE WAS RUMORED TO BE TAKING UP TO FIFTY PERCODAN A DAY.
FOR THE FIRST TIME, HE WAS TRULY STIFLED. THE BOTTOM WAS FALLING OUT.
WHAT TO DO.... WHAT TO MAKE...
("KOOL" WAS HIS BRAND)
I THINK IT'S TIME FOR "CLOWN".

JERRY WANTED TO MAKE A FILM ON AN IMPORTANT THEME — AND HE'D HAD EYES ON A PARTICULAR PROJECT FOR SOME YEARS.
CERAMIC PAPER WEIGHT
HITLER
CHURCHILL
THE THIRD REICH
PERCS
PRE-ROLLED JOINTS IN CIGAR BOX
FROM CUBA
"THE DAY THE CLOWN CRIED", A SCRIPT BY PUBLICITY FLACK JOAN O'BRIEN AND TV CRITIC CHARLES DENTON, TOLD THE FICTIONAL STORY OF AN UNLIKEABLE, UNSUCCESSFUL (AND GENTILE) GERMAN CIRCUS CLOWN NAMED KARL SCHMIDT WHO WAS SENT TO AUSCHWITZ FOR SATIRIZING HITLER AND WAS SUBSEQUENTLY USED BY HIS NAZI CAPTORS TO LEAD UNSUSPECTING CHILDREN INTO THE GAS CHAMBERS.
KOOL
LIKE MANY PEOPLE IN HOLLYWOOD, JERRY HAD HEARD TALES OF THIS REMARKABLE STORY, WHICH O'BRIEN HAD CONCEIVED WHILE SHE WAS SIMULTANEOUSLY READING ABOUT THE HOLOCAUST AND DOING PUBLICITY WORK FOR EMMETT KELLY. (SAD CLOWN CIRCUS LEGEND.)
MEIN KAMP
HITLER
DID YOU KNOW?.......
THERE WAS ALSO A ROMANIAN CLOWN NAMED YONELY IN A NAZI CONCENTRATION CAMP WHO REFUSED TO RETIRE HIS ACT AND ENTERTAINED FELLOW PRISONERS WITH HIS HUMOROUS PANTOMIME VIOLIN ACT?
SQUEAK SQUEAK SQUEAK
YONELY DID "MUSICAL TRICKS" ON ART BAKER'S SHOW "YOU ASKED FOR IT" IN 1951, PLAYING A TINY NOVELTY VIOLIN. HIS STORY COULD'VE BEEN THE KERNEL OF INSPIRATION FOR O'BRIEN.
THE "CLOWN" SCRIPT HAD AN OBVIOUS MIX OF HORROR, PATHOS, AND DRAMA, AND IT DREW THE ATTENTION OF SEVERAL IMPORTANT TALENTS OVER THE YEARS: MILTON BERLE, DICK VAN DYKE, BOBBY DARIN, AND JOSEPH SCHILDKRAUT AMONG THEM.
BOO-HOO! UNCLE MILTIE SEZ... BOO-HOO!
MY JEWISH FATHER WAS AN AUSTRIAN CLOWN... I KNOW A CLOWN'S PAIN...
♫ DREAM-LOVER LET ME HELP YOU LAUGH ♫
JERRY BEGAN RE-WRITING THE SCRIPT, TAILORING IT TO HIS PECULIAR TALENTS.
CLICK-CLACK
HE CHANGED HIS CLOWN PROTAGONIST'S NAME FROM "KARL SCHMIDT" TO..."HELMET DOORK".
TO PREPARE FOR PLAYING HELMET, JERRY, WHO'D BEEN PUTTING ON THE POUNDS THE LAST FEW YEARS, LOST 35 POUNDS....
ANOTHA BITE WILL KILL ME...
...ON A GRAPEFRUIT DIET!!
(AND PERCOCET....)
WITHOUT SECURING RIGHTS TO THE STORY, JERRY BEGAN SHOOTING IN SWEDEN. THE SHOOT WAS MISERABLE. THE SWEDISH ACTORS COULDN'T DO THE GERMAN ACCENTS. EVEN WITH JERRY FEEDING THEM LINE READINGS FOR THEM TO PARROT, IT WAS A MESS.
"VAHT VOULD YOU DO??"
"VAHT VOULD YOU DO."
NO!! "VAHT VOULD YOU DO??" DO A GERMAN FUCKIN' ACCENT!!
WE'RE SWEDES. WE DON'T DO GERMAN.

INSOFAR AS WE KNOW, THE MOVIE FOLLOWS THE SAME OL' JERRY LEWIS FORMULA. IN NEARLY EVERY CLASSIC JERRY PICTURE, THERE'S A MOMENT WHERE SOMEONE HAS A REALIZATION: THAT HE'S NOT AN IDIOT, AND, IN FACT:
THERE'S SOMETHING SPECIAL ABOUT THAT KID...
NOW, EVEN IN "CLOWN", JERRY HAS TWO NAZIS OBSERVE HELMET CLOWNING FOR THE KIDS BY A BARBED-WIRED FENCE. ONE NAZI OFFICER WANTS TO EXTERMINATE HIM FOR BEING A FOOL. THE OTHER GAZES AT HELMET'S ANTICS AND THE JOY IT BRINGS TO THE CHILDREN AND BASICALLY SAYS:
ZERE'S ZOMEZING SZPECIAL ABOUT ZAT KID...
WHOOPIE!
JERRY WANTED TO OPEN THE FILM WITH SOME OF HELMET'S ACT. THE GAG TRICKS JERRY SETTLED ON — LITTLE PUPPETS AND CIGARETTE TRICKS — WOULD'VE WORKED FINE ON TV IN CLOSE-UPS... BUT THESE WOULDN'T WORK IN A REAL CIRCUS. EVEN IN THE FIRST ROW, NOBODY COULD SEEM THEM.
IN THE FOOTAGE, JERRY SOUNDS MORE LIKE A JEWISH GUY FROM IRVINGTON, NEW JERSEY.
SOON, CHECKS STARTED BOUNCING AND THE PRODUCER, NAT WACHBERGER, WAS NOWHERE TO BE SEEN...
JERRY MANAGED TO GET THE FILM SHOOT BACK UP AND RUNNING, BUT HE HAD TO BLEED HIS OWN BANK ACCOUNT TO FINISH THE PICTURE. IT RUINED HIM FINANCIALLY AND SPIRITUALLY. THE FILM LOOKED INCREDIBLY CHEAP AS A RESULT.
HE DRANK BEERS IN THE L.A. EDITING ROOM, FURIOUS. PEOPLE GAVE HIM NOTES UP THE WAZOO.
BUD
SUNKIST
IT'S... A BIT... TOO... LONG....
EVERYBODY'S AN EXPERT. WHERE WERE THEY WHEN THE EMPTY PAGES WERE IN THE TYPEWRITER? WHERE WERE THEY WHEN WE WERE FREEZING IN FUCKING SWEDEN?
TOO LONG??! JESUS CHRIST ON A CROSS!!
HE SAVED THE MOST OF HIS HATRED FOR A YOUNG SWEDISH EXTRA WHO MADE THE MISTAKE OF TURNING HER EYES TOWARD THE CAMERA DURING A SHOT THAT HAD BEEN NEARLY IMPOSSIBLE TO GET RIGHT.
THERE!, SEE THAT?? VAMPING FOR THE CAMERA... SHE PULLED THE SAME SHIT IN ANOTHA SEQUENCE, REMEMBA?!!!? I TOLD HER TO KEEP HER EYES TO THE FRONT......
THAT IT WASN'T A BEAUTY PAGEANT. THERE'S NO ROOM FOR SHIRLEY TEMPLE IN A CONCENTRATION CAMP!!!
YEARS GO BY... "CLOWN" WAS SUCCESSFULLY SWEPT UNDER THE RUG FROM THE PUBLIC, BUT SPECULATION ONLY CONTINUED TO SWIRL.
CLOWN
CLOWN
ONE RUMOR WAS JERRY PROTECTED THE FILM'S WORK PRINT UNDER HIS BED WHERE NO ONE COULD FIND IT...

POST-SCRIPT: SWEDISH ACTOR HANS CRISPIN RECENTLY CLAIMED TO A SWEDISH BROADCASTER (SVT) THAT HE POSSESSES A COMPLETE VERSION OF THE FILM HE STOLE FROM EUROPAFILM, "CLOWN"'S PRODUCTION STUDIO, AND QUIETLY COPIED IT TO VIDEO.... HE PLANS TO "RESTORE" THE FILM FOR THE PUBLIC SOME DAY.... BUT..... **IS THERE A COMPLETE CUT?** WHAT JERRY DONATED TO THE LIBRARY OF CONGRESS WAS REPORTED INCOMPLETE AND OUT-OF-SEQUENCE —NEARLY IDENTICAL, WE CAN ASSUME, TO THE FORTY-ODD MINUTES THAT LEAKED IN 2013..... SOME OF THAT MATERIAL EXISTED ON A VIDEO TAPE BEFORE IT—ONE COPY LIVED AT THE LATE L.A. VIDEO STORE "MONDO VIDEO A GO-GO"... BUT I DIGRESS....

A COMPLETE "CLOWN."?
ONLY TIME WILL TELL...

2

ESSAYS & INTERVIEWS

Contents

未亡人は男好き
筆おろし
猥褻ネット集団
いかせて!!
の人妻たち
激しく淫らに
激愛撫
上映中
国際名画座
名画座入口

HEAVENLY KINGS, LUCKY GODS, AND THE JAPANESE PINK FILM

A primer on the explosively creative genre of Japanese Pink Film at its fin de millennium peak.

Written by
Gabriel Jandali Appel

Illustrations by
Mayumi Mitome

In Japan in the 1960s, when the tightly gated film industry was dominated by five major studios, a parallel independent space opened up for young aspiring filmmakers. This so-called "sixth studio" would become an arena for subversive politics and avant-garde exploration, unleashing films sold on salacious curiosity but filled with transgressive brio and freewheeling style. Pink Film, or *Pinku eiga*, is the name now given to this genre of independent softcore erotic movies—one that, though initially designed merely to titillate, would come to defy most common assumptions about adult cinema. If you wanted to break into the industry before middle age, this was likely your only route, with assistant directors on average able to direct their first feature after only three years of work, compared to a median of 15 years at the big studios. Moreover, so long as a director satisfied a few loose rules, they were allowed a level of creative control found almost nowhere else in Japanese cinema.

Those rules: a budget not exceeding three million yen, a shooting schedule no longer than five days, scenes filmed MOS (without live sound), and at least one bout of simulated fornication approximately every 10 minutes—though strict censorship laws banned the sight of even a lone strand of pubic hair, let alone penetration. Perhaps because sex wasn't explicitly shown, it was common for directors to substitute acts of brutality (as in the US "roughies" of the early '60s); taken as a whole, the genre contains a disturbing amount of nonconsensual sadomasochistic sexual violence perpetrated against women.

The films, their runtimes rarely exceeding an hour, were shown in dedicated Pink theaters and usually stacked in triple bills. These independent productions proved immensely popular following the runaway success of 1962's *Flesh Market*; by 1965, 44% of all films produced in the country were Pink, with 213 released that year alone. The result: an overnight industry providing real on-the-job training. What's more, while some Pink Films clearly lack redeeming social or artistic value, a number of them are noteworthy exercises in formal and thematic audacity. In the first Pink wave, the director Kôji Wakamatsu, a working-class ex-yakuza whose films are characterized by a brawler's belligerence, became something of a godfather to his genre confreres, collaborating with screenwriter and future Japanese Red Army member Masao Adachi, gaining praise at foreign festivals, and looking at sex and power through a politicized lens.

As the advent of VHS wreaked havoc on Japan's film industry through the '80s, Pink theaters endured, encouraging many civilian theaters to go Pink to stay in business. Several directors who got their start in Pink at this tumultuous time would go on to mainstream success, including Yôjirô Takita (from 1982's *Train Molester: Please Continue* to 2008's *Departures*), Kiyoshi Kurosawa (from 1983's *Kandagawa Pervert Wars* to 1997's *Cure*), and Masayuki Suo (from 1984's *Abnormal Family* to 1996's *Shall We Dance?*). In the face of the collapse of the studio system and broader economic stagnation in the '90s, the genre became a consecrated place of cinematic experimentation; for some critics, this was the golden age of the Pink Film.

The period saw the rise of four deeply idiosyncratic directors—Hisayasu Satô, Takahisa Zeze, Kazuhiro Sano, and Toshiki Satô—who would become known as *shitennô*: "The Four Heavenly Kings of Pink." The nickname allegedly began as a pejorative used by disgruntled theater owners who found their films needlessly challenging and overly artistic, but the Heavenly Kings, undeterred—and with the support of powerhouse producer Keiko Sato—together turned out over 100 radical films rooted in formal trickery, political protests, philosophical explorations, and, yes, a lot of weird fucking.

The Kokusai Meigaza (International Masterpiece Theatre) in the heart of Shinjuku, Tokyo, 2005. The venue permanently shut its doors in September 2012. Photograph by Jasper Sharp.

Keiko Sato, powerhouse producer behind the golden age of the Pink Film, who since 1982 has headed the production company Kokuei and kept it on the artistic vanguard of the genre.

Hisayasu Satô, director of approximately 50 Pink Films, infamous for his brick-to-the-face aesthetics, and one of few Pink directors to move freely between gay and straight-themed pictures.

THE FOUR HEAVENLY KINGS AND THEIR BIG SISTER

Keiko Sato aka Daisuke Asakura aka O-Nésan

Though not one of the Kings herself, Keiko Sato is perhaps the figure most responsible for the Pink Nouvelle Vague at the end of the '80s. She began working decades earlier, under the male pseudonym Daisuke Asakura (a pun that roughly translates as "We love it in the morning"). As she explained, "There were hardly any women in the industry in those days so we couldn't use a female name." She produced over 500 films for Kokuei—an early Pink Film production house that broke into the scene with the 1963 "female Tarzan" flick *Valley of Lust*—where she was known to her colleagues as *o-nésan*, Big Sister. Sato was employed as an accountant when, in 1962, her father, co-owner of Kokuei, called on her to join the family business. The request was born of emergency: Kokuei had attempted to circumvent a national censorship board (read: neglected to send a film to be cleared) and, as a result, nearly every Kokuei employee had been arrested. Sato took time off to help, enjoyed the work, and stayed on, becoming a producer. Twenty years later she was the company's president and owner and, at the helm, steered an armada of standout Pink Films into cinemas. She is known for championing acerbic scripts, compelling drama, and sui generis works—such as *Abnormal Family*, a Pink parody of the films of Yasujirō Ozu—and for her loyalty to developing directors. Without Big Sister, there might never have been any Heavenly Kings at all.

Hisayasu Satô

Hisayasu Satô has a well-earned reputation for extremity, outrageous sadism, and synapse-searing style, bolstered by his oft-cited provocation that he directs each film to "drive its audience mad, and to make them commit murder"—fitting words from an artist besotted with the radicalizing figure of Pier Paolo Pasolini, and one whose works include bestiality, amputations, sexual abuse, and ample gouts of blood, among other viscera. Take *The Bedroom* aka *Unfaithful Wife: Shameful Torture* (1992), in which he cast Sagawa Issei, the real-life cannibal and murderer referenced in The Rolling Stones' 1983 song "Too Much Blood" and the subject of Véréna Paravel and Lucien Castaing-Taylor's documentary *Caniba* (2017). But just as this controversial casting choice risks distracting from the film's bleak vision of emotional isolation and depersonalized sex, so too does Satô's penchant for excessive gore risk over-defining his body of work. Inspired by Nobel Prize-winner Yasunari Kawabata's novella *House of the Sleeping Beauties*, *The Bedroom* is set in a bizarre underground club where women willingly take sleep-inducing drugs and anonymous men

Takahisa Zeze, director of approximately 30 Pink Films, distinguished by a penchant for elliptical cutting and ambiguous narrative. Arguably the most cerebral of the Heavenly Kings, his work occasionally appears under the name "Jean-Luc Zeze."

do as they please with their unconscious bodies. The den of sin is lit with delirious neon, features a giant TV screen constantly playing static, and, as Satô often reminds the viewer, is under constant surveillance. When the POV of the peeping camera is shown, the artifacted video renders the sexual acts grotesque, a digital slurry of tongue, saliva, and stubble. Screens within screens recur in Satô's cinema, which parallels roughly contemporary studies in the video-age panopticon by Michael Haneke and David Cronenberg. There's the grainy snuff film footage of *RE-WIND* aka *Abnormal Sadism* (1988), in which the camcorder itself is revealed to be the murder weapon; and *Muscle* (1989), in which Takeshi's Itô gay porn magazine editor interrupts a photoshoot with his boyfriend by picking up a samurai sword and cutting off his arm, an act only seen upside-down, through the viewfinder of the large-format camera being used. After being released from jail, he obsessively hunts for a VHS tape of *Salò, or the 120 Days of Sodom* (1975), believing that Pasolini's final film may hold the answer to all life's questions—or at least a vision of apocalypse as strong as his (and Satô's) own.

Takahisa Zeze

If there is one figure who most clearly embodies the formal creativity of Pink Film in the '90s, it is Takahisa Zeze. His films are often obtuse, combining social commentary, references to academic theory and Eastern philosophy with elliptical editing and a coolly detached mise en scene. These elements are not surprising considering Zeze studied at Kyoto University, but that a graduate of one of Japan's most prestigious universities entered the low-budget porno industry—learning at the feet of Satô, in fact—is. Two of Zeze's finest films—*The Dream of Garuda* (1993), whose title refers to a Hindu deity (released as *Luxury Soap Technique 4: Secret of Agony*), and *Dirty Maria* (1998)—both chronicle the obsessive search for a lost woman, but *Vertigo* (1958) they ain't. *Dirty Maria* opens with three almost-wordless vignettes, giving the audience just enough to intuit out who the characters are: the

ROMAN PORNO VS. PINK FILM

The story of Nikkatsu Roman Porno, or what happened when one big, respectable studio went Pink.

In the early 1970s, Nikkatsu, one of the five major Japanese movie studios, was on the brink of bankruptcy and took the radical step of shifting all resources to the production of erotic films, dubbed "Roman Porno" (translated as "romantic pornography"), banking on the rising popularity of Pink Film. Although the contents of Nikkatsu product is similar—their first title was *Apartment Wife: Affair in the Afternoon* (1971), and the rule of one sex scene per reel roughly applies—they differ in one major respect. Backed by a studio machine, they were made with budgets on average three times that of an independent Pink Film, as well as a studio lot, dozens of directors and craftsmen on payroll, professional equipment, and Nikkatsu's vertically integrated theater chains and publicity machine. Like Pink Film, Roman Porno features early work by several directors who would go on to mainstream success, including Toshiya Fujita (from 1972's *August: Scent of Eros* to 1973's *Lady Snowblood*), Shinji Sômai (from 1985's *Love Hotel* to 1993's *Moving*), and Shûsuke Kaneko (from 1986's *Mischievous Lolita: Attacking the Virgin From Behind* to 1995's *Gamara, Guardian of the Universe*). The production of Roman Pornos officially ceased in 1988.

Kazuhiro Sano, director of approximately 15 Pink Films. The punk poet of the Pinks, whose films have a streak of rebellious romanticism that sets them apart from the blighted eroticism that dominates much of the genre.

Toshiki Satô, director of approximately 30 Pink Films, who, in spite of beginning his career with titles like *E-Cup Real Action Take Two: Rich and Ripe*, would become a director of surprising sensitivity and even, yes, delicacy.

soon-to-be-widowed husband is an upright, moral man; the soon-to-be-murdered wife is unfaithful; the murderer watches the victim at her place of work with an inscrutable expression. The next time we see the wife, she is a corpse being dragged across the floor. Zeze omits the murder scene—one of many actions, motivations, and events left as blanks for the viewer to fill in themselves, resulting in narratives that, in their artful elision, precise cutting, and indifference to psychology, are best described as Bressonian pornography. In *The Dream of Garuda* we follow not a mourning husband but a tortured perpetrator who begins seeing the face of the woman he raped in every woman he encounters. Searching for his actual victim, he hopes to cleanse himself of his guilty conscience, a salvation Zeze makes clear from minute one cannot be achieved. This is a move typical of a director who often focuses on unscrupulous characters at the outskirts of society while leaving his audience unclear if that attention is inspired by reverence, sympathy, pity, or disgust.

Kazuhiro Sano

Kazuhiro Sano began his career in the world of punk-inspired Japanese underground film, appearing in amphetamine-manic classics like Gakuryû Ishii's *Crazy Thunder Road* (1980) and *Burst City* (1982). Sano brought elements of Ishii's grubby, DIY, go-for-broke aesthetic to his Pink Films, featuring opening credits on handwritten cards, breakneck swish pans, and an abundance of black leather. *Under the Carp Banner* aka *Molester Obscene Peeping* (1992) opens with Sano himself as the biker jacket-clad Kunio, loitering around Tokyo with his girlfriend Rikako (portrayed by Sano's regular onscreen partner Kanako Kishi) as they eat KFC and drink Coca-Cola. Rikako suggests they visit her sister at the remote spa she runs, and when Kunio says he has no money, she replies, "Steal a car then." Boosting a Nissan SUV, Bonnie and Clyde take off, their exit from Tokyo accompanied by frenetic, cyan-tinted, handheld camerawork and a feedback-drenched guitar, which plays as they make love standing upright through the open sunroof. A culture-clash comedy of manners that ruminates on the fragmentation of contemporary Japan, it's a raucously funny film, with an unusual sense of zesty, feel-good libertinage in the inevitable softcore scenes. Though Sano's output as director is small relative to his fellow Kings, he did rack up three consecutive wins for Best Director at the Pink Grand Prix awards, the last in 1992, when he also won Best Film.

Toshiki Satô

Of the Four Kings, Toshiki Satô is likely the most palatable to a mainstream audience. Rather than the provocations of Hisayasu Satô (no relation), the polemics and formal experimentation of Zeze, or the gob-spitting romantic rebel rambunctiousness of Sano, Toshiki Satô's films strive to reflect something of average middle-class life in Heisei-era Japan, with more emphasis on emotion than sex. Many of his movies were marketed under the "Apartment Wife" series heading, portions of which could almost pass for respectable "women's pictures." His Pink Grand Prix winner, *Empty Room* aka *Apartment Wife: Moans from Next Door* (2001), opens with its heroine, Sachiko, inside an unoccupied apartment, listening through the wall to the sound of a couple having sex. She reaches under her skirt moments before a salaryman enters the room: the cuckolded husband of the woman next door, trying to carry on as if his wife's affair isn't happening under his nose. They discuss their respective plights: his unfaithful wife, her unloving husband. And then? They part, fully dressed. And though clothing will eventually be removed, thanks to the care that Satô shows his yearning-filled characters, the subsequent sex here carries an emotional weight that was rarely present in the Pink genre to this point—an attitude that would be embraced by the successors to the Heavenly Kings' thrones.

NEXT GENERATION: THE SEVEN LUCKY GODS

At the turn of the millennium, another group of Kokuei directors emerged as the latest Young Turks of "artistic" Pink Film. In homage to the *shitennô*, they became known as the *shichifukujin*, or "The Seven Lucky Gods of Pink Film": Toshiya Ueno, Shinji Imaoka, Yoshitaka Kamata, Toshirô Enomoto, Yûji Tajiri, Mitsuru Meike, and Rei Sakamoto. Learning their craft under the Heavenly Kings, they moved the genre beyond the reliance on misogynistic fantasies that mark so many of their mentors' films. "They seem to have little interest in dealing with violence—or, for that matter, with overtly political and social topics. Their films concentrate more on interpersonal relations and their characters are much more vulnerable," remarked Sato, still Big Sister to this new generation, in 2011. Imaoka's *Lunch Box* (2004) follows a mute woman's workplace dalliance, and her attempts to express her affection through the elaborate lunches she brings her beloved. The story, between couplings, is sensitively told through small interactions, the drama climaxing with one of her painstakingly prepared meals casually discarded in a trash bin. Tajiri's *Office Lady Love Juice* (1999) is a quiet romance between an older woman and a young man that mostly consists of intimate handheld two shots of the leads talking as their bond deepens, with the coitus almost entirely obscured in darkness. This isn't to say the *shitennô* didn't explore more ambitious—and unusual—projects, among these Meike's *The Glamorous Life of Sachiko Hanai* (2003), an espionage yarn about a sex worker who finds herself with a cloned copy of George W. Bush's finger. Restorations and the burgeoning DVD market brought greater foreign attention and festival runs for the Lucky Gods, with *The Glamorous Life of Sachiko Hanai* even getting a limited US release. Was this a matter of the Pink Film growing up, or being watered down? As Wakamatsu once said, "Movies can't really be called 'Pink' if they are being accepted by the general public. They've always got to be guerilla."

Metrograph A–Z
H Is for *Hammersmith Is Out*

Words by
Whit Stillman

"H" is for *Hammersmith Is Out* (1972)—one of the lamest comedies ever made and my start in film, playing (literally) *opposite* Elizabeth Taylor, Richard Burton, and Beau Bridges, then a hot young star, coming off the success of *The Landlord* (1970). I had taken the second half of my sophomore year off to study Spanish and "become a writer" in Cuernavaca, Mexico, where I had cousins. It was early 1971 and the Echeverría government was using paramilitary gangs to violently repress its opposition, as portrayed in Alfonso Cuarón's *Roma* (2018). I had written a dispatch on the events for *The Harvard Crimson* and was trying to write a bigger one for *The Village Voice,* where I had worked the previous summer.

It was a period of strange, ill-conceived movies getting tax shelter funding, and *Hammersmith* was one of these, financed by self-described "bored" industrialist J. Cornelius Crean, whose very name suggests the project's flavor. Though I had missed the shooting of an earlier scene for which young Americans had been wanted, the film's office coordinator took pity on me and sent me in for a waiter part. Mexican extras "with an American look" had been bussed in from Mexico City, all looking like burly members of an Irish rugby squad (reputedly descendants of Irish American soldiers who had defected to the Mexican side in the Mexican–American War). As I was *not* a burly redhead I somehow ended up in the precinct reserved for the film's stars and director, the charming Peter Ustinov. I was hiding behind the *Crimson* issue, observing the stars and trying to avoid expulsion, when he commented that it "looked like an 18th-century newspaper." Richard Burton had a most serious, impressive aura; one could see how Elizabeth Taylor might be underestimated, but what struck me was how clever and insightful she seemed, edging Burton in that. However, my golden hours were ending. The Mexican second assistant director was on to me and a terrifying bully: my first experience with the heaven and hell of assistant directors. A similar fellow was with us for part of the *Barcelona* (1994) shoot; he tried to tank the whole production.

Flashbacks came later, while watching a documentary on the Puerta Vallarta shoot for John Huston's *The Night of the Iguana* (1964), with Burton starring and the same bullying AD's shouts of "*Silencio!*" (The *Barcelona* AD resurfaced in 2002's *Lost in La Mancha*, volubly celebrating that shoot's cancellation.) On set in my waiter role I got some of Peter Ustinov's direction—but it didn't save the film.

CREATE OR PERISH: KHADY SYLLA

On the filmmaker's trailblazing portraits of daily life in Dakar and the loneliness of mental illness.

Written by
Cassie da Costa

Photographs by
Stéphane Weber

Khady Sylla was many things: a filmmaker, a writer, a scholar, a teacher, a daughter of water, a mother of two sons, and—in her own words—"mad." She was troubled by her mental illness, but not ashamed of it, and she analyzed its complexities in deeply personal, unconventional films that screened widely on television in Senegal, where audiences are more familiar with her. By and large, Western viewers are only now encountering her work: emotionally searing and formally daring projects that blend documentary and essay, which have charted a path for genre-defying, time-bending West African filmmakers to follow in her wake. In her cinema, movement becomes not only a rite but a necessity, a way to oppose society's confines. The result is an oeuvre teeming with escape hatches, portals, and magical transformations: a passage to overlooked or otherwise unseen worlds.

For Sylla, living was difficult to bear, but creating was a compelling force. "Khady, by the strength of water women, you are the river, you are the sea, you are the creek and you are the boat," reads the epigraph for *A Simple Word*, her elegiac family portrait posthumously released in 2014. It is one of her three key films, nonfiction works that show the force of language tearing through the screen. *Colobane Express* (1999), her feature debut, made with her sister and frequent collaborator Mariama, chronicles chaotic happenings onboard the eponymous bus service in Dakar. Arguments and negotiations erupt between drivers, passengers, and porters, forming a buzzing, electric street dialogue.

In *An Open Window* (2005), Sylla delves into her relationship with her friend Aminta Ngom, who is—in Sylla's words—"openly and defiantly" mentally ill. In voiceover she narrates Ngom's psychic anguish and recites self-penned monologues: lyrical, unsentimental, yet plaintive texts. She uses this device, to stirring effect, in *A Simple Word*, her final film, in which

she and Mariama attempt to trace their family's oral history while mapping larger cultural and political differences between village life and city life in Senegal. Repeatedly, Sylla speaks directly to the camera, her gaze piercing the screen, her face as commanding as her words.

Sylla's vital filmography, international co-productions largely funded by broadcasters such as Arte France or Al Jazeera, also includes two other short films: her 1997 drama *Les bijoux*, which follows a young woman as she prepares to meet a suitor, and the 2008 documentary *Le monologue de la muette*, about the mistreatment of Senegalese domestic workers at the hands of their employers. But Sylla was a writer first, publishing at least two novels and two novellas. Most of her books, including *Passagères*, *Marietou*, and *Les mains de couleurs*, seem to be out of print. Her only writing readily accessible to the public is the 1992 novel *Le jeu de la mer*, which translates to *The Game of the Sea*, a metaphysical tale about an imagined world concocted between two friends and the limitations placed on women within superstitious, patriarchal cultures. The novel, which was shortlisted for the 1993 Grand Prix des Arts et des Lettres du Sénégal, opens with dizzying imagery of the waves—carried by a mind and soul of their own—washing over a village. The friends spend much of their time sitting opposite each other at a table, playing a game of free association in which trinkets, gestures, speech, and song conjure stories imbued with their dreams, fears, and memories. One of their tales, however, penetrates the real. A character they've "written" escapes, and in an intersecting narrative, a police detective must deal with their unleashed creation as well as the petty complaints and prejudices of locals. The novel is at once fantastical and investigative, exploring the power of invention and authorship—a work in the tradition of those she worshipped such as Jorge Luis Borges and Sony Labou Tansi.

Sylla's bold, imaginative instincts flourished, understandably, given that the Sylla children benefited from early, robust exposure to the arts. As Mariama reports, their mother, Ouadja Sylla, worked for the historic newsreel service Actualités Sénégalaises under the directorship of Paulin Soumanou Vieyra. She was also secretary to Ousmane Sembène, the "father of African cinema" (and like Sylla, a novelist), subtitling works of his and of various ascendant filmmakers, including Djibril Diop Mambéty. The Sylla house served as a kind of salon, with frequent gatherings and screenings in the garden—a fertile environment for the sisters to develop curiosity about the moving image. Later, Sylla would count Mambéty among her mentors. Other influential filmmaker friends were the documentarian Rama Thiaw[1] and Safi Faye, a trained ethnologist who similarly focused her creative practice on the local, shifting between documentary and narrative depictions of Senegalese society.

Sylla's literary and cinematic voice, shaped by the primacy of spirituality, oral histories, and griot traditions, echoes throughout mid-century and contemporary African cinema. We might find its precedent, for instance, in several of Sembène's features that wed history and folklore, like *Black Girl* (1966), which has a certain twinship with *Le monologue de la muette* in its exploration of the inner life of a Senegalese maid, and pick up traces in Zambian filmmaker Rungano Nyoni's *I Am Not a Witch* (2017) and the French Senegalese director (and niece of Mambéty) Mati Diop's *Atlantics* (2019). The latter, like *Le jeu de la mer*, not only employs a similar sea motif but also interweaves the supernatural and a detective plot in its examination of capitalism's abuses. *I Am Not a Witch*, about a little girl accused of witchcraft and dispatched as punishment to rural Zambia to perform manual labor, recalls Sylla's depiction of misogyny in her novel, as well as in *An Open Window*.

Writing was indeed the origin point for Sylla's creative work, according to Mariama, but Sylla's path to the humanities was indirect. She was supposed to enroll in business school. Instead, she chose to attend a *hypokhâgne* (a preparatory program for admissions into an elite graduate school) for literature, then, in 1981, matriculated at École normale supérieure in Paris, where she studied philosophy on a scholarship from the Senegalese government. She returned to Dakar during her summer breaks, but remained in Paris after completing her studies. There, she taught literacy to migrant populations and wrote her novels, as well as a scenario for an unrealized film called *Entre ciel et terre* (Between Heaven and Earth) about farmers in Beauce, a region in north-central France. After she sent the ethnologist Jean Rouch a copy of *Le jeu de la mer*, he called her a week later, enraptured, hoping to adapt it into a film. She wrote a script in 1993, but he never followed through. This early taste of filmmaking inspired Sylla to pick up a camera of her own upon her return to Dakar in 1994.

Her first completed feature, *Colobane Express*, is a deft and playful foray into cinéma vérité. Sylla and Mariama used a proto-Steadicam system to rig the camera in place as they followed daily expeditions at close range: drivers and porters descend into fisticuffs over petty disagreements; riders express their frustration at suddenly canceled rides and misdirections. The sisters, along with director of photography Medoune N'Diaye, take a direct yet light-handed approach; with editor Cécile Fernandez's skillful sequencing, the flow of action within each scene is alternately trancelike and eruptive. The frenetic interactions on the bus service speak to a general dysfunction in Dakar. At one point, a group of girls board and start to talk about some paperwork they need to get sorted at City Hall—the process is taking so long that it has entered the realm of absurd. But, one of the girls says, what else can you do? You have to ride the bus, so to speak, and hope it gets you to your destination. Here, Sylla and Mariama are rapt, unobtrusive observers, offering a critique of the challenges in Senegalese society from within while also conveying

1. Khady Sylla's friend, Rama Thiaw—a filmmaker best known for her documentaries *Boul Fallé, la Voie de la lutte* (2009) and *The Revolution Won't be Televised* (2016)—said of Sylla, "She had her own singular and poetic way of filming. Unclassifiable and iconoclastic."

the humor and liveliness intertwined with the chaos and uncertainty of city life.

Unlike in her later films, we don't see Sylla in *Colobane Express*, but we do begin to get a sense of her artistic preoccupations: it's the people—and their relationships to one another, to certain objects, to themselves—who stand out. In one of many operatic scenes in the film, a rider chews on a piece of meat after offering some to an elderly man next to her (he declines). The bus lurches, and suddenly she begins to choke. The bus stops and she disembarks, along with several passengers who help her; after she regains control, the woman refuses to get back on the bus, blaming the service for her misfortune and fleeing down the road. The camera lingers on the abandoned bag of meat, left to rot on the street.

There are few extant interviews with Sylla, and even fewer written in English. Most of the information available today is the result of people discovering and championing her work. One such advocate is the filmmaker Johanna Makabi, who, as a student, first encountered Sylla as a subject in Joris Lachaise's documentary *Ce qu'il reste de la folie* (What Remains of Madness?, 2014). A few years later, Makabi had the chance to see *An Open Window*, which had won the First Film Prize at its FIDMarseille festival premiere more than a decade earlier. Sylla's films typically have received limited international exhibition otherwise. The first larger retrospective of her cinema to take place outside of Senegal was staged in 2024, in Amiens, before travelling this year to Paris and New York.

"CRÉER OU S'ANÉANTIR," SHE writes on a chalkboard in *An Open Window*: create or perish. She was living with schizophrenia; doctors had diagnosed her in 1994, a few months after she had shot her incomplete first film, *Phente*, in the Psychiatric Hospital of Fann, in Dakar. Sylla had already been recording the lives of the mentally ill in the city—she shares some of this experience in *Ce qu'il reste de la folie*—and it was through this work that she met Ngom, whose family had confined her inside their compound to prevent her from wandering off. But the film stock was overexposed and *Phente* was never finished. Clips from it were repurposed for the beginning of *An Open Window*; ghostly footage plays, as Sylla begins her monologue. "You look at yourself through a broken mirror," she says. "You see your fragmented face. Your face is shattered. And the one looking at you in the broken mirror sees the fragmented pieces of your face." Sylla stares directly into the camera as she speaks. "Which one of you will reconstruct the puzzle? Are you even on the same side of the mirror?" Here, Sylla's background in philosophy takes center stage, as both the camera and the spoken word deconstruct the idea of a sole, unified self. She is and isn't herself. Ngom is and isn't Ngom.

Like the two friends in *La jeu de la mer*, Sylla and Ngom establish a world in common. Sylla interviews

DAUGHTER OF WATER

Written by
Johanna Makabi

I discovered African cinema during my studies, but outside the classroom, as these films were not part of the curriculum. I was deeply moved by Ousmane Sembène's *Black Girl* (1966), where I saw Dakar—the city of my Senegalese heritage—in black and white. Actress Mbissine Thérèse Diop, who must have been around my grandmother's age, embodied a story that profoundly touched me, one I could identify with. Freedom or death—that is what these images cried out. Later, *Touki Bouki* (1973), from director Djibril Diop Mambéty, told me the story of my parents' youth, their departure, the choice of exile made by the post-independence generation. I came to better understand my mother's aspirations.

But Khady Sylla was the missing piece. When I was an anthropology student seeking a perspective separate from the vision of the white French anthropologist and filmmaker Jean Rouch—whom Sembène criticized for filming Africans as if they were insects—I found Khady. Khady, it turned out, looked at herself as an insect, just as I did. She dissected her society, her place in the world, and in an act of freedom decided to show everything. That is what stirred me: unfiltered, direct, facing the camera, in her own distinctive articulation, Khady spoke about what it means to be a Black woman.

Rimbaud once wrote, "The Poet becomes a seer through a long, immense, and reasoned derangement of all the senses." Meanwhile, Audre Lorde declared, "Your silence will not protect you." In many ways, through her work, Khady also became a seer, breaking the silence to immerse us in the poetry of daily life in Dakar, bringing us face to face with those on the margins, like Amy, the young maid, in *Le monologue de la muette* or the passengers of *Colobane Express*. Khady filmed people with tenderness and sensitivity, immersing herself so deeply that, in *An Open Window*, she emerged as her own subject. She turned the camera into a tool of clairvoyance, revealing those whom society ignores, those we no longer see. She reminds us that the ebb and flow of the waves—an allegory she so artfully employed in her work—just like the beating of our hearts, is both ordinary and extraordinary.

Khady is my "rich" aunt, my big sister who left home—the one I watched wither away in immigration, the one who pursued her freedom instead of finding a husband. She is the one who could never entirely explain the bitter taste life takes on when you are a Black woman longing for freedom. Khady's films are, for me, a lesson in humility and a manifesto of rage. I have made her words in *An Open Window*—"create or perish"—my mantra.

Khady Sylla, captured by her then partner, the French press photographer Stéphane Weber, smoking a cigarette on vacation in Saint Louis, 1994. Right: In another of Weber's portraits, Sylla strolls among the flowers in the Bois de Vincennes, 1992.

Ngom, who was emotionally ostracized by her concerned, suspicious family. Ngom, in turn, is leery of her friend's inquiries. Since Ngom isn't permitted to leave the grounds without a chaperone, Sylla arranges for her to, at least temporarily, escape her confinement by offering to accompany her. But this is only a superficial reprieve, for the film reveals Ngom's lasting wounds as she recounts the devastation of her infant daughter's death and the disintegration of her marriage. From outside, the camera observes a boarded-up window, symbol of Ngom's lost freedom.

Sylla worked together with cinematographers Charlie Van Damme and Francóis Kotlarski, as well as editor Amrita David (who also edited and co-wrote Alice Diop's 2022 legal drama *Saint Omer*), to create a wrenchingly intimate yet unsentimental portrait of two women at odds with society and themselves. "I had a lot to say about Aminta and my own journey," Sylla told the FIDMarseilles journal. "I wrote [the script] as if dictated by a muse, like when I write poetry. One of the film's challenges is to portray a fragmented consciousness, damaged by illness." Throughout *An Open Window*, the filmmaker unflinchingly discloses her own psychic turmoil, speaking of the loneliness and agony of her experience with mental illness, made more complicated by a country where her condition is highly stigmatized and misunderstood. The friends, in overlapping and distinct ways, speak through each other. Ngom's musings are nonsensical to her family, but Sylla insists on listening. She recognizes herself in them. "I was experiencing that invisible pain, more than invisible, that pain so hard to identify," says Sylla. "How do you explain it to someone who has never felt it?"

How does one locate, and then transmit, a sense of something so fractured, so beyond language? Sylla, perhaps in response to her own question, eventually became detached from life. "Now I feel like looking at the world through the eye of a camera, to capture images like dreams," she says in *A Simple Word*. "I need a third eye, a mechanical eye, the mirror eye which is the only thing that can make me feel joy. I do not love life. I only love movies and literature." Here, she prefers to remain at a distance. In the film, Sylla and Mariama travel from Dakar to Barale, the rural village where they find a sort of refuge from the noise and claustrophobia of the city. Sitting on the side of the road, resting, is their grandmother, Penda Diogo Sarr. Sylla and Mariama help her up and follow her back to her home; the sisters want to know their family tree and what happened in the village long before they were born. In a voiceover, Mariama speaks of the "ancient world," traceable only from the stories being shared by her grandmother and other family members. Sylla, who passed on October 8, 2013, aged just 50, seems somewhat vacant in the film—she stares out a van window, takes notes, watches the faces of her elders with alternating attention and remoteness. Even when she looks directly into the camera, you can feel her retreating. She's already passing.

LIMELIGHT: JOÃO CÉSAR MONTEIRO

Written by
Nick Pinkerton

Illustration by
Jasper Jubenvill

After years of being almost entirely unavailable on home video, even in the director's native Portugal, the films of João César Monteiro, are emerging into public view again, with new restorations touring the US in the fall and a forthcoming Blu-ray box set from Cinema Guild. One would love to believe this will lead to wider recognition of Monteiro, who died in 2003, as one of the most original, obstreperous filmmakers of late 20th- and early 21st-century European cinema, but given the obstinate, bearish nature of his directorial personality, and the gleeful perversity, displayed with a flasher's bravado, of even his best-known work, smart money isn't riding on it.

Monteiro's active years as a filmmaker spanned a little over three decades, in which he produced films both uncommonly variegated and governed by a highly individualistic but consistent internal logic; they can be isolated into a number of periods or modes, as is done here, but all belong to the same project of restless exploration, self-critical revision, and compulsive wrestling with knotty questions concerning the nature of cinema itself. He never struggled to find a distinctive voice as a writer and director, though finding an audience proved more difficult, a situation that changed only slightly with the release of 1989's *Recollections of the Yellow House*, the first of several films in which Monteiro added lead actor to his on-set responsibilities.

Playing out in the grottier districts of Lisbon, *Recollections* is a film in which coarse, protean, peasant bawdiness sits cheek by jowl with erudite esoterica. Monteiro's body of work is defined by this volatile compound—and a blithe dismissal of the gap between the lower classes and "high" culture posited by received wisdom, which makes shared human heritage the exclusive deer park of an intelligentsia. A voracious autodidact with a vast knowledge of all fields of art across all eras and an intractable allegiance to Portugal's poor, Monteiro never pandered in the name of accessibility, an attitude that, then as now, leaves one open to accusations of "pretension"—implicit in this the idea that one respects audiences by treating them as gormless dolts.

He was born João César Monteiro Santos on February 2, 1939—nearly 14 years after the coup d'état that supplanted the First Republic with the *Ditadura Nacional* ("National Dictatorship"), and six after António de Oliveira Salazar, newly President of the Council of Ministers, established the *Estado Novo* ("New State"). His hometown, Figueira da Foz, a popular tourist destination on the central Atlantic coast, was then a city of some 50,000 souls. His father was a liberal landowner from nearby Tavarede; his mother, a maid 16 years the father's junior. Monteiro's patrimony was sufficient to pay for college in Lisbon, where he arrived as a teenage erotomaniac and, according to a later autobiographical self-portrait, was swiftly "expelled after contracting a very dangerous venereal disease." A tendency towards dissolution ran in the family: "Having finally managed to squander his entire fortune in satisfying his brutal appetites," writes Monteiro, "my handsome father died of a heart attack, leaving me, perplexed and penniless, scratching my head."

Delivered from the blessings of higher education and parental expectation, Monteiro struck out on his own. After self-publishing a book of verse, 1959's *Corpo Submerso*, and making a brief detour in Paris, during which he logged an audience with François Truffaut, Monteiro was back in Lisbon. A regular at Café Gelo, meeting spot for the capitol's surrealist contingent, he was drawn into the orbit of Alberto Jorge Seixas dos Santos, a critic and director of the ABC- Cineclube de Lisboa, who helped Monteiro to find vocational training as assistant director on Perdigão Queiroga's 1962 *O Milionário*. A scholarship led to an indifferent stretch at the London School of Film Technique, where Monteiro routinely skipped class to spend his days in front of Paolo Uccello's *The Battle of San Romano* at the National Gallery. ("The English were not born for cinema," he later wrote. "In fact, I still don't quite understand why the English were born.") After this disappointing sojourn, he returned to Portugal to encounter the first flowering of Novo Cinema, the local equivalent of the various "Waves" that crashed across Europe in the 1960s, here producing a new crop of films that would gradually redefine what was possible and permissible in the national cinema.

1. PORTRAIT OF THE ARTIST AS A YOUNG CRITIC

In this charged atmosphere of budding cinephile culture, the versifier turned his pen to criticism, and by the mid-'60s Monteiro's byline surfaced with regularity in the pages of *O Tempo e o Modo* and, later, in the more established *Diário de Lisboa*.[1] As a critic, Monteiro was, from jump, truculent, eccentric, prone to grandiose statements—on D.W. Griffith's 1919 *Broken Blossoms*, Monteiro writes, "cinema discovers its interiority"—and obviously under the influence of the take-no-prisoners style associated with *Cahiers du Cinéma*. His 1968 entry for their annual poll of the year's 10 best films includes three titles: Jacques Tati's *Playtime*, Jerry Lewis's *The Big Mouth*, and André Delvaux's *One Night... A Train*. ("Moral of the list," he writes, "You like fewer and fewer films each time.")

One senses that, like the *Cahiers* cohort, Monteiro approached writing about films as a way of articulating how he might make them himself, but his first attempt got no further than shooting two days of an unfinished 16mm project. This was followed by perfunctory work in television advertising, screenwriting, subtitling (for Jean-Marie Straub and Danièle Huillet), and somewhere in the mix, a three-day stint in a mental hospital. Screen actor-turned-producer Ricardo Malheiro, whose company, Cultura Filmes, was underwriting a series of shorts on artistic luminaries, would give Monteiro his second shot behind the camera. The resulting *Sophia de Mello Breyner Andresen* (1969) is a portrait of the Porto-born poet renowned for her literary output as well as her principled opposition to the Estado Novo, a 17-minute short showing Andresen with her five children and then-husband, at leisure in their home on the Algarve coast and its beaches, plashing in the surf with relish.

Monteiro is obviously taken with his subject, but the film is no overawed hagiography: after a scene of Andresen reading her most famous children's story, *The Girl from the Sea*, one of her offspring criticizes her lack of a "natural" tone when reciting; later, as she muses on her work's philosophical underpinnings, two daughters sabotage her monologue by turning on the record player. Rather than undercut Andresen's dignity or razz her self-seriousness, such moments confirm a passage of her work that she's seen reading: "To say that the work of art is part of culture is rather scholarly and artificial. The work of art is part of the real and it is destiny, fulfillment, salvation and life." Posthumously, Andresen has been hoisted up as a pillar of the Portuguese canon, interred in the National Pantheon alongside presidents, footballers, and *fadistas*, but Monteiro's film gives us something more than an idealized effigy—the Grand Woman of Letters as a flesh-and-blood woman, her artistic practice inextricable from her quotidian life and the pleasures of the natural world.

Monteiro next returned to the scraps of his earlier, aborted film, which, along with new footage, became a 34-minute cri de coeur, *He Who Awaits Dead Men's Shoes Dies Barefoot*. The '65 rushes, silent save for a rattle of a projector and Monteiro's narration, form a preamble describing the failure of the initial shoot. The c. 1969 footage that follows—by all visible evidence tackling the same story with new actors—represents the first surfacing of a fascination with twinned and mirror-image narratives that would carry through Monteiro's career. (A favorite Monteiro trick shot, in which a character appears to address the viewer head-on in a looking glass reflection, also makes its debut here.)

The film's subjects—young men without work, money, or romantic companionship, wasting their days in cafés exchanging epigrams amidst a stultifying, dead-end atmosphere of conservatism—recall those of Jean Eustache's *Santa Claus Has Blue Eyes* (1966), though the idlers here are stuck in Lisbon in the senescent years of Salazar's regime. Luís Miguel Cintra makes the first screen appearance of his storied career, including several returns to casa Monteiro, as Livio, introduced dreaming of a world beyond Portugal ("A bottomless pit, an asshole one can't escape from," per the opening voiceover) and, more immediately pressing, puzzling over where to find a few *escudos* to take a girlfriend out. His pal Mário (Carlos Ferreira) hatches a scheme to make off with the hand-me-downs of a recently deceased general by buttering up his widow, after which, finding nothing they can expropriate into their own wardrobes—the narrow dress shoes pinch Livio's feet—they pawn the bundle to pay for Livio's somewhat desultory dinner with his date, who slips through his fingers by the film's end.

A magpie collection of quotations and allusions, the film is an introduction to Monteiro the pastiche artist. Livio reads aloud from *Os Lusíadas*, Luís Vaz de Camões's 16th-century epic poem and cornerstone of Portuguese literature; an insert shows a hand scribbling swaggering morsels from Jean-Luc Godard ("Cinema is a fraud") and Arthur Rimbaud's "Mauvaise Sang"; save for a brief verbal exchange, the only words heard in the last six minutes are literary excerpts, from Jorge Luis Borges and Margarita Guerrero's *Book of Imaginary Beings*—concerning a coming rebellion of "mirror people" currently confined to their specular realm—and Franz Kafka's *The Trial*.

With Monteiro—eager, like Livio, for escape—travelling frequently, editing *Dead Men's Shoes* took the better part of two years, and the film hardly set the world on fire when complete. Undaunted, Monteiro began a feature-length project in the summer of 1972, initially titled *The Sacred Family*—a tip of the hat to Marx and Engels?—and known today as *Fragments of an Alms-Film*. It offers a first glimpse of the director on-screen: wearing a leather jacket, cigarette holder dangling louchely from his lips, he displays his middle finger to the camera.

Scraps of World War II archival footage bookend Monteiro's aptly titled *Fragments*, a film shot through with short, dissonant digressions—an orange accompanied by Francis Ponge's lyric ode to the fruit; a zoom past an elderly woman seated in a ruined building—evincing Monteiro's delight in blindsiding juxtapositions and non sequiturs, as well as his growing dissatisfaction with clean linear narrative. Something resembling a storyline does, however, emerge. This concerns the cloistered domestic existence of João (João Perry), his wife, Maria (Manuela de Freitas, a staple of Monteiro's cinema) and their young daughter. The three are only all seen together in one scene: João, wearing a plastic pig mask and squatting toad-like on an end table in the living room, refuses to engage with Maria's visiting parents, tut-tutting mouthpieces for bourgeois order. Long takes, some running the 11-minute length of a 35mm mag, recur: of father and daughter indulging in tumbling horseplay, of husband and wife in episodes of intimate groping, alternately anguished and blissful. Such heightened attention to bodies in uninterrupted, turbulent motion recalls the Jacques Rivette of *L'Amour fou* (1969), while the film concludes with a quotation from another *L'Amour fou*, André Breton's 1937 manifesto, spoken in voiceover after Maria has put a bullet in João: "Above all, let the idea of the family be buried!" (Notably, Monteiro's wife, Margarida Gil, who would become a prominent filmmaker in her own right, was an assistant director on the film.)

Fragments was to have been followed by a free adaptation of Shakespeare, but Monteiro's *The Tempest* dissipated with the clouds of Estado Novo governance. After years of military engagement with African colonies fighting for independence, increasingly unpopular both abroad and at home—the slogan "People of Portugal: Africa is burning" is heard in *Dead Men's Shoes*—and a concurrently rising tide of pro-democracy agitation, a nearly bloodless military coup on April 25, 1974, the "Carnation Revolution," put an end to 48 years of corporatist dictatorship.

Monteiro's artistic response to these events was *What Shall I Do With This Sword?*—the nearest thing that he would ever make to an engagé work of militant cinema. It was filmed in the period of uncertainty between the revolution and the ratification of the new Constitution of the Portuguese Republic on April 2, 1976, a stretch that included attempted coups, mass expropriation of private land, economic turmoil, the ripple effects of Portugal's exit from its African colonies, and the political violence of the "Hot Summer" of 1975, during which civil war appeared inevitable.

Sword? opens with a view from one of the turrets of Lisbon's hilltop Castelo de São Jorge, behind the barrel of an old bronze cannon pointed towards a military vessel anchored in the broad Tagus River. This is the supercarrier USS Saratoga, part of a NATO flotilla present to participate in a series of naval exercises dubbed "Locked Gate"—scheduled months before the revolution but interpreted in its aftermath as a show of force toward a country threatening to drift away from the US sphere of influence.

Monteiro's perspective on Portugal's looming "allies" is expressed via parallel montage that moves between the fleet and images from F.W. Murnau's 1922 *Nosferatu* in which Max Schreck's Count Orlok arrives by schooner, accompanied by a cargo of vermin and the Black Death. Only the underclasses are heard from in the film—tillers of the soil and factory hands, a zaftig streetwalker who strikes up an easy rapport with the off-camera Monteiro, even the visiting seamen, who appear more clueless than sinister—a choice that testifies to Monteiro's sympathies, though his film doesn't traffic only in easy agit-prop sloganeering. A blustery, desk-pounding speech from a 72-year-old veteran lefty is followed by a gathering of revolutionaries from the soon-to-be-independent African colony of São Tomé and Príncipe discussing, among other things, the obscene gap between their wages and those of their white co-workers. The purpose of the juxtaposition is not to suggest the Portuguese worker *hasn't* been exploited, but that various forms and degrees of exploitation are propagated by the colonialist and capitalist system, distinctions which must be better understood if, to paraphrase the graffiti that concludes the film, proletarians of all countries are to unite.

Top: Margarida Gil, João César Monteiro's wife and future director, defends the mouth of the Tagus, and Portugal herself, from a NATO fleet in 1975's *What Shall I Do With This Sword?*—his most militant work as a solo director. He is also one of many uncredited contributors, including visiting Brazilian Glauber Rocha, to 1975's *The Guns and the People*, a boots-on-the-ground document of the Carnation Revolution.

Bottom: Monteiro evokes Florentine painter Paolo Uccello's *Saint George and the Dragon* in a scene from 1981's *Silvestre*. At left is Maria de Medeiros; at right, Luís Miguel Cintra.

1. João César Monteiro's greatest period of sustained activity as a film critic, however, came during Fernando Lopes's 10-month, 37-issue stewardship of *Cinéfilo* in 1974, in which Monteiro achieved notoriety for both his insouciant prose and for recommending football matches in the listings section.

The question posed by the title of Monteiro's film—shades of V.I. Lenin's 1902 pamphlet *What Is to Be Done?*—connects to its leitmotif image, that of Gil, dressed in the mail and tunic of a Crusader, broadsword in hand. The images of the female warrior and of Lisbon's 16th-century Belém Tower, where she is last seen, the traditional point of embarkation for those Portuguese seamen, celebrated by Camões, who built its empire, are loaded with jingoistic implications—the exhortations to remember a heroic past that were stock-in-trade of the Estado Novo—but here their meaning is ambiguous. The "sword" of Portugal has been put to dubious use through the centuries; could it serve a nobler purpose in time to come? It was to the country's collective memory, a memory in which its possible futures might be descried, that the next distinct phase of Monteiro's filmmaking was dedicated.

2. INTO THE PAST

Whatever hopes Monteiro had once held out for Novo Cinema—Paulo Rocha's *The Green Years* (1963) and Fernando Lopes's *Belarmino* (1964) had made particularly strong impressions upon his return from London—appear to have curdled by the mid-'70s. In his introduction to a 1974 interview with António Reis, a figure of outsized importance to the older Monteiro and the Portuguese filmmakers who came of age after the revolution such as Pedro Costa and João Pedro Rodrigues, Monteiro describes anticipating Reis's latest film as "another punishing chore"—but the encounter proved a tonic. Monteiro was rhapsodic over *Jaime* (1974), Reis's 35-minute tribute to Jaime Fernandes, a peasant who, towards the end of a life substantially spent in confinement at Lisbon's Miguel Bombarda Hospital, began to produce dense ink-and-pencil drawings representing an exotic anthropomorphic and zoomorphic bestiary. Every bit as significant was the impact made on Monterio by Reis's next film, 1976's *Trás-os-Montes*, co-directed with Margarida Cordeiro and filmed in the eponymous northeastern mountain region with a cast of local villagers, following the filmmakers' long immersion in the customs, folklore, and the vernacular idioms of the Terra Fria. A return to the foundational legends and heritage of its setting, a film with the dirt of Portuguese soil underneath its fingernails, *Trás-os-Montes* indicated the into-the-past trajectory that Monteiro would follow—inasmuch as such a stubborn one-off could ever be said to "follow" anything—in a suite of films comprising features *Trails* (1978) and *Silvestre* (1981) and a trio of 1979 shorts, *The Love of the Three Pomegranates*, *The Two Soldiers*, and *The Mother*.

Heavily populated with nonprofessional actors, these five works are based on interpretations of the *Contos Tradicionais Portugueses*, a collection of folk tales published in 1957 by the poets Carlos de Oliveira and José Gomes Ferreira. Monteiro, typically, adds his own rich layers of literary and art-historical allusion; in the midst of the story of Branca-Flor, a gentle daughter of the Devil who escapes her father through elopement with a shepherd, recounted in *Trails*, we hear a lengthy extract from Aeschylus's *Eumenides* in which de Freitas plays the role of Athena, addressing a phalanx of village women playing the parts of the Furies, who reply to her in the polyphonic singing style of the Alentejo region. Discussing *Silvestre*, in which 15-year-old Maria de Medeiros portrays a young woman who dons knight's armor in order to rescue her kidnapped father, Monteiro cited the influence of the cross-dressing Katherine Hepburn in George Cukor's 1935 film maudit *Sylvia Scarlett*. Across these works, Monteiro develops a visual grammar of flattened planimetric perspectives indebted to Italian painting of the quattrocento and earlier—if Uccello is the presiding spirit of *Silvestre*, which features a tableau vivant recreation of the painter's *Saint George and the Dragon*, Giotto is that of *Trails*, with its games of scale between stunted architectural backdrops and foregrounded figures.

Though they draw from the same well of folklore, each of Monteiro's medieval films its own curiously shaped vessel. They aren't all even strictly "medieval": *Trails* has two narrative strands, one period, one contemporary, and while *The Two Soldiers* has its share of fairy tale goings-on (an ailing king, an enchanted tree whose leaves restore lost sight) and traditional iconographies (the skirl of *gaita* bagpipes; hydrocephalic *cabeçudo* costumes), its comrades-in-arms look like refugees from the Great War's trenches... or Godard's bleak battlefield travelogue *Les Carabiniers* (1963). The action of *Trails* moves from Trás-os-Montes to Beira to Alentejo and the Atlantic Ocean, and this *plein air* film is very much invested in the rugged splendor of the Portuguese landscape and the primal myths that sprang from them. *Silvestre*, by contrast, is a largely studio-bound vision of the age of chivalry, employing front projection and painted backdrops—if *Trails* evokes tales told before a blackened hearth, *Silvestre* suggests canvas, stained glass, and the tapestry mill. It continues Monteiro's excursion into deliberate artifice in *The Love of Three Pomegranates*, both of which suggest the possible influence of Éric Rohmer's *Perceval le Gallois* (1978), which plays out against a backdrop of cardboard castles and fiberglass rivers. But Godard and Rohmer were French, and, as the critic João Bénard da Costa observed in an enthusiastic contemporary review of *Trails*, a French filmmaker "who care[s] more about what they have to say than what the viewer would like them to say" could reasonably hope for a sizable audience. The 1980s would be almost over before Monteiro found as much, a decade spent largely adrift.

3. OUT TO SEA

Five years passed between *Silvestre* and Monteiro's next feature, 1986's *Hovering over the Water*—and Monteiro's stock was running so low when *Hovering* was finished that it wouldn't receive a commercial release in Portugal for 10 years. After the largely inland pursuits of his medieval films, *Hovering* brought Monteiro back to the Algarve coast of *Sophia de Mello Breyner Andresen*, a work that ends on the sound of beating waves and Andresen intoning, "When I die, I will return to reclaim the moments I did not live by the sea." And while, in his 1997 *The Hips of J.W.*, Monteiro mocks the Portuguese cult of the open water, mythologized by artists from Camões to Andresen ("Don't give me that mystical sea shit!" he groans), he wasn't wholly immune to the lure of the beaches and quays, and the mysterious, fatal depths beyond.

At the center of *Hovering* is one Laura Rossellini (Laura Morante), a young Italian widow who, after a lengthy absence, has come to summer at her late husband's 17th-century manorial home, kept company by her two preadolescent children, their housemaid, and her sisters-in-law, who occupy the house year-round. While sunbathing Laura spots an inflatable life raft containing a pistol and a handsome, stripped-to-the-waist American, Robert Jordan (Philip J. Spinelli), near death from exposure and a head wound. Hearing news of the assassination of PLO member Issam Sartawi at a nearby congress of the Socialist International—a real-life event that dominated headlines in the spring of 1983—she, despite suspecting the Yank's involvement, provides him shelter, bringing trouble in the form of emotional

Top: Laura Morante in a trick mirror shot in João César Monteiro's *Hovering over the Water* (1986).

Bottom: In 1989's *Recollections of the Yellow House* Monteiro's on-screen alter ego João de Deus returns to haunt the streets of Lisbon in a sequence inspired by F.W. Murnau. In a piece published in 1966, Monteiro observes: "Nosferatu is the bearer of the plague, an epidemic fatality that invades and rots everything that is alive."

2. The de Deus cycle also includes two shorts—*Lettera Amorosa* (1995) and *A Walk with Johnny Guitar* (1996)—that are not discussed here for reasons to do with space rather than quality.

and sexual entanglements and the arrival of some of his unsavory former associates (Monteiro plays one).

Something like Pier Paolo Pasolini's *Teorema* (1968) reworked as a meditation on Euro-American relations, *Hovering* is a film of rueful romanticism, intoxicated by beauty and shot with the serene, muted coloration of a Piero della Francesca *fresco*. Hereafter, Monteiro's work would assume a decidedly less picturesque, urban focus, as exemplified in *The Last Dive* (1992)—commissioned as the "water" entry in a cycle of films about the elements—a nocturnal trawl through Lisbon's fleshpots. As the film opens, callow youth Samuel (Denis Gomes) contemplates the Tagus with a glint of suicide in his eye, his reverie interrupted by a middle-aged man, Eloi (Canto e Castro), a former sailor and now full-time debauchee who, diagnosing Samuel's intentions, drags the shy, sullen lad out for a final spree in the company of a trio of escorts—the girl reserved for Samuel is a mild-mannered blonde deaf mute Esperança (Fabienne Babe) who happens to be Eloi's own daughter.

The premise may suggest a racy odd-couple comedy—a Lusophone *The Last Detail* (1973) with a touch of incest for flavor—but Monteiro isn't interested in matters such as psychological nuance and character development that are the hallmarks of Hollywood humanism. The reasons for Samuel's despair are not spoken of any more than are those for the suicides in Bresson's films; nor is the revelation that lifts his despair articulated any more than the changes of heart in Murnau's *Sunrise* (1927) or Roberto Rossellini's *Journey to Italy* (1954). Monteiro's focus, as with that of these forebears, is on telling a simple story via modes of expression that are uniquely cinematic, on exploring and complicating the relationship between sound and image, specifically, and even, in the film's centerpiece, removing the aural element entirely. This occurs after the quintet sit for an outdoor entertainment: the ballerina Catarina Lourenço's "Dance of the Seven Veils," a 10-minute *pas des deux* with the moving camera, caught in a single take, accompanied by the music of Richard Strauss's *Salome*; following a cut to the old sailor's gawping daughter, the dance is then repeated down to the smallest gesture by Babe, who goes through her motions in total silence—the silence in which she would have witnessed the performance.

Unusual among his later films in its occasional employment of documentary-style handheld camera, *The Last Dive* functions as a vivid document of not just Lisbon's polluted port but a disappeared city further ashore: one can see the grimy old Mercado da Ribeira, since gussied up as a Time Out® market; the old Red Light District on Rua Nova do Carbalho, seen thronged with sailors on shore leave in *Sword?*, today sanitized into a tourist photo op; the streets of Alfama, packed for the annual celebration of the city's patron saint. It is here that Monteiro makes a cameo, hovering outside a public toilet occupied by Esperança, scampering in as she exits, pulling a wad of toilet paper from his blazer pocket. Viewers of *Recollections*, the film he'd made immediately before *The Last Dive*, might reasonably suppose that this furtive, rodentlike little man was up to something insalubrious.

4. PLAYING GOD

Monteiro has always been a palpable presence in his own films, at first as a disembodied voice, then as a recurring bit player; in addition to previously cited examples, he appears as a jabbering hermit and the leader of a trio of banditti in *Trails*, and as the King of Portugal in *Silvestre*. In the lean '80s, he also appeared in the films of others: opposite Fernando Rey, briefly, in João Mário Grilo's *A Estrangeira* (1982); at a poker table in Gil's first feature, *A True and Faithful Account* (1987), which he co-wrote. His most substantive role came in 1988's *Doc's Kingdom*, directed by American expat Robert Kramer, whom Monteiro met when Kramer and his associate Spinelli, future star of *Hovering*, arrived in Portugal to screen *Milestones* (1975). In *Doc's Kingdom*, Monteiro is taverner "João César," dispensing drinks to Paul McIsaac's ex-radical exile and advice to his estranged son, played by Vincent Gallo. This gradual escalation of in-front-of-the-camera activity culminated in Monteiro's star turn in *Recollections*, and it is this film and the two other features in which he plays the recurring character João de Deus—*God's Comedy* (1995) and *The Spousals of God* (1999)—that established Monteiro internationally, *Recollections* earning him the Silver Lion at the 46th Venice International Film Festival.[2]

João de Deus, per Monteiro, was imagined as "a free being… allowed to do practically anything," a desiccated sensualist obedient only to the law of desire. His aristocratic freedom does not come, however, with the security of the aristocracy. João, as he is introduced in *Recollections*, is a curious combination of ascetic and voluptuary, tramp and dandy, a shabbily dressed freelance journalist scraping by from gig to gig, spending solitary evenings in the austere chamber he occupies in a boarding house run by a performatively prim and proper de Freitas. The lone decoration on his room's otherwise bare walls is a poster depicting Erich von Stroheim as the mountebank Polish hussar in *Foolish Wives* (1922), an indicator of a luxuriantly perverse inner life beneath a drab exterior, as well as a penchant for dress-up that finds ample expression in the trilogy, which sees de Deus adopting the guises of officer, gentleman, revolutionary, and madman.

Monteiro's reluctant decision to play de Deus himself proved an inspired one for, as well as being a gifted physical comic—his signature move is disposing of cigarette butts with a deft side kick that sends them spinning off his heel—he is a compellingly odd screen presence. He speaks his lines with an almost funereal, deadpan solemnity. His chest is sunken, sallow; his limbs, dry kindling; his hands, long, elegant, and unusually active, given to gestures like those of a manic symphony conductor or a priest—the kind you'd warn your kids about—offering benediction. His monumental skull and bladelike, Beaky Buzzard nose appear to account for approximately half his body weight, and lend him a more than passing resemblance to Court Orlok, a matter played up late in *Recollections* when de Deus predatorily prowls a Lisbon wreathed in cobalt blue German expressionist fog.

Monteiro's scruffy on-screen alter ego has garnered comparison to Chaplin's Little Tramp, though de Deus is closer to Chaplin-the-man in his ephebophilic predilections, rarely reciprocated. In *Recollections*, these are directed at his landlord's daughter (Teresa Calado), whose sudsy bathwater he covertly quaffs, extracting an errant pubic hair with wonderment. In fact, more than any of the commonly suggested cinematic parallels, the on-screen persona developed by Monteiro recalls the spindly, fetish-fevered character of "R. Crumb" as seen in the American artist's comics, a compulsively masochistic self-exhibitionist always on the edge of mortal decay who makes no attempt to sugarcoat the misogyny that shades his worship of women. Unlike the Tramp, ageless under white pancake makeup, or even the eternally adolescent, capering Groucho, whom Monteiro recalls with his spectacles and schmear of moustache, João de Deus is distinctly middle-aged, beset by the decrepitude that seeps into a 50-year-old man's body after a lifetime of neglect: night shivers, sore gums, a persistent smoker's cough, a stiff leg, a mysterious nagging soreness in the testes... His comportment is modest, deferential, that of a man past the age of expectation, if not desire. Among the first lines we hear him speak, off-camera: "I shall be old soon. Then it will all be over."

And yet many adventures lie ahead for João de Deus, who finds himself on the street after an ungallant attempt at the target of his lust, and shortly thereafter a ward of the Miguel Bombarda Hospital—as seen in Reis's *Jaime*—where one of his fellow patients is none other than Cintra, reprising his character from *Dead Men's Shoes*. (The warp and weft of intertextual references in Monteiro only grows denser the deeper one travels into his filmography.) Exhorted on his release from lockup at the close of *Recollections* to "Go and give them work," João, at the opening of *God's Comedy*, appears to have followed this dictum, now semi-respectably employed as the neat-freak manager of the Paraíso do Gelado ice-cream shop whose owner (de Freitas, back in a new form) negotiates a merger with a French company while he devotes himself to his collection of pubes. Temptation, this time in the form of the daughter of a neighborhood butcher, again leads to a fall, and de Deus is back wallowing in penury at the beginning of *God's Wedding*, only to be elevated to the elite ranks of the superrich by a "messenger of God" (Cintra) wearing the uniform of a naval officer who gifts him a suitcase stuffed with American dollars. The contents are enough for our hero to buy himself the title of baron, a palace to match his newfound status, and a buxom baroness (Joana Azevedo) with whom he struggles to consummate his union before finally, perhaps inevitably, landing back in the clink, where Monteiro bids de Deus goodbye in a smutty parody of the final scene of Bresson's *Pickpocket* (1959).

Along with such highbrow references, Monteiro's God trilogy is united by a new, distinct approach to staging that includes the engineering of intricate sight gags. A proselytizer for Lewis and Tati back in '68, Monteiro, along with his Georgian friend Otar Iosseliani, was largely responsible for keeping the Tati tradition alive through the 1980s and '90s. In the first post-credits shot of *The Spousals of God*, running slightly over seven minutes, João arrives at a park bench, prepares himself a frugal repast of bread and sardines, disposes of it as inedible, chugs a beer, snatches a branch from one nearby tree, uses it to modestly shield himself as he micturates on the trunk of another, has his exchange with the messenger, engages in a celebratory jig, and then takes a look at the pay dirt—a scene-setting both elegantly simple and packed with filigreed detail. Later, sitting down to lunch with the cigar-chomping Mother Superior at a convent cafeteria, ectomorph Monteiro makes a sublime drawn-out gag of piling almost the entire contents of a massive steaming tray of smoked sausage stew onto his plate and then scarcely touching a morsel.

Their humor tied to the satisfaction of animal appetites and breaches of fusty decorum, the João de Deus films also draw on the popular tradition of 1930s Portuguese comedies of working-class life, offering pungent evocations of the tatty fringes of Lisbon, a city of florid-faced old men fingering greasy playing cards, market stalls manned by profane female fishmongers, and snack bars where laborers line up to bolt *pregos* on their breaks.

Monteiro's final film, *Come and Go* (2003), would have made the de Deus trilogy a tetralogy, following our antihero to Ethiopia, but Monteiro had been diagnosed with the cancer that would ultimately kill him before its shoot began in the summer of 2002 and so, by necessity, his filmmaking life ended where it had begun, in Lisbon. Monteiro's character here, João Vuvu, is a different animal from de Deus: a widower and father, neither prince nor pauper, not a rampaging sex pest but a courtly dirty old man, content to spend his days entertaining a parade of bemused women, riding the 100 bus to the Jardim do Príncipe Real, and awaiting his end in the shade of a Mexican cypress, the same one Cintra appears seated under in *Dead Men's Shoes*. Vuvu is not a Monteiro alter ego, exactly, though one is tempted to think he's a bit closer to his creator than de Deus is, and the knowledge of Monteiro's illness hangs over every moment that he is on-screen—outside of Derek Jarman's *Blue* (1993), what other film addresses eternity with such clarity? (Monteiro remained as churlish on the brink of death as he was in life: Vuvu is slowed, not by cancer, but by complications from being penetrated by a torpedo-sized strap-on.) Discussing the role played by Monteiro's "evanescent body" in his work, the director Fernando Lopes would posit, "He sacrificed himself to his cinema"—which makes *Come and Go* something like Monteiro-the-martyr's cinematic Stations of the Cross. Four-and-a-half months after its maker's death, the film had its Cannes premiere. He is risen!

5. SECOND TELLINGS AND LAST RITES

A ransacker of the storehouses of culture, Monteiro's practice was informed not only by cinema but by literature, painting, and music.[3] A statement Reis made in conversation with Monteiro, is borne out in the latter's corpus: "Cinema is an art that touches all the others, without being their sum." For all of his engagement with the full range of the arts, Monteiro knew cinema to be a sovereign state. One imagines that the man who said of his *Sophia de Mello Breyner Andresen* that it "represents above all the proof, to those who want to understand and accept it, that poetry can't be filmed" would find something suspect in the words "lyrical," "painterly," or "literate" when applied to a film, which, after all, can only succeed when being "cinematic." In his final years, the problems of the adaptation and reinterpretation of extant texts—by August Strindberg, by Robert Walser, and by Monteiro himself—comes increasingly to the fore, resulting in some of the most contentiously received works in a career that was hardly lacking for polemical dustups, as well as some of the richest.

Monteiro's interest in bifurcated narratives and counterposed reflections reaches an apotheosis in the confounding, coruscating *The Hips of J.W.* For its first half hour, the film limits its scene almost entirely to the atrium of a dilapidated building in which a libertine God (Monteiro), surrounded by lithe female angels, bickers with his brother, Lucifer (Hugues Quester), about how to manage their dominion of humankind. The applause of a heretofore unseen audience alerts us to the fact that we have been watching a play. The text, performed, as it was written, in French, is from the opening of Strindberg's 1897 *Inferno*; the stage directions—God, our absentee landlord, keeps popping off to exercise his privilege of *droit du seigneur* with his angels—are Monteiro's alone.

After the show, Quester's Jean de Dieu discovers a Portuguese man sleeping one off in the bowels of the makeshift theater; he's the dead ringer of the actor playing God, being none other than Monteiro, but insists he's in fact an old sea salt by the name of Henrique. After he holds court on his passion for John Wayne—the "J.W." of the title—what follows is something like a condensed auto-remake of *The Last Dive*, in which Jean confesses to suicidal

Top: "As it was in the beginning, is now, and forever shall be." 2003's *Come and Go*, João César Monteiro's posthumously released final film. The director/star sits in Lisbon's Jardim do Príncipe Real.

Bottom: One of a handful of images in Monteiro's scandalous *Snow White* (2000), depicting the dead body of the author of the source text, the Swiss writer Robert Walser, near the grounds of the Herisau asylum where he spent his final years. Manoel de Oliveira, to whom Monteiro had not always been kind as a critic, would be one of the film's most vocal defenders.

3. By the time of his death, João César Monteiro had amassed a personal library of more than 5,000 albums, and the soundtracks of his films give some clues to his predilections: grand opera, folk music from rural Portugal to Mali, Dimitri Tiomkin's score to *Rio Bravo* (1959), Karlheinz Stockhausen...

ideation, Henrique drags him out for a final bender and, after a night that includes Henrique relieving himself on a nightclub stage, he takes the plunge into the Tagus, leaving Jean among the living. De Dieu rejoins his troupe, including Pierre Clémenti and Azevedo, at a country manor, where they rehearse a new play that adds a mythical element to de Dieu's brush with the hoi polloi, with Clémenti—doing a spry Monteiro impression—taking on the role of the silver-tongued Henrique, vying with Quester's de Dieu for the favors of Azevedo's Ariane.

To summarize: the freely interpreted performance of a philosophical-religious dialogue, written by a psychically distraught Swede at the end of the 19th century, finds a distorted reflection in the nocturnal adventure of a bourgeoise Frenchman and a Portuguese in late 20th-century Lisbon, then is refracted and further distorted by a troupe of Franco-Portuguese actors in a tranquil environment of well-appointed comfort. Add a late appearance in *The Hips of J.W.* by João de Deus that further complicates all we've seen, and you have a dizzyingly complex work concerning the transmutation of art into lived experience, and vice versa, and the anomalies found in translation—for example, the anarchist Henrique's explanation for his idolization of Wayne, that lumbering hidebound conservative: "He was everybody's favorite target, the scapegoat who must be eliminated."

The last cinematic adaptation undertaken by Monteiro was the most controversial film of his career, initiating a national debate concerning public funds going to cinema subsidies. This was 2000's *Snow White*, a work that, for the great majority of its runtime, consists of black film leader—for audiences outside of Portugal, enlivened by subtitles—over which the Swiss German writer Walser's verse *dramolette*, made up of dialogues between Snow White, the Queen, the Prince, and the Huntsman, picking up *after* the familiar action of the story, is recited by actors. (As an admiring Walter Benjamin wrote in 1929, Walser's approach to popular fables is to "start where the fairy tale stops.")

Was this, as many commentators took it to be, an empty provocation, another middle finger from the aging punk? Contrary to a popular critical canard, almost no one goes through the trouble of making a film with the principal motive of irritating people; personal compulsions are far more compelling spurs, with any discomfort caused to those one dislikes a fringe benefit. The excising of sound from the dance in *The Last Dive* finds its dialectical counterpoint here, and there is evidence Monteiro had been toying with the idea of a "blank" film decades before *Snow White*. Monteiro, who had submitted a traditional shooting script for *Snow White* to the appropriate financing bodies, later stated he decided to scupper his plans after a reading, on the first day of production, from the Spaniard Francisco de Quevedo's satirical text *The Joys and Misfortunes of the Asshole*, which inspired him to make a film "from the perspective of the blind 'eye' which does not see."

Snow White was an immediate scandal, with news cameras present at its Lisbon premiere to capture predictably divisive reactions, as well as press Monteiro—the scapegoat who must be eliminated—for explanations. "What did you want? A telenovela?" responded the pugnacious director, before launching into a tirade against a state-subsidized television that "pays no service to the community." What about the critics? "The critics can go fuck themselves." And the public? "The Portuguese public can go fuck themselves." One only needs watch Monteiro's films to know this was an expression of profoundest affection.

BOOTH GIRLS

WORKING WOMEN IN CINEMA'S GLASS HOUSE OF DESIRE

BY ELENA GORFINKEL

PHOTOGRAPHS BY LANGDON CLAY

In Wayne Thiebaud's 1964 oil painting *Booth Girl*, an impassive woman stares ahead, encased in a freestanding, Deco-era movie ticket booth, its base a cornflower blue. The edges of her starched white uniform, with its mandarin collar, and of the stall itself, give off an electric, tubular hum of marquee neon lined by alternating colors, orange and fuchsia and garnet and lime. She is surrounded by an abstracting white space. Her posture is stiff and inanimate, her gaze direct but opaque. A yellow light emanating from the top rim of the booth casts a glow across her face. The painting gestures towards the generic, a study in clinical stillness—ground zero for fantasy, the tabula rasa of the empty movie screen. Fill in the blanks.

THE "BOOTH GIRL" was born along with the cinema. The theater's structural arrangement—street to frontage, lobby to screening room doors, screen to projection booth—inductively places her as the figurehead of the ship's bow. Her ceremonial location situates her as silent transactor of the spectator's hope for admission into cinema's palace. Through a flick of the wrist and other economical gestures, she deals her hand: swiftly counting cash; passing over a paper ticket stub, perhaps some change, to the moviegoer; securing smooth, frictionless entry into celluloid reverie.

THE BOOTH GIRL'S geniality and very existence has long been central to the cinema's consolidation as commodity. Early film industry magazines and exhibitor handbooks, such as a 1920 edition of *The Moving Picture World*, instruct that the ticket-booth worker must de facto be a young woman, "good looking," "clever and intelligent," "infused with the spirit of the institution," also, "cool, courteous and very rapid." A cinema management guide, published by a Chicago-based theater corporation in 1926, asserts that cashiers should "radiate and reflect the spirit of pleasure and welcome to our patrons" and "transmit to your patrons the refinement and graciousness of the feminine touch."

This "feminine" presence secures the street-level seductions of the dream factory. Film's spangled lure is communicated via the visage of the young woman, an open invitation to sample the delights therein. (It is perhaps notable that in the period Thiebaud painted his booth girl, his best-known paintings were enticing renderings of glazed ice cream sundaes and platters of pastel frosted cakes.)

Below the surface, though, the conflicting decadence and fraudulence of the culture industry lurk. The British-born, New York transplant Mina Loy's montage-evoking poem "On Third Avenue" (1942) summons some of these ambivalences:

> like a reliquary sedan chair
> out of a legend, dumped there,
>
> before a ten-cent Cinema,
>
> a sugar-coated box-office
> enjails a Goddess
> aglitter, in her runt of a tower,
> with ritual claustrophobia.

Loy hints at the multiplicity and power of the ticket booth girl: Goddess and captive, frosted confection in a plastic-sleeved box, at once shop window and diorama of what the cinema offers projected on the screen inside.

Writing from the vantage of the "girl in the glass house" in a film fan magazine in 1919, Helen G. Smith, a New York City–based theatre employee, laments that "when I climb daily into my glass caboose in front of the chief amusement center, I feel like the main

exhibit at the aquarium." The movie booth: at once cash nexus, and, as per Smith, "private as a goldfish bowl."

A DECADE LATER, Thiebaud's avatar-like box office worker reappears, in mimeographed black and white, on the cover of the 1973 double issue of *Women & Film*, one of the foundational second-wave feminist film journals. Stripped of the painter's candied palate, with its nostalgic chromas of postwar prosperity, this figure is more starkly defined. Is her dead-eyed stare less existentially ambiguous, and instead a clear cautionary tale, a mark of women's containment by cinema's grand architecture? Perhaps it is the shadow cast by feminist critiques of cinema as an apparatus of patriarchal norms. Enclosed in the structure of a multivalent system—a way of looking, a commercial industry, a product of unseen toil—the booth and its resident are reduced to metonyms of "the movies," *tout court*. Yet what of the booth girl's own unique status as laborer, spectator, subject?

A SUITE OF DISTINCT and distinctly stylish films made from the 1980s onwards maps these possibilities, tracing the booth girl outside of her box. They show her migration, tracking how, in the decades since Thiebaud's painting was completed, the movie theater where she is employed has become a porn movie theater—perhaps encapsulating a train of thought articulated by many critics, among them, Fredric Jameson, that, "the visual is essentially pornographic, which is to say that it has its end in rapt, mindless fascination"—and she has become an itinerant trickster of a sort. The porn booth girl is no longer contained, but slips away, infiltrating both the auditorium and the world beyond it. These films all play with the founding fantasy of the booth girl as a mediator of onscreen spectacle. But she is also a participant-observer, a phantom, and an undesignated guest.

Placed at the entrance of the porn theater, physically separate from but still closely associated with the flesh peddled onscreen, the porn booth girl is both surplus and cipher. To the (largely male) spectators who creep in from the street, magnetically drawn toward the moans echoing from within, she ostensibly functions as preview, sizzle more than steak. *Variety* (1983), Bette Gordon's feature debut, based on a screenplay by novelist Kathy Acker, is perhaps the most iconic depiction of the porn booth girl on-screen. Christine (Sandy McLeod) resigns herself to working in the ticket booth of the titular theater upon the suggestion of her friend Nan (photographer Nan Goldin): down on her luck, she needs to pay her rent. The Variety Photoplays, a real-life theater on Third Avenue that showed porn, soft- and hardcore, alongside grindhouse, B- and C-grade films in the 1960s and 1970s, fascinated Gordon. Though later immortalized by Samuel Delany in his 1999 book *Times Square Red, Times Square Blue* as a fertile domain of gay cruising, of oft-anonymous and intimate social contact, it is presented by Gordon as largely a straight porn house, at the heart of Times Square's then-robust red-light district. (The theater also appears in 1976's *Taxi Driver*, with the unimpressed concessions counter girl played by Diahnne Abbott.) Made at a time of heated feminist debate about sexual representation, including the Women Against Pornography movement's opposition to its place in public culture, Gordon sought to explore the porn theater as a fictive site for feminist curiosity and critique.

In the director's reimagining, Christine's occupation of the booth cracks open her own personal transformation. Seated in her glass house, an interior mirror placed in the corner of her workstation registers and reflects Christine's gaze, directing it inward as much as outward, magnifying the necessity of her visibility: viewer and viewed. She soon ventures out from behind the glass, an act that bestows her with the radiating potency of

a border crosser; even as she courts the dangers of subterranean spaces made for straight male pleasure, shuttling through peep shows, adult bookstores, and as far as Yankee Stadium—which offers another form of overdetermined, overlit spectatorship—she retains some kind of invisibility cloak. With the stealth of a spy, she pursues Louie (Richard M. Davidson), an enigmatic businessman and frequent visitor to the theater, who takes her on a date and just as quickly departs, possibly returning to a life of crime. Christine's *Vertigo*-like investigation of the mysterious object of her inchoate desire coincides with a process of self-eroticization. Becoming a Hitchcockian voyeur, she steps out of the booth and into her own noir movie, now the agent of her own fantastic mise en scène.

Of Christine's transfigurations, the most radical occurs at the level of language. Set against the candid, warm conversations that Christine engages in with other women at Nan's bar, where friends and workers from the area trade tales, a more exaggerated form of speech is used elsewhere as a striking counterpoint. When meeting with her square journalist boyfriend (Will Patton) at the diner for lunch, Christine abruptly breaks into a stilted, mechanical monologue. She enumerates explicit sex scenes with hypnotic detachment, as if they were florid descriptions of the porn films that she observes at work. Her flat recital ruptures the realist surface of Gordon's film, providing a more Brechtian enunciation that shows up the farce inherent to these pornographic scenes.

Less than the images that Christine glimpses, it is the sound emissions—the grunts, ohh's, and exhortations of "I'm coming!" that stream through the screening room doors—which rouse her curiosity. She listens, repetitively, to the obscene messages left by an anonymous caller. As she sinks deeper into her fantasy, she goes so far as to ring up Louie and extort a meeting from him, articulating aloud her desire for pursuit and control. Meanwhile, the visual field suggests something illusory, deceptive, exemplified in the film's ambiguous final shot of the empty street corner where Christine and Louie are supposed to meet, a site of uncertainty with shades of Antonioni's *L'Eclisse* (1962).

SURPASSING MUTE VOYEURISM, the booth girl in these films emerges as an agent of talk, gossip, yarns, and apocrypha. She trades in secreted, hidden knowledge, in pilfered longings. It is she who sees the porn theater patrons in the light, and they submit to being seen by her, a stranger witnessing their concealed yearnings.

One superb example: Marie-Claude Treilhou's *Simone Barbes or Virtue* (1980)—her first film, produced by Paul Vecchiali's company Diagonale, restored in 2022 and given a second life—which proposes, in place of a booth girl, a rangy usherette. This is not the introspective usherette of Edward Hopper's 1939 painting *New York Movie*, a detached onlooker absorbed in her own thoughts; nor the pious usherette of William Wyler's *The Good Fairy* (1935), a destitute teen waif who spins utopian yarns for fellow orphans, directing moviegoers to their proper entrance with the pointing of a large scimitar; nor the curmudgeonly, aged ticket-takers that one finds popping up throughout early cinema. Considerably more loquacious and world-weary, yet hungry for life, the titular Simone Barbes is played by Ingrid Bourgoin as a version of herself (she had been employed alongside Treilhou at the Pigalle porn cinema where the film was shot). She is a constantly gabbing, argumentative woman—as per Treilhou, "a perpetual fireworks display."

Simone and her co-worker (Martine Simonet) pass each shift in the faded amber-hued lobby of the former Cine-Vog Montparnasse cinema (revivified for the production). Between stints of directing customers between the three screening rooms, the pair

chat among themselves. Just as often they snap back at their demanding, twitchy patrons, with Simone serving up jaded, hilarious readings of each guest's faults, rebuffing their occasional misogyny or homophobia. When a loiterer lingers, Simone retorts, "You know this isn't a charity!" After deodorizing a "stink" in theater two with a spray air freshener, she gloats, "You could set them on fire, they wouldn't notice. Talk about concentration!" In the glaring light of the lobby, the sounds of canned fucking waft out each time the door opens, as the bored usherettes share a pâté sandwich or drink liqueur smuggled in by Simone from the bar next door. Above the women's heads hang sculptural wall neon, several sets of golden outlined eyes that function as quotation marks, satirizing the space. Extending this reflexivity, a pretentious Belgian porn director (film historian Noël Simsolo) comes to see his own film playing and later emerges bewailing the disgraceful projection of his art. With the arrival of ever more eccentric patrons, along with Simone's needling of her lovesick colleague, the flow of banter verges on slapstick.

After her shift ends, Simone wanders across Paris by night. Unlatched from her ritual location, the booth girl becomes a totemic agent, a newly asserted presence in terra incognita. Simone visits her waitress girlfriend at a cheekily mid-century lesbian nightclub where an alternate world opens up—another register of illicit spectacle, performance, hustle, sentiment, and grift, inflected by the convivial spirit of a 1930s hectic screwball comedy, home to a pair of female sword dancers, an all-woman cabaret band performing anachronistic belters, and louche guests.

In Simone's final passing encounter, she exits the club and is propositioned by an older man (*Cahiers du Cinéma* critic Michel Delahaye) from a car. She agrees to a ride, taking the wheel of his Volvo in what seems at first to be a pickup. Largely undisclosing, they look for a suitable end to the night as Simone opens up, tells him a riddle. As the melancholic "Sérénade Toscane" sung by Jacques Herbillon is heard, his face confesses tumultuous emotions. He weeps. Half of his false mustache peels off. Coupling foreclosed, this booth girl lassoes the doldrums of night. They careen into another shape, as street lights, nearing dawn, blink off.

"TAKE TEMPTATION OUT of Your Ticket Booth!" So crows a full-page advertisement for Caille Ticket Office's mechanical devices in *Moving Picture World*, 1916. In the image, a young woman is pulling the thread of a ticket-dispensing reel, while a small devil figure points his scepter at the roll. The advertised device automatically counts the number of tickets sold, promising to stamp out the enticement of theft from the wandering impulses and waning willpower of the booth girl. Even here her innocence and pliable naïveté yields to chanced deception when the gleam of cinematic lucre beckons.

MORE THAN HALF a century later, the ticket-taker who succumbs to this latent temptation is Chantal Akerman. In 1972, having premiered her first short film, *Saute ma ville*, at Oberhausen, she moved from Brussels to New York, and found work at the 55th Street Playhouse, an arthouse that also featured gay porn in the early days of gay liberation.[1] During a run of Fred Halsted's urban fisting trance film *LA Plays Itself* (1972), Akerman began

1. Several of New York's prominent gay porn cinemas were owned by the cigar-wielding lesbian producer and distributor Chelly Wilson, whose likeness seems to be homaged in the figure of an anonymous booth woman in Allan Moyle's 1980 teen runaway musical queer fantasia *Times Square*. One of Chelly's famed movie palaces features in Jack Deveau's 1978 orgiastic *A Night at the Adonis*, in which the real-life usherette, a young Black woman named Bertha, plays a self-reflexive bit part.

to pinch from the box office, giving only half of a ticket stub to each patron and thus effectively pocketing half the takings. She swiped $4,000 for the making of her films *La Chambre* and *Hotel Monterey* (both 1972)—sublime studies of place, self, and duration—until being let go three weeks later.

She describes the job in the book *Autoportrait en cinéaste* (2004), reflecting on the moment she realized her sudden secret fortune:

> That day I had the idea of filming the hands of every man who bought a ticket for the cinema between noon and seven in the evening. I thought it might make an interesting film. And then I thought about it some more and decided that it wasn't a very good idea after all.

IN JACQUES NOLOT'S *Porn Theatre* (2002), the second feature from the actor/director and Roland Barthes's former lover, the booth girl becomes a mature woman (Vittoria Scognamiglio), an unnamed bisexual bachelorette who raspily voices a grizzled philosophy of life lived in adherence to one's own predilections, holding court from her booth. She is analyst and interlocutor of the denizens of this waning porn palace in its last days—the site itself a since-shuttered porn theater also in the Pigalle district, Le Mery, on the Place de Clichy. Her open booth is positioned in the corner of the cinema lobby, a space that also briefly harbors junkies and pigeons, and through which sauntering trans sex workers, drag queens, and genderfuckers come and go, descending the stairs to the single screening room, alongside men seeking an eyeful, a blow job, or simply a nap.

The booth woman sips whiskey, providing a choral commentary on a dog-eared life of erotic experience, of male and female lovers, estranged, dead, and departed, while encouraging the doting young projectionist to sexually experiment, to avoid any future regrets about not having tried everything once. They are joined at their makeshift bar by a regular, an unnamed 50-year-old man (Nolot himself) who has survived decades of living with HIV, and of seeing lovers and friends pass, visiting the porn cinema armed with a wad of cash, wearing a fake wedding ring to reassure the closeted men among his liaisons. He reads aloud a prose poem that he composed, reflecting on time's passing and life's frailties. Eventually, a threesome peeks into view.

Porn Theatre quietly reveres the sexy booth woman, who is openly desired by the projectionist. (A compelling inversion of this form of pitching woo is found in Tsai Ming-liang's 2003 melancholic drama *Goodbye, Dragon Inn*, in which booth girl Chen Shiang-chyi yearns, unrequited, for Lee Kang-sheng's elusive projectionist at the Fu-Ho Grand; she leaves him the anonymous gift of a hot sweet bun during the Taipei theater's final screening, after which they likely never meet again.) In Nolot's film, the transformation of the booth girl from silent ornament to his madam-like sparkling conversationalist extends through to the implied protection that her presence offers to the trans women who wander, work, and exultantly fashion themselves in the cloistered space of the porn theater.

Even as the films glimpsed on the Le Mery screen are straight porn titles, the explicitly gay male and nonbinary queerness of the sex acts in the aisles and vestibules of the cinema defuses and diffuses, centrifugally. This different sense of pleasure in looking, yoked to activities of gay cruising and sex work, is paralleled by the booth woman's spirited storytelling. In the screening room, several trans women carve out the space and make it theirs, offering themselves up, as if sacrificially,

for the taking. One woman disrobes demonstratively, changing from her femme street clothes to lingerie, marking a shift from lounge to bedroom, all while standing up amid the shaggy cinema seats, visible to the shadowed men who soon engulf her. Another regal queen in a gold dress places herself at the nexus of many gazes as she walks in front of the screen on which cis hetero bodies ecstatically grind on, a halo or penumbra that provides cover for all that takes place here in the dark.

IN DELANY'S BOOK on Times Square, he recounts an invitation he makes to his inquisitive friend Ana, to visit a porn theater with him and observe his routine. Occasionally propositioned by men, she adjusts her eyes to dimly lit rows and balconies. She finds her footing mostly by watching the cruising patrons, but her exploration momentarily extends to touch. During a pause, Ana reaches in, as do other onlookers, to briefly grasp a leather-clad man's cock—who has been fucking and getting fucked by Delany. (The leather man frowns when he realizes the hand is a woman's.) She succumbs to the lure of the porn theater as ground for social and sexual contact, a feeling in the dark.

The remembered detail of Ana's act of touch chimes with Delany's later claim that in another world the porn theater, as erotic site of both spectatorship and embodied practice, should and could be used and made available to all. "What waits is for enough women to consider such venues as a locus of possible pleasure." This waiting world is one that these films, however gingerly, peer into.

DOES THIS IMAGINED woman, given entrée to roam in the space of the porn theater, exemplify the ultimate queer feminist fantasy? The booth girl seems to chase a dream of relative anonymity, tacit invisibility, femme voyeurism, and cruisy solidarity, indulgences taken in the impure sociality of sex and cinema, of all that exceeds what happens on-screen, in the glowing rectangle held aloft. These films, staged to take place in once-active porn cinemas, foreground their near-extinct habits, summoning the specters of an urban unconscious of lust that is sedimented in the crevices of its walls and the shadows of its flickering images. Today, ticket sellers or booth girls are disappearing from cinemas; in many multiplexes around the world, they have been rendered obsolete, replaced by a lifeless, silent touch-screen machine.

AKERMAN'S PORN BOOTH girl film documenting the daily parade of male hands purchasing theater tickets was never made. What would it have looked like? Would it have resembled the images of banknotes and hands beyond agency in Bresson's *L'Argent* (1983) and its indictment of capitalism, or would it have been something more messy, surreptitious, vulnerable? Akerman, a lesbian, furtively observing the hands of incipiently gay men buying access to a heterotopia, an ephemeral world nested within another. Hands as erotic implements, scenes of disclosure, absent touch, micro-confessional. Hands bear and hold as much anonymity as cocks.

In *Porn Theatre*, Sconamiglio does in fact reach for and grasp multiple patron's hands on the edge of her booth. She is unafraid to make memory in the flesh. Imparting her lifetime of amorous knowledge with various past lovers to her trainee-in-waiting, the pink-faced projectionist, she divulges: "I couldn't bring myself to steal in those days. So I stole feelings instead."

The purest, most apposite looter of the picture palace, the booth girl in these films ultimately asks: what pleasures are there for the taking, ready to be seized, and what pleasures are meant to be stolen?

ENTHUSIASMS: GARY INDIANA

Films cherished by the late novelist, essayist, playwright, and actor, as described by Indiana and friends.

Words by
Gary Indiana
and Friends

Photograph by
Ulrike Ottinger

Lending an ear, Montréal, Canada, November, 1982. Gary Indiana was meeting up with Ulrike Ottinger and star Magdalena Montezuma, in town for a screening of their *Freak Orlando* (1981) at the 11th edition of the Festival du nouveau cinéma.

When Gary Indiana died last October, aged 74, we lost one of our finest advocates for cinema. It wasn't just his inimitable way with words. Reading him, you understood that the stakes were real: nothing less than a world being terrifyingly and depressingly remade around him by corporate overlords (a perspective increasingly absent from cultural criticism). Yet Indiana also understood, per his words, that "the most troublesome illusion about art is the popular belief that 'real' art is heavy, ponderous, and boring." Three years ago, he had presented a series of films at Metrograph—films that he loved, or that were on his mind. His initial longlist encompassed 10 titles: Billy Wilder's *A Foreign Affair* (1948), Georges Franju's *Head Against the Wall* (1959), Luis Buñuel's *The Young One* (1960), Bryan Forbes's *Séance on a Wet Afternoon* (1964), Louis Malle's *Lacombe, Lucien* (1974), Mike Hodges's *Black Rainbow* (1989), Claire Denis's *I Can't Sleep* (1994), Jacques Nolot's *Before I Forget* (2007), Tom Shankland's *The Killing Gene* (2007), and Mati Diop's *Atlantics* (2019). It's a glimpse into his interests at the time: grief, murder, insanity, visitors from the afterlife. But this genre-hopping selection also speaks to Indiana's diverse tastes, his disdain for fads, and his all-in devotion to the art and people he deemed worthy, i.e., the qualities that made him such an original critic.

Alongside his novels, plays, and art essays, he covered cinema for *The Village Voice*, *Artforum*, and *East Village Eye*, and wrote two standout BFI Film Classics monographs, on *Salò, or the 120 Days of Sodom* (1975) and *Viridiana* (1961). He also acted, appearing in films on both sides of the Atlantic—for directors belonging to the New York underground such as Michel Auder and Jackie Raynal, as well as for German arthouse stars Christoph Schlingensief, Dieter Schidor (whose cursed 1985 production *Kalt in Kolumbien* would become the source material for Indiana's novel *Gone Tomorrow*), and Ulrike Ottinger, who here shares her portrait of Indiana carousing ahead of a festival screening.

Extending this spirit, we have selected three excerpts from Indiana's criticism: on the films of Andy Warhol (which Indiana favored over Warhol's paintings, writing that one of the *Maos* "reminded me of a gold American Express card being brandished at Zabar's to pay for three bagels"); the operatic, ennui-drenched *La Paloma* (1974), starring Indiana muse Ingrid Caven; and *The Garbage, the City and Death*, the controversial play by Indiana's art hero Rainer Werner Fassbinder, later adapted to screen as *Shadow of Angels* (1976, also by Swiss director Daniel Schmid). These texts are followed by a series of recollections by Indiana's friends, describing some of the films that he so memorably recommended to them.

GARY INDIANA

Bike Boy
Andy Warhol
1964

One of the most liberating experiences of my life was seeing *Bike Boy* at a theater in Cambridge. I was with some ultrastraight but sensitive, tolerant Harvard boys who froze in horror after the first two minutes. Viva was in a bathtub with a man, telling him if he wanted to make plastic sculptures he should just do it and shut up about it. "We're into other things, now," she whined. As I watched this film I thought: "That's for me."

It's bizarre that Warhol's films have been out of circulation for so long. Or perhaps not so bizarre. When Warhol said, in his last interview, that the films "are better talked about than seen," it occurred to me that a certain crust of the haute monde might have been less welcoming to Andy if it had been exposed to his movies. Which, I believe, compose his richest body of work. Who will ever forget Ondine, with his face buried in Joe Dallesandro's underpants, in *Loves of Ondine*? Or Ingrid Superstar's recipe recitation in *Bike Boy*? The draft dodger's soliloquy, or Viva's epic monologue, in *Nude Restaurant*? Taylor Mead scampering about in *Lonesome Cowboys*: "Oh you jingle, and you jangle, but you seldom wrangle..." I haven't seen those films in 20 years, and I remember every frame. I've already forgotten *E.T.*

Warhol's films are gloriously erotic, as sculpture is erotic. They're honest. Pornography—which every American should enjoy at least as much as having Edwin Meese for an attorney general—is dishonest. Perfect faces on perfect bodies do not blissfully couple without any problems, in real life; they only do that in California. When Ondine's about to get into Little Joe's BVDs, the bathroom door flies open and in walks Brigid Polk, demanding to know what that cheap little hustler is doing with her husband. Sexual pleasure is immanent in the Warhol movies, a possibility; but pornographic fulfillment is always shown as a deluded ambition. Real people are too complicated.

La Paloma
Daniel Schmid
1974

I like Daniel Schmid's idea that we are all private radio stations transmitting on our own frequencies, sometimes audible to each other, sometimes not. Personally, few blue-ribbon cultural products occupy my consciousness with anything like the force of my own imagination or experience, and those that do, like *La Paloma*, seldom belong to the upper reaches of any established canon. I am indifferent to any argument that a "greater" work should affect me more profoundly, or that there exists a legitimate authority to declare one thing "major" and another "minor." In the end we have only our experiences and we feel them with the particularity of monadic creatures. Why this film and not another? The intense perfection of its metaphor, possibly; something gorgeous in its refusal to coalesce around a conclusion that is less than hallucinatory; the sublimity of Ingrid Caven, whose voice and persona have always evoked for me the most sardonic and melancholy reflections.

Romance involves us in abjection and absurdity. Beyond a point we have no choice about it. We do violence to ourselves by pursuing it and equal violence by squashing our feelings. It's a souvenir of the last century, and not the worst one. The protagonist of *La Paloma* is a dull man who becomes interesting through his infatuation. For one moment in his life he is truly alive. I can't answer the question of whether his fixation is "worth it," and because I can't answer it, *La Paloma* continues to haunt me as the paradigm of certain disappointments.

Garbage, The City and Death
Rainer Werner Fassbinder
1976

Not a week has passed since his death that I haven't wished Rainer Werner Fassbinder were still alive. If he had moved to New York, as he sometimes planned to, I'm almost certain he would have made movies about artists, art, money, and real estate, movies about careerist hustlers and flim-flam promotion men dolled up as critics and dealers, movies about cash flow as the source of aesthetics, and everything else, in our patriotic time. Alongside *An Early Frost*, we might have had a speculative fiction in the manner of *The Third Generation*, about how a major chemical company invented AIDS for germ warfare purposes, and how a biological experiment got out of control, and the means by which the resulting havoc came to be blamed on the most despised minority groups; yes, Fassbinder could have managed a fiction like that quite convincingly, and perhaps uncovered an interesting notion: if the right wing didn't invent AIDS. It might as well have, since it works so well as an instrument of state policy.

Fassbinder understood the modern world in the least deluded terms available. He showed how capitalism organizes all human beings into victims and exploiters, prostitutes and pimps; he saw the historical mechanisms in which victims become empowered by the guilt of their oppressors to victimize others in their turn. This is a central theme of *Garbage, The City and Death*, a play that was banned in Frankfurt 10 years ago and is now being banned again, for alleged anti-Semitism. (One of the two sympathetic characters in the play is called "A Rich Jew.") The most vociferous allegations come from Joachim Fest, editor of the *Frankfurter Allgemeine Zeitung* and, ironically enough, author of the only exhaustive study of Hitler that barely mentions the Final Solution.

Certainly Fassbinder intended to provoke people with his naming of characters in this work, but the internal properties of the characters play against their surface "identities." The tallest character is always called "The Dwarf"; the former concentration-camp exterminator, Herr Müller—instead of going to South America with money from the American CIA like Klaus Barbie—gets up in drag every night and sings in a nightclub. The city of *Garbage, The City and Death* is run by gangsters who carve up the town into zones of real estate speculation, preying on the underclass that serves their libidinal cravings. On the surface, social problems have been solved, because everything has been rationalized. Everyone knows his place; the scum on the bottom will be destroyed, the scum on the top will profit. Fassbinder's play anticipated the Reagan '80s. It paints a world where no one needs to talk anymore because everyone feels the same fear, and even this fear has been turned into merchandise. *Garbage, The City and Death* should not be banned to placate a hypocritical "morality."

JANIQUE VIGIER

Dark Victory
Edmund Goulding
1939

Bette Davis, when asked why she smoked, is said to have answered, "Darling, if I didn't smoke, I wouldn't have had a career." In his 2003 novel *Do Everything in the Dark*, Gary gives that line to one of his characters—not his alter ego Miles, though Miles might well have said it. Gary often said it himself. Davis appears only in that novel, but all of his work partook of her, as it did of personae, stagecraft, illusions, schemes, vedettes, fatalism. In the stark, sentimental melodrama *Dark Victory*, Davis plays Judith Traherne, a vain socialite who lives for her horses and her parties. She's young and she's received a bad prognosis; she knows how the whole thing is going to turn out. She lights up constantly and holds her cigarettes low, deep in her fingers. A lesson in poise. Gary liked watching Davis smoke as much as he liked a cigarette.

BRUCE HAINLEY

The Boy Friend
Ken Russell
1971

Why was this movie Gary's *favorite thing in the world?* Backstage downtime and preening, or the onstage shenanigans? Knowing musical phantasmagoria and kaleidoscopic tutelage? Purposeful lapses in accents? Rapid shifts from backwater "let's-put-on-a-show" theater to swooning cinematic extravaganza? Ridiculous fawning over a scouting Hollywood director named De Thrill? Tap-dancing Tommy Tune, decked out in raccoon, then a loony cut to chorus girls in negligees beckoning from a thick bramble of his coat's fur, the sexiest mites in the world? Glenda Jackson on crutches, a reality effect with glycerin tears? *Vo-de-o, vo-de-o, vo-de-o*? Or maybe just Twiggy, at first an unsure understudy, finally glowing as the harlequin Pierrette; her voice tentative, then, as Gary's friend Jean-Jacques Schuhl admired, "Clinical. Icy irony of the music of Wolfgang Amadeus Mozart coming from another room quite far away"?

CHRISTIAN LORENTZEN

Nada
Claude Chabrol
1974

As he told the Athens-based magazine *Polar* in 2020, Gary first encountered the work of the French novelist and screenwriter Jean-Patrick Manchette, who would become one of his favorite authors, at a festival of experimental shorts in Cambridge, Massachusetts, in 1968, when he was 17 and saw *Le Socrate* (1968), directed by Robert Lapoujade from a screenplay by Lapoujade, Manchette, and Colette Audry. *Nada* was the first of Manchette's novels to be adapted as a feature, and one of the few of those adaptations that Gary rated. "Chabrol's film of *Nada* shows a smart grasp of what Manchette was up to—his books are meant to be fun, absurdist romps with serious implications, not humorless political tracts," Gary said. The story of a gang of disillusioned leftists who kidnap an American ambassador named Poindexter from a Paris brothel (on Rue Manchette) and take him to an abandoned mansion in the countryside only to be massacred by an overwhelming detachment of Interior Ministry goons, *Nada* is a parable of revolutionary impotence in the face of state savagery. Contrast one of the gang killing a cop with a slingshot that makes a bullseye of his forehead as they escape the brothel with the gratuitous bloodbath of the climactic mansion raid: the cartoonish gore brightens the moral imbalance. Like Manchette in his novels, and indeed Gary himself, Chabrol somehow keeps up a light touch as everybody goes down.

MATTHEW FOLDEN

Color Me Kubrick
Brian W. Cook
2005

As Bruce Hainley noted in a steady-handed obituary for Gary, published by *Texte Zur Kunst*, "When he was feeling blue, he often watched *Color Me Kubrick*."

Joe Spencer and Viva in Andy Warhol's *Bike Boy* (1964). Gary counted catching a screening of the film in Cambridge, Massachusetts, as "one of the most liberating experiences of my life."

Drum majorette-styled dancers tap their little hearts out on the stripes of the red, white, and blue in a Busby Berkeley–inspired sequence from Ken Russell's austere, understated *The Boy Friend* (1971).

Cook's film is an excellent entry in the canon of con-man cinema, with John Malkovich pumping ample juice into his characterization of real-life swindler Alan Conway. While perhaps not an antidote, the film's gallivanting mood pairs well with the blues. When Gary programmed his series of films for us at Metrograph in 2022, his initial selection, ultimately whittled down to four, did not include *Color Me Kubrick*. Maybe having a new book out had kept him in good spirits. Maybe he just forgot to include it. A few months afterwards, and periodically over the following two and a half years, Gary cajoled me to try and organize a screening of *Color Me Kubrick*. Maybe the initial omission, or a million other things, had gotten him down. The last time he requested it, I noticed he didn't cajole quite as heartily, having gotten distracted, mid-sentence, by the cute boy beside me. Seems he had a couple ways to deal with the blues. I wish that we'd had a copy of *Color Me Kubrick* always available in the projection booth (along with a cute boy), ready to be screened for Gary at any time. We owed him at least that much.

SAM MCKINNISS

O Lucky Man!
Lindsay Anderson
1973

O Lucky Man! is a modern English picaresque co-written by and starring Malcolm McDowell. It appears in the tradition of William Hogarth's *A Rake's Progress*, the 18th-century painting series depicting the decline of a profligate. Swap Hogarth for Victor Vasarely as set dressing, then cross it with *Sympathy for the Devil* (1968), since the narrative action periodically cuts to scenes of former Animals keyboardist Alan Price singing and playing the film's original soundtrack with his band in a London recording studio, à la Godard and the Stones. Gary relished all things Hogarthian, so he liked this very funny, three-hour-long movie. We watched it together on DVD one afternoon several years ago at his place, a happy memory. It helps that '70s-era McDowell was such an enticer. Lovely Helen Mirren also stars. We follow their vicissitudes through luck and misfortune, played for laughs under capitalism despite all its pitiful cruelty. Quoth Price: "Poor people are poor people and they don't understand."

HEDI EL KHOLTI

That Old Dream That Moves / Nobody's Hero
Alain Guiraudie
2001 / 2022

I go through emails you sent me over the years. It's like a rabbit hole. TikTok videos, YouTube links, streaming recommendations... I find gems about Jacques Nolot's *Before I Forget* (2007), and Bertrand Bonello's *Nocturama* (2016)... About *Tár* (2022) and Ryan Murphy you write: "hilariously awful" and "grotesquely bad," that:

> even negative reviews of either thing seem oblivious to the blatant intellectual and sociological dishonesty embedded in them, their totally false representations of human beings, and revealing the true ugliness of these things would be beyond the pale for most publications, which just grade them on their reviewers' notions of consumability. Cate Blanchett has finally become unbearable...

I find movie dates we made: *I Am Not Your Negro* (2016), *Parasite* (2019)... I suddenly remember when you left Maurice Pialat's *Under the Sun of Satan* (1987) at the Royal in West LA to smoke a cigarette and missed my favorite scene: the nighttime walk with the alarmingly average-looking devil, played by Jean-Christophe Bouvet. When you stayed at my house, we got into the habit of watching a movie every night. I remember we watched *Arrival* (2016) after smoking a joint and you kept laughing, with that infectious laugh of yours, and called the spaceship "the giant turd in the sky," and it kind of did look like one. We also watched *Miracle Mile* (1988), which I hadn't seen since it had come out. I have a soft spot for it, LA in the '80s, before I moved here: the performances, the inventiveness, the nihilism. You had never seen the movie, and loved it.

I find an email from 2014, after the Hammer Museum honored both Barbara Kruger and Quentin Tarantino. You write:

> I've actually always hated Tarantino. Really hated him. ... I don't have any interest at all in any of the movies showing now. The directors who are working steadily these days repulse me, even ones that started off good like David O. Russell or P.T. Anderson. They were never on the same level as Buñuel, Fassbinder, etc., etc., never struck me as having any compelling vision if that's the word, I also hate Scorsese and his ilk... on the flight from Havana to Toronto they had a nauseating menu of movies, I watched a half hour of *Bridge of Spies* because everything else looked even worse—and was reminded that Spielberg is the worst of all of them, everything he does is just a pile of sugar-coated crap.

The notion of a filmmaker with a "compelling vision" makes me think of our shared enthusiasm for Alain Guiraudie. We watched Guiraudie's *That Old Dream That Moves* around 2015. It never properly came out in

Malcolm McDowell as "Mick" Travis, a clueless Candide bouncing about "postcolonial" late 1960s and '70s Britain, runs for cover in Lindsay Anderson's 1973 opus *O Lucky Man!*

the US but I had a bootleg. You were blown away. The way the film tracks the delicate flux of libidinal energy between working-class bodies—middle-aged men who suffered the indignities of hard physical labor—at their post, or in the shower room of a soon-to-be-decommissioned factory. The way Guiraudie sets the film in a naturalistic socioeconomic reality without ever burdening it with some predetermined sociological agenda. You bought every available DVD on Amazon of his films. We talked about them on the phone and you told me to watch Fassbinder's *Eight Hours Don't Make a Day* (1972).

A year later when I decided to publish Guiraudie's first novel, *Now the Night Begins*, I sent you the translation, which you read right away. You were enthralled by the prose, the pacing, the pure mischief of it, and offered to blurb it. You wrote something great:

> The genial perversity of Alain Guiraudie's *Now the Night Begins* is something rare and fascinatingly energized, a metaphysical and moral slapstick that points to the arbitrariness of all authority and the fluidity of all desires. In its way, the most elegant, certainly the most hilarious brief for anarchy that anyone has written in a long time.

The novel came out but sadly did not attract much attention. It didn't help that Guiraudie didn't want the cover to have any connection to his most well-known film, *Stranger by the Lake* (2013), which shares some of the plot, settings, and characters of the novel, though produces a vastly different outcome. We settled on a really great painting by Paul Klee that Guiraudie loved. On the phone I relayed to you the plot of *Rabalaïre*, Guiraudie's 1,040-page second novel, and translated some passages on the spot. I lamented the fact that I couldn't publish it—it would be too expensive to translate even if someone would take it on. On your trip back from Mexico last year we watched his last film, *Nobody's Hero*, and we both were in awe of it.

I learn that Guiraudie's new movie, *Misericordia* (2024), is playing at the Nuart on the Westside. He's doing a Q&A and invites me to the screening, so we can finally meet. The traffic is bad and I'm feeling pretty anxious but I don't know why. I used to see movies at the Nuart all the time when I lived in the neighborhood. When did I last go? Maybe *Enter the Void* (2009)? The theater has been renovated since and they serve wine now. Sadly the screening is not sold out. It would have probably done better on the Eastside where most of the audience lives. Guiraudie says great things in the Q&A. He says the film is personal, and speaks about the crushes we have on our friends' parents when we're young. I remember some of mine. When it's over we talk for a while in the lobby and it's pleasant. I surprise him by asking him to sign my copy of *Now the Night Begins*. On the way home, I'm still anxious, I don't know why, and then register your absence.

A visit to the custodians of the cult filmmaker Paul Morrissey's archives.

Written by
Michael M. Bilandic

Studio Photographs by
Aaron Cheung

Interior Photographs by
David La Spina/Esto

Paul Morrissey in bed, a piece of furniture to be used for sleeping and nothing else. A character in his unproduced *Baby Street* might be speaking for his creator, who disapproved of non-procreative monkey business: "If you can't have sex in a normal way you shouldn't do it at all!"

Despite his permanent status in the court of underground film royalty, it's not always easy to be a devout Paul Morrissey disciple. These days, the director's name is too frequently met with confusion, misinformation, or, worst of all, silence. I was recently pontificating on his greatness to a Zoomer actress, opining as to why I so admire Morrissey's body of work, an assortment of formally wild provocations and radical humanist satires, when I realized—too late—that the whole time she had thought I was talking about the *musician* Morrissey. I guess it's a fair mix-up, considering both Morrisseys are known for their Irish Catholic upbringing, snarky wit, ambiguous sexuality, and often unpopular politics. The cover of the debut Smiths record from 1984 even features a still of a shirtless Joe Dallesandro from Paul Morrissey's first solo directorial feature, *Flesh* (1968). Not long after that conversational debacle, I found myself chatting with a much older, blue-chip visual artist who told me with utter confidence that Morrissey-the-singer named himself after Morrissey-the-filmmaker as an homage to his favorite director. This is clearly ridiculous as The Smiths' frontman was literally born Steven Patrick Morrissey.

Nowhere is the confusion regarding Paul Morrissey's work and legacy greater than when the name Andy Warhol comes up. The legendary Pop artist had ensconced himself in New York's avant-garde film scene by the mid-1960s with epics like *Sleep* (1964) and *Empire* (1965)—*Sleep* being five hours of footage of the poet John Giorno sleeping; *Empire* being an eight-hour static shot of the Empire State Building. It was later in 1965 that Morrissey entered Warhol's inner sanctum and started collaborating on the films, adding new layers of narrative and humor (often to the annoyance of the experimental old guard).

Morrissey quickly became a co-director on game changers like *My Hustler* (1965), *Chelsea Girls* (1966), and *Lonesome Cowboys* (1968), the last a low-budget burlesque Western centered on five gay cowboys. Not only did these films represent a moment where the underground broke out into the artistic semi-mainstream, but they debuted a whole new set of larger-than-life personalities: the Superstars. Inspired by the classical Hollywood star system of the '30s and '40s, Warhol and Morrissey launched the careers of their eccentric, stylish friends: Viva, Holly Woodlawn, Candy Darling, Ondine, Taylor Mead, Edie Sedgwick, Gerard Malanga, and countless others. These brilliant but ramshackle films—frequently indulging in libertine sexuality and amphetamine-fueled soliloquies on all manner of topics—don't have title cards, which has led many to assume that Warhol was the lone artistic force behind them. To further complicate Morrissey's already unclear role in this edgy world, the strait-laced workaholic additionally took on the responsibility of overseeing day-to-day operations at The Factory, co-founded *Interview Magazine*, and managed both the singer Nico and the Velvet Underground. No one job title encompasses Morrissey's frenzied activity in this period; his fingerprints are all over countless era-defining creations.

In 1968, Warhol was shot by *SCUM Manifesto* author Valerie Solanas in a failed assassination attempt. While Warhol was convalescing, Morrissey took firm control of the filmmaking ventures at The Factory and immediately directed *Flesh*, which he followed up with *Trash* (1970) and *Heat* (1972). These three films established the brooding, hunky Dallesandro as a leading man, raked in money, and played at venues uptown, downtown, and all around the world, even at Cannes. But the films were still produced by Warhol, a far bigger celebrity; his name was placed on the promotional materials in gigantic letters with Morrissey's tucked below. This trend continued when Morrissey directed *Flesh for Frankenstein* (1973) and *Blood for Dracula* (1974), a pair of gory camp variations on the classic monster tales starring a young Udo Kier. These films were frequently shown as *Andy Warhol's Frankenstein* and *Andy Warhol's Dracula*. It's an uncomfortable truth that when most people think of Warhol movies, they're just as often actually thinking of Morrissey movies. Even though he went on to direct seven more feature films on his own over the following decades—including a remarkable trilogy of gritty New York portraits: *Forty Deuce* (1982), *Mixed Blood* (1984), and *Spike of Bensonhurst* (1988)—this constant association and entanglement became a source of growing anxiety for Morrissey. He felt like he was being erased from his own life story.

Born in Manhattan in 1938, Morrissey's biography is a wild ride of contradictions. In a milieu overflowing with sex, drugs, and rock 'n' roll, Morrissey remained an openly reactionary conservative—castigating the lifestyles portrayed in many of his films while still approaching his subjects with an abundance of humor and empathy. He was too "normal" to assimilate into the hedonism-worshipping art world of the '60s yet far too outré for mainstream Hollywood. He never fit into any specific movement, and proudly saw himself as too independent to be lumped in with so-called independent filmmakers. This division only intensified after a bad accident in 2009 and continued through to his death last October. So when I was offered a chance to sift through his (largely unseen) personal archive, my jaw dropped. Would it be possible to finally connect the dots and tell a version of Morrissey's life based on fact over speculation? Could this shadowy figure come any closer into focus?

I showed up at Morrissey's Upper East Side home on a windy January afternoon. Though he had passed away a few months earlier, his apartment remained largely unchanged. Only a block from The Metropolitan Museum of Art, the prewar residence is its own museum of sorts, with every square inch occupied by ceramics, romantic Turner-esque seascapes, and glamour shots of Old Hollywood starlets. There was nothing modern to see here, and certainly no Warhols on the wall. It was like entering a world free from the debased hand of contemporary culture—or at least that's how Morrissey might have described it.

I was greeted at the door by Morrissey's niece, Marisa Crawford, who tended to the ailing filmmaker in his later years, and runs his film trust. In 2023, she brought on board the archivist Michael Chaiken to help carefully catalog Morrissey's artifacts and make sense of it all. (Chaiken has previously worked on the archives of Norman Mailer, the Maysles Brothers, Isabella Rossellini, and Bob Dylan.) We sat down at a dining table scattered with original scripts, film negatives, and assorted memorabilia. I tried to play it cool—despite being only a few feet from Dallesandro's ponytail, which had been discovered in an envelope, and Nico's original handwritten lyrics for her 1968 album *The Marble Index*. Together, we perused this secret history of underground culture and chronicled some of Morrissey's fascinating career.

MICHEAL M. BILANDIC: Marisa, when did you figure out that your uncle was not just your mother's younger brother but a legendary filmmaker at the vanguard of New York City bohemia?

MARISA CRAWFORD: Well, the white dog from *Trash*, Caesar, became our family pet, and I knew that he was from Paul's movie. My mother was very close to Paul. Even though she was raising a family in Highland Park, New Jersey, she would often go to New York and take us along. Paul had a house on East Sixth Street. Joe Dallesandro was living there with his wife and baby.

MMB: As a toddler, you were essentially crossing the most coveted velvet rope in town to schmooze with the Warhol Superstars.

CRAWFORD: People like Nico, I didn't see them as weirdos, I just thought we had a beautiful life. But Paul was protective of us. He had this group of friends he was so tolerant of—but, at the same time, we weren't allowed to have sugar or listen to what he called "trash music." He wanted a different direction for us.

MICHAEL CHAIKEN: Paul was essentially a working-class Irish kid. Jesuit educated. A lot of people put on these airs of being contrarian, but for Paul it was something very deep and there from the absolute beginning.

MMB: He stated numerous times throughout his career how lucky he was to have received a "traditional" and "common sense" education from his Catholic school days.

CHAIKEN: I wouldn't say he was a practicing Catholic, though. His idea of the church was more from the time of Julius II, when the church was a patron of the arts, and giving Michelangelo commissions to paint. He was in love with beauty.

MMB: It feels only natural that he would wind up working with Warhol, whose views on beauty and religion seem fairly aligned. For someone who was so tapped into the proto-counterculture, though, he displayed an unusually high respect for institutions, order, and authority early on. Following his graduation from Fordham University in 1959, he enlisted in the Army.

CHAIKEN: He served at Fort Benning and then Fort Dix in the early 1960s. In letters to friends, he talks about how much he likes it: *It's a little boring but I get to go off base and go see movies.* But he was lucky, he could easily have been drafted into Vietnam. He was in the Army Reserves right up until he was discharged in the summer of 1965, when they were about to shoot *My Hustler*.

MMB: In 1960 he moved to the East Village and opened the Exit Cinema, a storefront cinematheque on Fourth Street where he hosted a screening series and started making silent shorts, like *About Face* and *All Aboard the Dreamland Choo-Choo* (both 1964).

CHAIKEN: The Exit Cinema lasted about a year. It was a cross between an apartment, a gallery, and a microcinema. He rented films from places like the New York Public Library. He was kind of doing what Amos Vogel was at Cinema 16. [The New York City–based film society that screened films from 1947-1963. —Ed.] Paul would mix the programs. He'd show a film like *Icarus* (1960)—he was the first person to ever show a De Palma film—then a wartime documentary next to an animated short. The cinema became successful enough that people would congregate outside, and eventually the cops shut it down. This is before Jonas Mekas had Anthology Film Archives, even before the Film-Makers' Cinematheque.

CRAWFORD: To him it made sense, renting a store and living in the back. He was always resourceful, and never cared what people thought.

CHAIKEN: An interesting thing about his early shorts, and certainly about his photography, is that there was already a parity between what he was doing and what Warhol was doing. Both were heavily influenced by early cinema, silent cinema. The way Paul used lighting was similar to the way Warhol did in the *Screen Tests*, which later, Paul would help him shoot. There's a parallel in the aesthetic, and even the subject matter; Paul's *Like Sleep* (1964), is about junkies, you know, shooting up, shot with chiaroscuro lighting. It's similar to what Paul and Warhol became famous for together right after.

MMB: I love that even though he was sharing bills with all the Film Culture–endorsed 16mm avant-garde filmmakers, his references are completely different than those of, say, a Stan Brakhage.

CHAIKEN: He said that stuff was wallpaper to him. He was much more interested in the one-reeler. I mean, for Paul, Hollywood in the '30s and '40s into the early '50s was like Valhalla... So when Exit Cinema shut down, Paul needed to find work. He tried to get a job at DDB and other ad agencies, like *Mad Men*. But the only job he was able to get is with the City of New York Department of Welfare out of the East End Welfare Center on East 108th Street. For a few years—this is '61 to '64—Paul worked there. Looking at that material in the archive—we have field books with all his notes from knocking on people's doors—you realize the character Michael Sklar plays in *Trash*, that was Paul's job! He'd go to tenements and have to follow up: "How are you doing? How is the money being spent?" He hated that job.

MMB: It feels extremely plausible to view that job as a genesis for his particular brand of humor: satirical portraits of people on the margins. Not to mention his politics, which regarded urban liberalism through a fairly harsh lens. Prior to his tenure at the Department of Social Services, he was a little more malleable—I was surprised to see a photo of him campaigning for JFK in '60—but after he worked for the city, you don't catch much of a glimpse of that again.

CHAIKEN: One hundred percent. It must've been very sobering, and somewhat frightening, and probably a bit funny for him, too, to witness. But a lot of his issues weren't with the cases he was assigned to. It was the bureaucracy that drove him crazy. He was submitting detailed field reports and watching nothing happen, and then writing long letters about how the welfare officers are absolute morons who aren't doing anything for these people.

He either quit or got fired, and around this time, in June of '65, the Astor Place Playhouse did a retrospective of all of his early short films. Warhol was also showing *Vinyl* (1965) and *Poor Little Rich Girl* (1965) that same week. And on June 20, Gerard Malanga, one of the Warhol Superstars, came to see Paul's films. Because Malanga stars in *Vinyl*, he told Paul, "You should meet Andy." So, Malanga was actually the matchmaker.

MMB: The next thing you know, Paul and Warhol are collaborating on films nonstop. It's the start of an intensely productive period for them, leading to *Chelsea Girls*, *I, a Man* (1967), *Imitation of Christ* (1967), and *The Loves of Ondine* (1968). How did this come about?

CHAIKEN: Warhol saw Paul's films, liked them, and said, "You're really good, you can keep shots in focus." And the thing that attracted Paul to Warhol, which Paul was moving towards, was the use of sound, because all of Paul's early shorts are silent. He was like, "Wow, Andy actually has sound equipment. He can afford all this." So, Warhol invited Paul to The Factory. The first film they worked on together is *Space*, which was filmed in July of ' 65. It stars Donald Lyons, Danny Fields, the folk singer Eric Anderson. Edie Sedgwick's in it, too. There's like 15 people in this film. Warhol was like, "Paul, how do I fit everybody?" Paul said, "Well, you can just pan the camera." That was mind-blowing for Warhol. The next film they worked on, which I think has really stood the test of time, is *My Hustler*.

That was the first film where it was like, "Wow, Paul is part of this thing." Warhol realized quickly that Paul was a resourceful, can-do human being. And, you know, he wasn't on drugs. He was obsessed with work and with films; he had this huge knowledge of not just filmmaking but film history. Warhol brought Paul in to essentially manage the film activity at The Factory, but also to be The Factory's publicity director. That's why Paul had his hands in so much stuff.

Warhol had two essential people running The Factory at that time: Paul, who was almost the VP, and Fred Hughes. The painting stuff was Hughes's wheelhouse. He dealt with people like Leo Castelli and Henry Geldzahler. Paul wasn't interested in modern art; he was interested in helping Warhol get his name out there and helping with the films. In Warhol's head, the idea was, "If we make these crazy films, and they start showing and I become notorious, that'll help sell my paintings."

MMB: Right, the films add value to the art, even though they don't necessarily bring in money.

CHAIKEN: But that flipped because of *Chelsea Girls*; *Chelsea Girls* made some money. And then *Flesh*, *Trash*, and *Heat* made an obscene amount compared to what they cost to make. Later, in the '90s and 2000s, when Paul was on a tear saying that Warhol did nothing, a lot of people chastised him for that. But the archive lends credence to a lot of what he was saying because he kept all the correspondence, all the receipts. It's Paul's name on a lot of the contracts. The one thing that becomes abundantly clear, though, is that Warhol, because of what he had already achieved by 1965, had given Paul this unbelievable venue to pursue the things he wanted to pursue. They were like twin brains. They were very simpatico at that moment.

MMB: I'm itching to delve into the Velvet Underground chapter.

CHAIKEN: Right. Around the end of 1965, Paul had the idea that Andy could make money on the films by putting them into some kind of rock 'n' roll context. They'd already been talking to a Broadway producer, Michael Myerberg, who was planning to open a disco with an enormous dance floor in an airplane hangar in Queens. Paul and Andy proposed

Top: Sylvia Miles basks in the southern California sun while Joe Dallesandro avoids it between takes on the set of *Heat* (1972). Photo taken by Paul Morrissey.

Bottom: Rogues' gallery, left to right: Billy Edgar, Jimmy Maddows, actor unknown, and Patrick Schoene, on the set of *Madame Wang's* (1981).

An ardent antiquer, Paul Morrissey's former home is filled with evidence of his passion for collecting, from glossy prints of glamorous Golden Age Hollywood stars—especially a ubiquitous Greta Garbo—to vintage hand-thrown pottery.

doing some kind of multimedia event there. It just so happened that Malanga and Barbara Rubin were filming the Velvet Underground at the Café Bizarre and Malanga had no idea how to operate sound. He called Paul. Paul went, just to help out, saw the Velvet Underground, and thought, "These guys are perfect. They even have 'underground' in their name. If we can get them to play music for our night, we could show the films too." Paul was thinking of the Velvet Underground only as an engine. So one of the first things Paul did, outside of helping Andy direct *My Hustler* and set up distribution of The Factory films, is that he got him involved with the Velvet Underground. All of this happened very quickly. By January 1966, Warhol, Paul, and Lou Reed, on behalf of the band, formed a company called Warvel, Inc.–the Warhol Velvets–and signed a management agreement. Warhol was essentially the bank, and Paul was the day-to-day manager of the band. And that first performance at the Film-Makers' Cinematheque in February 1966 became the staging ground for the Exploding Plastic Inevitable.

MMB: That alone is mind-blowing.

CHAIKEN: The other thing that happened is that Paul met Nico in late '65 or early 1966. She was in *La Dolce Vita* (1960) and had a single out in the UK, so people knew her. But Malanga brought her to The Factory, where Paul saw her and was like, "Look at this woman!" He thought the Velvet Underground were fantastic. But they were ugly and they didn't really do anything, they just stood there screaming about heroin. So, he's like, "We'll get Nico in the band, and people can stare at her." He was the one who pushed Nico on them and saw it as a package.

MMB: Paul's connection to Nico is really interesting. It seems to go on way past the Velvet Underground.

CHAIKEN: Way past. Paul's lifetime connection to the Velvet Underground was largely through Nico, whom he truly loved and cared for. She lasted less than a year in the band. When she got squeezed out, Paul became her manager. Nico lived with Paul for a little while, too.

MMB: I didn't realize Paul shot the cover of her 1967 debut album, *Chelsea Girl*. The slides from that shoot of her gazing out the window, looking all forlorn, they're so beautiful. Marisa, what's your memory of Nico and the Velvets?

CRAWFORD: I knew her from a very young age. I remember her coming up to Highland Park with her son, Ari, when he was very little, and my mother buying us matching wool sailor outfits. And I remember the band performing. Paul would get people on the floor to dance. He went outside, saw someone like Eric Emerson trying to get in and asked, "Can you dance? You can come in if you dance." It was all just part of the thing he was orchestrating.

CHAIKEN: Paul co-conceived and named the Exploding Plastic Inevitable and ran it for that season at The Dom in the East Village. Then, when the Velvet Underground went on tour, he went with them. He was the one keeping all the books. There are records in Paul's archive of who got paid what, what Malanga got paid to do the whip dance in Chicago, you know? [$207 –Ed.]

MMB: I saw Max's Kansas City bar tabs, too. I know *Chelsea Girls* was conceptualized there, on napkins. It's just an incredible history of the New York counterculture at the time.

And this is basically the dawn of what becomes known as independent film.

CHAIKEN: It was around when they started shooting *Chelsea Girls*, which Paul had a huge hand in. All the stuff with Nico, with the colored lights, he shot on his own. People revere the Velvets nowadays, but back then, the real turning point for Warhol and Paul was the fact that *Chelsea Girls* actually played uptown, it was a major event. What really launched Andy Warhol Films was the legitimate success of *Chelsea Girls*.

An important point, too, is that Paul was saying, "You need some narrative thread. It can't just be *Empire*. It can't just be *Eat* (1963). That's wallpaper that the Velvet Underground can play over. If you want people to come and continue to see these movies, we need a thread of a plot. It doesn't have to be sophisticated, but a thread of something."

MMB: Even if it was just a series of vignettes set in different rooms of the Chelsea Hotel, presented in split screen. That was a big step forward.

CHAIKEN: 1967, the year after *Chelsea Girls*, was the beginning of these quasi-sexploitation movies, like *I, a Man* and *Bike Boy*, that use the same techniques of the early Warhol films but there's a little bit of a plot to help audiences carry themselves along.

MMB: And then Warhol got shot by Valerie Solanas in '68, which ushered in the next phase. Paul took the production reins and received sole director and screenwriter credits for *Flesh*, which stars Dallesandro as a street hustler.

CHAIKEN: Unlike the later films, though, the dialogue was largely improvised, so there's no physical scripts for those early Dallesandro films. And that stuff, all the production materials, is one half of the archive. The other half is the actual films. We discovered Paul had a storage space in New Jersey, and we found boxes of outtakes. The shoots were very economical. Paul was like, "We're going to do this on a Saturday and shoot for three hours using available light. We'll shoot when the sun goes down and take advantage of the sunset." The outtakes for *Flesh* all fit into a single box.

MMB: And he somehow even saved Dallesandro's ponytail, which he fit into a letter-sized envelope! So these films are made for next to nothing and get full-on national releases, becoming cult hits.

CHAIKEN: Well, *Flesh* cost a few thousand dollars, and it was a sensation. It played at MoMA, it played internationally. Three million people saw *Flesh* in Germany alone.

MMB: And the final title in the Dallesandro trilogy, *Heat*, played at the New York Film Festival and at Cannes. The name Paul Morrissey was starting to become a singular brand.

CHAIKEN: The one that broke, though, was the second, *Trash*. That film really was the beginning of a viable, independent commercial cinema; it got caught on that wave of *Putney Swope* (1969) and *Gimme Shelter* (1970). It played college campuses, but also arthouse cinemas around America. Dallesandro was becoming an icon. Paul, too. He said again and again in interviews that he wanted to rebuild the old Hollywood studio system of Darryl Zanuck and David O. Selznick. It was intentional that

Human waste. Continuity Polaroids taken on the set of *Mixed Blood* (1984), in which Alphabet City is depicted as a dog-eat-dog urban hellscape.

he found faces like Dallesandro, Geraldine Smith, Jane Forth, Candy Darling... Paul himself was always willing to melt into the background. He cared more about the people in front of his camera and capturing their true personalities than directing them. For him, it was all about casting. He wanted to create this Superstar star system that would get young people interested in movies and movie stars again. He'd almost totally given up on Hollywood cinema by the '60s. He thought once Method acting took over, it was all downhill from there.

MMB: I know he loved John Wayne and Clint Eastwood.

CRAWFORD: He would laugh so hard in the *Dirty Harry* movies.

CHAIKEN: Well, he loved the fact that Wayne onscreen was the same as Wayne offscreen. Wayne's not trying to affect anything, he didn't go to acting school to learn how to emote. Guys like Eastwood and Wayne are a little more amplified onscreen, but they're playing essentially the same character in every movie.

MMB: Yeah, and he loves the comedic device of a quiet loner surrounded by—

CHAIKEN: A bunch of people who won't shut the fuck up!

MMB: Now, somehow in the middle of all this he co-founds *Interview Magazine*, in 1971?

CHAIKEN: He started it with Andy and John Wilkinson. But he wasn't writing for the magazine. Paul's contribution to *Interview*, really, if you've seen the early issues, they're full of old Hollywood photo stills—all those were Paul's.

MMB: Paul and Warhol then made *Women in Revolt* (1971), *Heat*, and the Paris-shot farce *L'Amour* (1972), which features, among others, fashion designer Karl Lagerfeld. And then Paul traveled to Rome to make the two films that he's arguably most famous for: *Flesh for Frankenstein* and *Blood for Dracula*.

CHAIKEN: That was kind of Paul's move out of The Factory. Because he had been there from '65 to '73, every day. Then, when *Flesh*, *Trash*, and *Heat* found success, the Italian producer Carlo Ponti got interested and said, "You want to make a movie? How much money do you think you need?" Paul told Ponti, "$100,000." Ponti's like, "$100,000? I'll give you $200,000." That was more than Paul had ever spent on anything, let alone a movie. He said, "If you give me $200,000, I can make two movies." So he very quickly shot *Frankenstein* first, then *Dracula*.

MMB: I saw Udo Kier talk last year, and he's unbelievably funny. He described getting cast in those after meeting Paul on an airplane.

CRAWFORD: Paul met everybody on transportation.

CHAIKEN: When you get to *Frankenstein*, in terms of what's in the archive, the writing starts to double. The first instance of anything resembling a script is *Frankenstein*. But Paul didn't write it out as a script; he wrote it as a treatment, almost like a short story.

MMB: I heard Kier demanded that he have real lines to say.

CHAIKEN: That's right. They were writing the script almost as they were filming, the day of... My sense is that Paul was like, "Okay, The Factory era is in the rearview mirror." He wanted to go to Hollywood and get into more traditional ways of making movies.

MMB: And these films were hits.

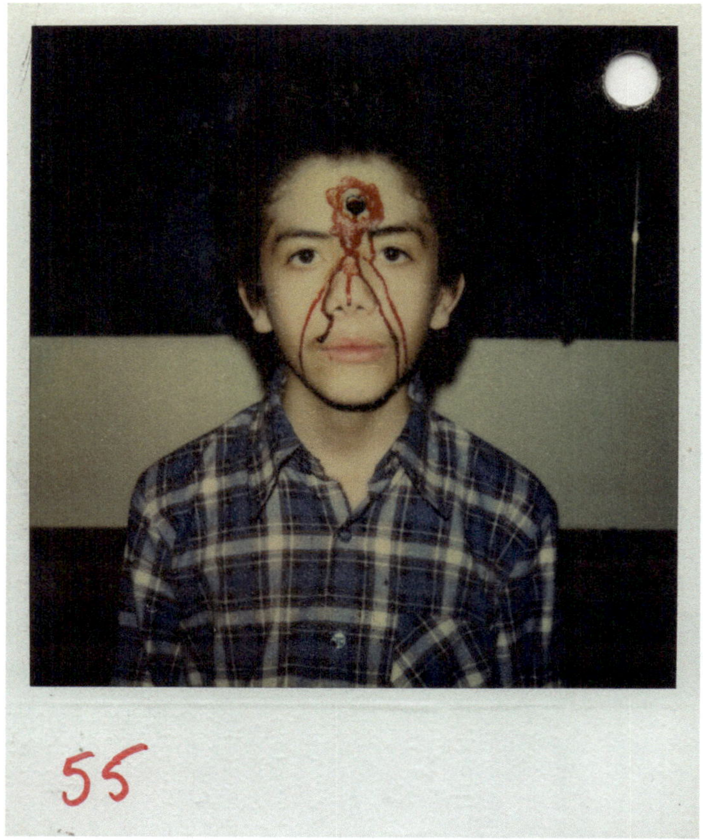

CHAIKEN: *Frankenstein* was hugely successful, more so than *Dracula*. They had the 3D element, which Paul thought was gimmicky, but he was like, "Alright, I'll try it."

MMB: Then he comes back to America. When did he move uptown to this apartment?

CRAWFORD: 1974.

MMB: Where would he write?

CRAWFORD: He would work at the end of this table, sitting in this old dentist chair without the headpiece. He'd be on the phone, papers everywhere. He had his routine: he'd have his tea and cake; then he would come here and work all day; then he'd sit in his "Greta Garbo room," a room filled with Greta Garbo photos where his TV was, where he'd have dinner and watch Turner Classic Movies; then he'd go to his bedroom to read.

CHAIKEN: At that point, Hollywood became interested, because they realized, "This guy can make movies for not a lot of money." Paul tried his hand at making another horror film, but in the studio system; that's how you get *The Hound of the Baskervilles* (1978), which was shot in England and turned into an unmitigated disaster. Paul couldn't get along with Dudley Moore. It wasn't a happy experience for anyone involved.

MMB: You see this fork in the road in a lot in careers: do you keep pushing for a big studio career or keep doing what you know?

CHAIKEN: After *The Hound of the Baskervilles*, he didn't really complete anything. He was like, "I'm going to move to Hollywood and try my hand at making Hollywood films." So—with Warhol as co-producer—there was a year or so when he tried to play the Hollywood game, and he couldn't do it. This is where the Warhol thing became a double-edged sword for Paul. He realized that Warhol was the greatest producing partner because he would just give him the money and leave. Now Paul had to deal with Hollywood assholes who wanted total control over everything, who won't leave him alone. Paul was like, "I can't play that game." So when that all fell through, he quickly got *Madame Wang's* (1981) together, which is his take on the LA punk movement. It's microbudget and doesn't even really come out.

MMB: I think it's his most underrated film, and quite possibly his funniest.

CRAWFORD: He had a great apartment in LA and was hanging out with George Cukor all the time. He was interviewing Cukor for what was going to be a book of conversations between himself and Cukor, accompanied by Cukor's personal letters—that was the other big project happening simultaneously with *Madame Wang's*—but he burned out on Hollywood and came back to New York.

MMB: It is kind of hilarious because that is the narrative of *Madame Wang's*: someone shows up in LA, gets annoyed by everyone, and goes back home. His last film, *News from Nowhere* (2010), has almost the same structure too.

CHAIKEN: Very soon after making *Madame Wang's*, he saw Alan Bowne's *Forty-Deuce* as a stage play. The play got panned in the press, but Paul loved it. He and Gary Indiana both thought it was brilliant.

MMB: And then he adapted it into his film of the same name, starring a 23-year-old Kevin Bacon as the leader of a bunch of foul-mouthed young gay hustlers roaming Port Authority. Paul's 1980s New York trilogy is a spectacular run, though the films rarely screen—I mean, *Forty Deuce* never screens.

CHAIKEN: I think those are his best films. That's the fulcrum of his genius. All the lessons he learned working with Warhol, and from *Chelsea Girls*, he applied to *Forty Deuce*, but to better effect because he was a more skilled filmmaker. He knew exactly how to shoot *Forty Deuce* with two screens and how to make it work. [The second half of the film uses a split screen —Ed.] But he started to have serious issues with the producers—it wasn't like working with Warhol—and he had a lot of problems with the distribution.

MMB: It's also very cool to see his collection of *New York Post* clippings here. One of the biggest misconceptions I had about him was that he was really out there in the streets, writing these scripts from firsthand knowledge. When in reality it feels like a lot was just snatched from headlines. There's an article about the drug pulley system used in *Mixed Blood* and another about a class taught in a public-school bathroom, which he used so memorably in *Spike of Bensonhurst*.

CRAWFORD: He made up worlds that were like nothing he lived but that he thought were funny. He did this when shooting a scene in the kitchen for *News from Nowhere*. The lead actor was supposed to be a junkie mother, and my nephew played her son and my daughter played her daughter. Paul set up a bed in the kitchen near the dishwasher and the kid is cold. So the mother says, "Here, get a sweater," and she opens the dishwasher to get their clothes. Nothing makes sense, but Paul thought, "a drug addict!"

CHAIKEN: All the things they were making fun of in the '60s and early '70s, the sex and drugs, by the '80s all that stuff had become establishment religion. And Paul was horrified.

MMB: I'm sure John Waters deals with this every day; it must be surreal when you create a satirical body of work that then becomes reality, where everyone looks and acts like characters from your movies. One of the things that really struck me, reading through Paul's interviews, is how contemporary his takes on identity, sex, and the anxieties of urban life sound now. I think he lays down some interesting paths for how to use humor to address this unease. He said that you don't want to mix politics and film, that politics is for lawmakers and journalists and film is for creating more emotional narratives.

CHAIKEN: On the surface the New York trilogy might not seem very political, but it is. But to your point, again and again—as people began to realize he wasn't some sort of crazed libertarian left-wing freak, he's actually a Reagan conservative—he would tell interviewers, "Yeah, all that is true, but I don't think cinema is the place for politics." He cared deeply about his characters and about the people he put in his films. He didn't feel the need to interject his own politics into them. Even if a film was about someone who's living a life that he was completely opposed to, he wanted to find a kind of empathy.

CRAWFORD: I remember he got a call: "We're doing a gay film

festival and want to include your films." And he was like, "I don't do gay films, I do films about people." Like, these are just people.

CHAIKEN: I don't think he wanted these films to be labeled as anything. Again and again, he said, "I'm pro-humor and I'm pro-human." The only way he could deal with Mayor Ed Koch's New York City in the '80s was to do it as some sort of outlandish comedy. It's grim, but it's comedy nevertheless.

MMB: Then, in 1985, we got *Beethoven's Nephew*, which is the weird outlier in his filmography.

CRAWFORD: I haven't seen it since the original screening, but I was so impressed by Paul working on that level of production. And the costumes!

CHAIKEN: The last half hour, in terms of his filmmaking techniques, is probably his most sophisticated... he uses these long, spiraling tracking shots against Beethoven's Ninth Symphony, the most purely expressive moment in any of his films.

MMB: It must have been exciting for him to finally celebrate classical music instead of "trash music" like rock 'n' roll, too.

CHAIKEN: In interviews, he's said it's his most personal movie. You can see it in Beethoven's tortured character. Beethoven has all these unresolved contradictions in his life and is kind of curmudgeonly, but is also obsessed with his sister's son. I think Paul saw a lot of his own story in the character.

MMB: Then, finally, we got *News from Nowhere*, a small-scale production that reunited him with Viva.

CRAWFORD: The movie started production, then he had the accident.

MMB: That was in 2009, right? He was hit by a U-Haul while crossing the street near his apartment and briefly fell into a coma.

CRAWFORD: When he finally did get around to finishing the film, I felt like it wasn't the same person making it. He didn't want to promote it or bring people in. He shifted to a more insecure Paul, if you can imagine.

MMB: We should really talk about Montauk. The 28-acre estate, made up of several houses, that he and Warhol had there was a mythic getaway. *News from Nowhere* was filmed there, and it's a recurring locale throughout his life and career.

CHAIKEN: Paul found the Montauk estate. He bought it with Andy in '71 with the money they made from *Trash*.

MMB: A who's who of the time stayed there: Mick Jagger, Elizabeth Taylor, Truman Capote, the Kennedys... It's

Left: Teaser poster for *Spike of Bensonhurst* (1988), from a photograph by Shonna Valeska. The film's star, Sasha Mitchell, would shortly become a teen heartthrob thanks to his recurring role on the ABC sitcom *Step by Step*; the poster offers the promise of sex appeal.

Right: Walls hung with art dating from before his birth, Paul Morrissey's apartment was a sanctuary from a contemporary world he found obscene and laughably absurd.

unbelievable, looking at these photos. Do you have any particularly wild memories of your time there, Marisa?

CRAWFORD: Well, Paul wanted me and my sister Christina to come out there with the Mamas & the Papas when John Phillips was renting the main house and working with Paul on *Man on the Moon* [the short-lived Broadway musical —Ed.]. Denny Doherty was there, and Michelle Phillips and her stepdaughter Mackenzie Phillips—this was a few years after *American Graffiti* (1973) had come out; she was still a teenager—and I was 10 or 11. My sister and I went with Paul to have dinner at the house with all of them. I went to use the bathroom and the door was ajar: Michelle was in a silk robe over the toilet, bare butt out, stoned out of her mind. Meanwhile, Mackenzie was like, "Come with me!" She showed us her wardrobe and all these tube tops, which my sister and I got dressed up in, and she offered us sangria and Harvey's Bristol Cream. As soon as Paul got wind of that, he pulled us up to the second house. I remember vomiting all night. He was yelling, horrified, like, "Don't be like them!"

MMB: The Montauk house, which had been decorated by the former owners and maintained by Paul—there was lots of Val-Kill furniture, for example—was very much in line with his aesthetic, his love for old, handmade works that organically showcase function over form. As is this apartment.

CRAWFORD: He had started collecting the Arts and Crafts movement stuff in the '60s, he was very inspired by their ideas.

MMB: It's astonishing how someone who was at the epicenter of modern art in 1960s New York refused to collect anything contemporary. I was reading an article that has Paul at a thrift store buying a cookie jar, and the interviewer says, "Oh, I heard Warhol collects cookie jars, too." Paul responds, "He doesn't collect cookie jars. I collect cookie jars. He's just heard me say I collect cookie jars." But when I was looking at the Warhol estate auction, I saw Warhol owned thousands of cookie jars—so was he just copying Paul?

CRAWFORD: Warhol was very much like a child, he was like, "Oh yeaaaah. I want cookie jars, too." And his house was like a hoarder's palace, though I never went in.

MMB: There's a subplot in *Madame Wang's* about doorknob collecting. Was that something Paul was into, too?

CRAWFORD: Oh my God, yeah. Paul spent a lot of time at swap meets. He sent my sister Christina home from LA with a suitcase full of doorknobs after that shoot. The crazy things he'd have us do. We loved Uncle Paul.

PRIMARY SOURCES: INSIDE THE PAUL MORRISSEY ARCHIVE

Priceless artifacts from the improbable life of a good Catholic boy who got a job at the Factory, journeyed into the Velvet Underground, and reinvented the American film comedy.

Paul Morrissey, July 1967, photographer unknown. By the end of the month Morrissey, with Andy Warhol, had shot *I, a Man.* The film, which features Tom Baker, Ultra Violet, Ingrid Superstar, Nico, and Valerie Solanas, opened the following month at the Hudson Theater on 141 West 44th Street. In June of the following year Solanas attempted to murder Warhol, and very nearly succeeded. It was during Warhol's recuperation that Morrissey received his first credit as sole director on a "Warhol" film, 1968's *Flesh.*

W-1

THE CITY OF NEW YORK
DEPARTMENT OF WELFARE
250 CHURCH STREET
NEW YORK 13, N. Y.
DIGBY 4-8700

JAMES R. DUMPSON
COMMISSIONER

March 5, 1965

Mr. Paul Morrissey
111 East 10th Street
New York, New York 10003

Dear Mr. Morrissey:

On February 5, 1965, we wrote to inform you that you still owe the Department $10.67 for 14 unauthorized telephone calls to New Brunswick, New Jersey, which you made between August 11th and October 23, 1964. You did not claim that February 5th letter from the post office.

This is to inform you that unless we receive a check or money order from you in the amount of $10.67, action will be taken to recover this sum.

Please let us hear from you at once.

Very truly yours,

DIVISION OF PERSONNEL MANAGEMENT

Lena Payne

By: Lena Payne

Fieldwork notebook dating from the time of Paul Morrissey's job as an investigator for the East End Welfare Center at 309 East 108th Street in East Harlem, and a letter from his employer demanding recompense, to the tune of $10.67, for "14 unauthorized telephone calls to New Brunswick, New Jersey." Morrissey was in the employ of the City of New York Department of Welfare from 1961 to 1964. By the end of his tenure President Lyndon B. Johnson had begun to roll out a series of domestic reforms collectively referred to as the Great Society program, one aspect of which was what Johnson called, in his 1964 State of the Union Address, a "War on Poverty." Several of Morrissey's films depicting life lived, as he saw it, by the urban underclasses, testify to his opinion concerning the likelihood of successfully ridding the world of privation through legislation.

Paul Morrissey poses behind the shuttered doorway of his storefront cinema/living space at 36 East Fourth Street, the vitrine of which advertises screenings of 1960's *Icarus*, the debut film by the youngest son of orthopedic surgeon Anthony F. De Palma, an esteemed faculty member at Philadelphia's Jefferson University: Brian was then a sophomore at Columbia University, making this first foray into filmmaking. Though Morrissey, in later life, was reliably contemptuous when speaking of "avant-garde" or "underground" cinema, it was in the avant-garde underground that his filmmaking career began, with Morrissey screening his silent comedy shorts for downtown crowds. "Like many Hollywood studio heads," he said, "I began in the Lower East Side as the operator of a Nickelodeon." Photograph by Paris Asta.

Left to right: Lou Reed, Edie Sedgwick, John Cale, Moe Tucker, Gerard Malanga, Sterling Morrison, Andy Warhol. Photograph by Paul Morrissey, which was then used on the flyer for the Andy Warhol, Up-Tight show, which ran from February 8-13, 1966, at the Film-Makers' Cinematheque at 125 West 41st Street. The multimedia event would be the first public performance by The Velvet Underground with Nico and also the premiere screening of Warhol's *More Milk, Yvette*, a tribute to the ill-starred romance of Lana Turner and Johnny Stompanato starring Mario Montez, né René Rivera.

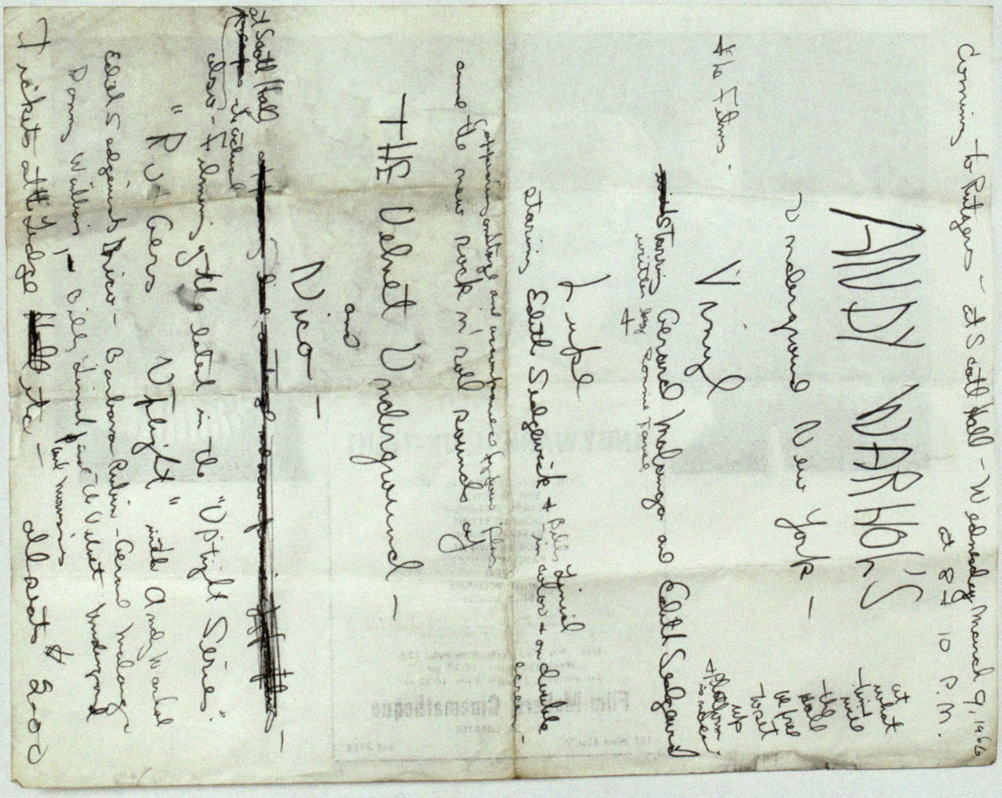

Original flyer for Andy Warhol, Up-Tight, front and back. On the advert for the Velvets' first public performance with Nico, Paul Morrissey is drafting promotional material for a forthcoming gig, a March 9, 1966 appearance at Rutgers University's Scott Hall in New Brunswick, New Jersey. The band's playing was accompanied by screenings of the Morrissey/Warhol films *Vinyl* (1965) and *Lupe* (1966), as well as footage of the Velvets and Nico. Guitarist Sterling Morrisson would recall of the show: "At Rutger's we were all dressed entirely in white. The effect, with all the films and lights projected on us, was invisibility." An altercation between a member of the Warhol entourage, photographer Nat Finkelstein, and campus police on the day of the concert caused a stir around town, and resulted in a capacity crowd of 650 turning out for both the 8pm and 10pm performances.

Morrissey and Nico, née Christa Päffgen, photographed on the concrete block facade of the Ennis House in Los Angeles' Los Feliz neighborhood. The structure, designed by a Frank Lloyd Wright then in thrall to Mayan architecture, was erected in 1924, and plays a prominent role in William Castle's 1959 *The House on Haunted Hill*, as well as other, lesser, films. Of the Warhol contingent's early excursions to California, actress and Exploding Plastic Inevitable dancer Mary Woronov would remember: "We dressed in black leather, they dressed in wild colors. They were like 'Oh wow man, a happening!' We were like reading Jean Genet. We were S&M and they were free love. We really liked gay people, and the West Coast was totally homophobic. So they thought we were evil and we thought they were stupid."

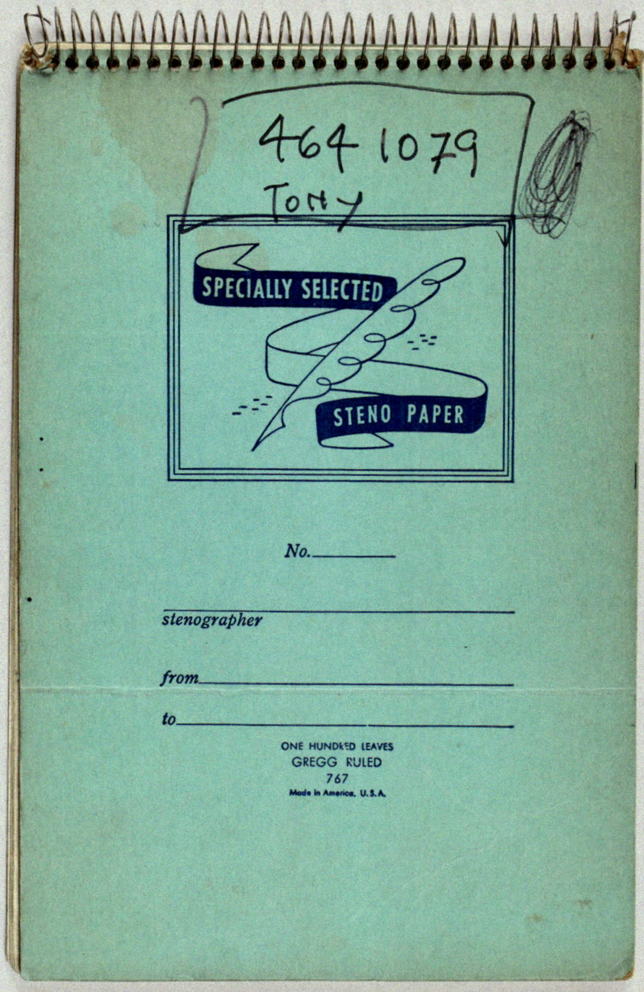

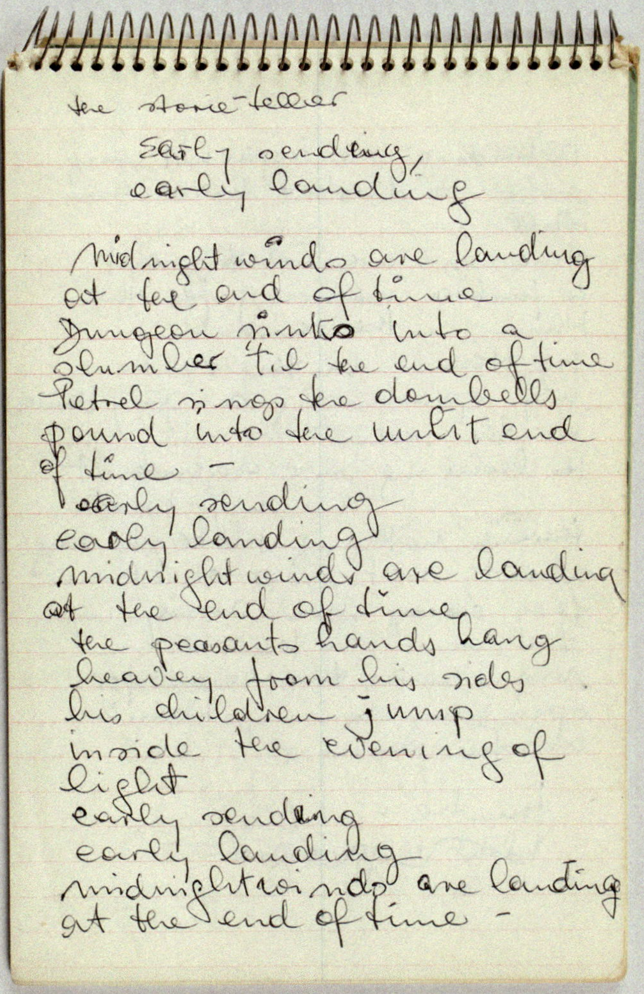

Steno paper spiral notebook, "One hundred leaves of Gregg ruled paper," formerly belonging to Nico. Contents include drawings, poems, and the lyrics of songs that Nico would record on her 1968 *The Marble Index* LP ("Frozen Warnings," "Facing the Wind" and, seen here, "Evening of Light"), as well as lyrics to "I Can't See Your Face in My Mind," which would feature on The Doors' 1967 *Strange Days* LP. The superimposed photographs of the chanteuse, one in color, one in black and white, that grace the cover of her 1967 debut LP *Chelsea Girl* were both taken by Paul Morrissey.

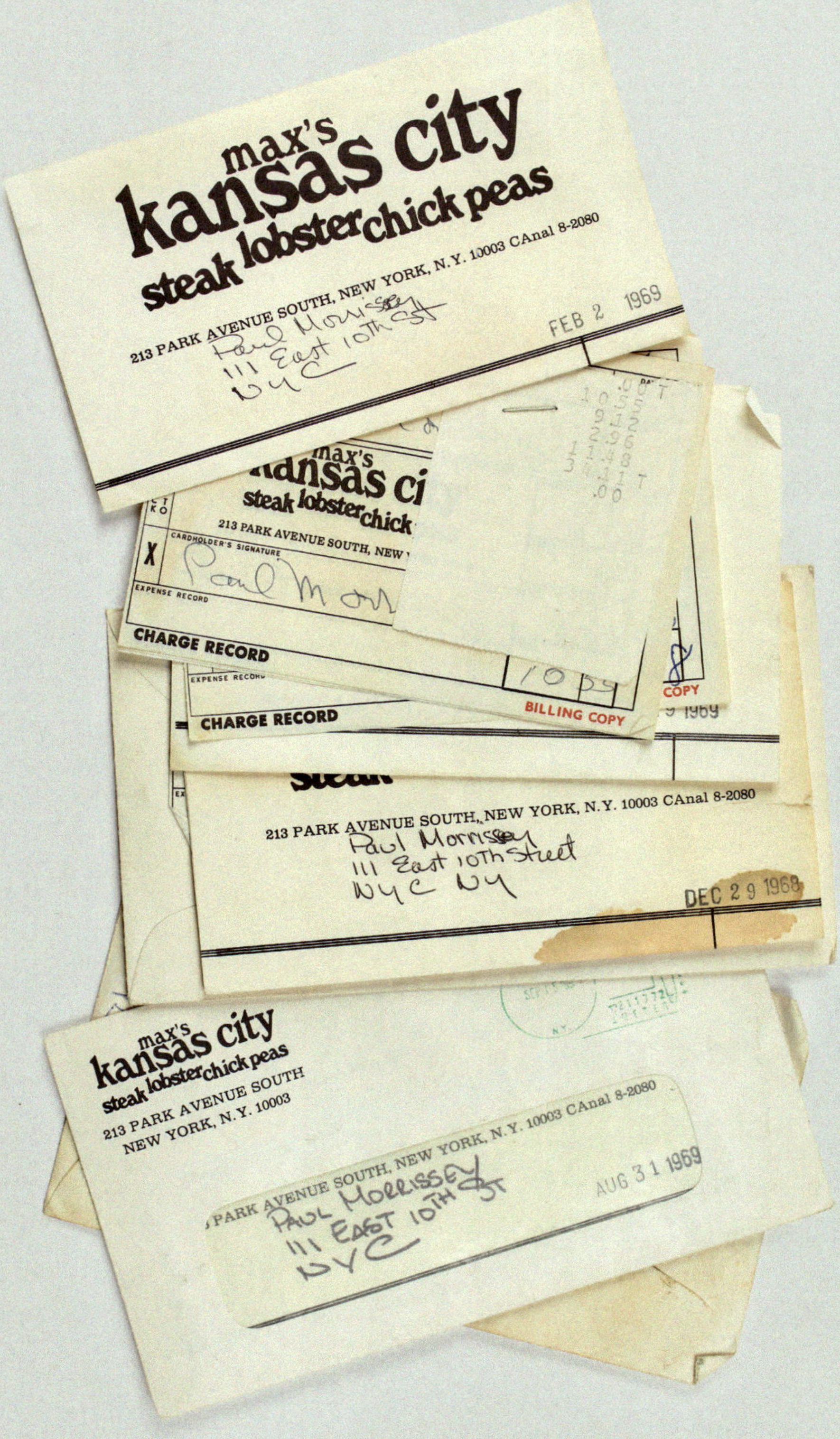

Receipts from Max's Kansas City, the nightclub and restaurant located at 213 Park Avenue South, opened and operated by Mickey Ruskin, which was for some time the designated watering hole of the Warhol crowd. Paul Morrissey, as manager of the Velvet Underground and, generally, the most level-headed guy in the Factory mob, was responsible for settling tabs. Not depicted is a "Balance Past Due" notice, addressed to Morrissey's apartment at 111 East Tenth Street, for the sum of $195.21.

Joe Dallesandro's ponytail, from an envelope date-stamped "Dec '72," on which the words "Joe Dallesandro's long hair" are written in Paul Morrissey's hand. That month, the Factory held its first ever Christmas party, which Dallesandro and his son, Joe Jr., attended. In March of the following year Dallesandro, now close-cropped, was in Rome filming *Flesh for Frankenstein* and *Blood for Dracula* with Morrissey.

Original print ad maquette, c. 1971, for Paul Morrissey's *Women in Revolt*, cut and paste-up on board. Though a great believer in improvisation on set, at least during this period of his career, Morrissey was in every other aspect of his work obsessed with fine-print detail and maintaining control over his artistic output, attributes that would make him that rarest of rarities: the financially successful "underground" filmmaker.

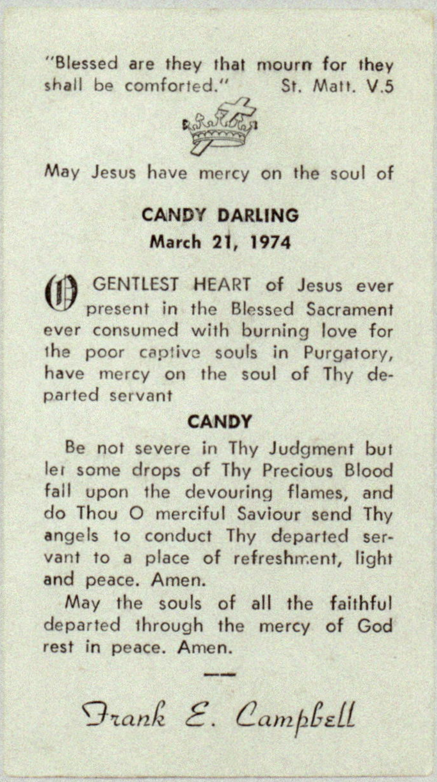

"Blessed are they that mourn for they shall be comforted." St. Matt. V.5

May Jesus have mercy on the soul of

CANDY DARLING
March 21, 1974

O GENTLEST HEART of Jesus ever present in the Blessed Sacrament ever consumed with burning love for the poor captive souls in Purgatory, have mercy on the soul of Thy departed servant

CANDY

Be not severe in Thy Judgment but let some drops of Thy Precious Blood fall upon the devouring flames, and do Thou O merciful Saviour send Thy angels to conduct Thy departed servant to a place of refreshment, light and peace. Amen.

May the souls of all the faithful departed through the mercy of God rest in peace. Amen.

—

Frank E. Campbell

Prayer card from the funeral of Candy Darling, the Massapequa Park, Long Island–raised transgender actress who appears in Paul Morrissey's *Flesh* and *Women in Revolt* (1971), and was immortalized in song by the Velvet Underground's "Candy Says" and the second verse of Lou Reed's "Walk on the Wild Side" ("Candy came from out on the island...") Darling died of lymphoma on March 21, 1974, aged 29; services were held at the Frank E. Campbell Funeral on 1076 Madison Avenue at 81st Street, where Judy Garland had lain in state only two years earlier.

At Cinecittà studios, on the set of *Blood for Dracula*, 1973, photographer unknown. Paul Morrissey looks to star Udo Kier; Kier gazes out to eternity; Joe Dallesandro looks to the camera. The film, which with *Flesh for Frankenstein* marked Morrissey's first excursions into genre movie terrain, would earn an enormous amount of money, almost all of which, to hear Morrissey tell it, was pocketed by producer Carlo Ponti.

On the set of *Forty Deuce* (1982), photo by Mandy Vahabzadeh. Paul Morrissey appears deep in thought while consulting with a pre-stardom 21-year-old actor Kevin Bacon, reprising the role—that of a contingency minded, ferally opportunistic rentboy named Ricky—that he'd originated on the off-Broadway stage, and which had earned him an Obie Award earlier that year. Morrissey's meeting of minds with *Forty-Deuce* playwright Alan Bowne, later his co-writer on *Mixed Blood* (1984) and *Spike of Bensonhurst* (1988), was a reinvigorating shot in the arm for the filmmaker, creatively. Bowne died in 1989, from complications related to AIDS.

NEW YORK POST, WEDNESDAY, JUNE 10, 19

Love among the ruins

By STEPHEN M. SILVERMAN

THE scene is not a pretty one: the Lower East Side of the near future resembles war-torn Beirut. It is a quarantined enclave of the diseased, multitudes of victims suffering in various

Bowne adds: "Love to the death."

Among many fatalistic prophesies, "Beirut" suggests that the government will be forced to monitor lovemaking, that patients who test positive will be branded, and that Hollywood has died, literally, from a dearth of stars.

14 ★★

NEW YORK POST, WEDNESDAY, DECEMBER 16, 1987

SCHOOL OF SHAME!

By PAT SMITH
Brooklyn Bureau Chief

TOP school officials and Brooklyn Borough President Howard Golden went back to class yesterday — in a bathroom.

Class in a bathroom in B'klyn

Board of Education president Robert Wagner, vice president Irene Impellizzeri and Golden visited Walt Whitman IS in Flatbush, a building so crowded that one class is held in a bathroom.

"This school was designed for 1200 elementary students," Golden said. "Instead, it is being used by more than 2100 junior high students.

"It's a disgrace. There's no planning."

As he spoke, Jean Derac gave special bilingual instruction to five French-speaking students.

They were crammed into a 10- by 15-foot tiled bathroom where sinks still line one wall.

Patches on the walls and floor showed where toilets had been removed to make room for desks.

Another room was divided into two classes by a row of five-foot-high cabinets, leaving five feet open to the ceiling.

"What this means for kids in terms of disruption of learning and the signals we send them . . . is a disgrace," Wagner said.

No provision had been made for the population increase in the area, fed by French and Spanish-speaking people from the Caribbean, Wagner said.

A 14-room addition to the school will take at least two years to complete, Wagner said. "We'll try our best, but I don't want to make any promises."

New York Post: Don Halasy

Brooklyn Beep Golden, flanked by Board of Ed's Impellizzeri (left) and Wagner, inspect classroom in a bathroom.

New York City born-and-bred, Paul Morrissey was morbidly fascinated by the social and moral disintegration of his hometown—or, at least, an idea of that disintegration as propagated in the local tabloids through the 1980s. Morrissey would dutifully snip, collect, and file for future use the most gruesome, sensationalistic reportages of societal breakdown in the five boroughs as documented by the *New York Post*, *New York Magazine*, and other publications, in envelopes labeled, for example: "Cuomo ties to mafia + Farrakahn/School Class in Toilet." The "Class in Toilet" detail would be memorably incorporated into *Spike of Bensonhurst* (1988). Also pictured is the *New York Post* review of *Beirut*, Alan Bowne's dramatic response to the AIDS crisis in New York City.

An underlying theme of Paul Morrissey's work—never "underlying" in his outspoken interviews—is his abject horror at what a brutish, indifferent, individualist, profit-and-pleasure-minded system does and will continue to do to people... particularly the young and vulnerable. This piece of Nancy Reagan "War on Drugs" era propaganda was anything but a joke to Morrissey, who scorned drug use and the popular culture that, to his mind, glamorized and encouraged it.

Paul Morrissey at Montauk, at Eothen, the property he co-owned and managed with Warhol until the latter's death, photographed by John Fitzgerald Kennedy, Jr. In a 1974 *Hustler* interview, Morrissey expressed his unguarded enthusiasm for the family of the 35th President: "I think the Kennedys should run the country, period. When they're not we should expect the nation to look like the shit hole that it does look like."

IMAGINARY CINEMA: PAUL MORRISSEY

Written by
Nick Pinkerton

A guided tour through the reams of unproduced scripts and undeveloped treatments in the Paul Morrissey Archive.

Right: Paul Morrissey, in a candid moment, awaits the arrival of the muse. Paris c. 1985. Photograph by Ewa Rudling.

"I have now reached the point of looking upon the world as a spectacle to be laughed at." These are the words of Gustave Flaubert, written when the future author of *Madame Bovary* was all of 15 years old, in an 1838 letter to his friend Ernest Chevalier. They also happen to describe the position of another artist who was, like Flaubert, both entirely of his time and intractably opposed to it, committed to the ceaseless ridicule of a contemporary scene that seemed to keep him in a permanent state of dyspepsia and mortified mirth: Paul Joseph Morrissey.

From his earliest published interviews to his very last, Morrissey, born 1938 in New York City, never wavered in the withering contempt he voiced for the post-Sexual Revolution, post-electrified guitar permissive society that had turned its back on the wellspring of tradition and the habits of self-restraint represented by his Catholic schooling, for which he always gave effusive thanks. (Is there such a thing as a distinctly Catholic sense of humor? Morrissey's ironically distanced perspective on the follies of mortal man seems to me a thread connecting his work to that of such disparate comic artists as Evelyn Waugh and Muriel Spark.) It is one of the peculiar paradoxes that define Morrissey's art and life that he rose to prominence by virtue of his various roles in Andy Warhol's Factory, an institution whose mainstream notoriety would be unimaginable without the same social upheavals that Morrissey decried. Adamantly anti-drug and anti-rock, he was the original manager of the opiate-and-amphetamine-friendly Velvet Underground. A lifelong bachelor and proclaimed celibate who volubly scorned the licentiousness of popular culture, he made, under the aegis of Warhol, films that were deemed pornographic in their frank explicitness. A self-defined reactionary conservative, he maintained affectionate working and personal relationships with trans actresses—Candy Darling, Jackie Curtis, and Holly Woodlawn, among others—whom he repeatedly cast in female roles, and made a film almost entirely with Latin American actors, 1984's *Mixed Blood*, at a time when such a prospect was anathema to Hollywood. Outrageously opinionated in interviews, he insisted time and again that his individual political leanings had nearly no role in his filmmaking practice. A foundational figure in the emergence of the modern American independent film in New York, his primary inspiration was the star system of the Golden Age Hollywood studios and, in spite of his underground credentials, he always maintained that his intention was to make "commercial" films. In publicity photographs Morrissey invariably wears a thin, pert frown, while profilers rarely fail to note that his denunciations and lamentations are punctuated by fits of giddy laughter. A pessimist, perhaps, but a downright jolly one.

To these myriad contradictions, another is added by Morrissey's archives, whose organization, a formidable task that began near the end of his life, has continued following his death last October, and continues still. Morrissey began his career as a vocal critic of the scripted movie, issuing statements like the following, from a 1971 interview for the Philadelphia underground newspaper *The Daily Planet*: "Everyone else who makes a film tries to tell the actors how to act and tries to give them dialogue to memorize, to repeat, to make them parrots, to cut off all their own originality and to channel their originality through the written dialogue." At the same time that he was making this declaration, however, Morrissey was already trying his hand at composing conventionally recognizable scripts, and this proselytizer for the preservation of on-camera spontaneity would be a staggeringly prolific author of screen stories for nearly his entire working life, the result being that his personal effects contain scores upon scores of treatments and scripts—some for finished films, a great many more for the 30-plus projects that were never made, with some of the latter fleshed out in multiple complete drafts, others having progressed no further than the first whiff of inspiration.

It is the artifacts relating to the films which were not to be that I've concerned myself with here, having passed several afternoons in front of the faux fireplace-styled electric heater in the living room of the former Morrissey home on 81st Street in the Upper East Side, poring over hundreds of pages representing the sum total of Morrissey's what-might-have-been output.

A screenplay alone, it should be noted, is something less than a freestanding work of art. The manuscript of an unpublished novel is, after all, still a species of novel, while an unproduced screenplay is something distinctly lacking finality, and consequently sadder, in a "For sale: baby shoes, never worn" sort of way.

Throughout his life Morrissey would insist, monomaniacally, on the capturing of performance being the crucial element of the alchemy of filmmaking: "We're not making movies," he said of his Warhol-era output, "but movies of people." What was meant by this was that the employment of elements of cinematic style—photography, editing, soundtrack, et al.—was deferential to the all-important act of bringing across an actor's personality on the screen; given these stated priorities, the sense of incompletion one feels in sifting through Morrissey's stillborn projects is particularly acute. But more than just offering grounds for conjecture, the trails he left behind offer scholars and admirers alike intriguing and heretofore largely unreported glimpses into his persistent preoccupations, the range of targets he trained his satirical scorn on through the years, and the unusual contortions that an independent filmmaker doing his best to keep a seat at the table in an unforgiving industry may occasionally be called upon to perform. In most cases, the contents of the archive offer few clues as to why these projects didn't move forward: a financier's "yes" leaves a paper trail; a "no," generally, does not. As to which were the victims of producers' indifference or other external misfortunes, and which their author lost his initial enthusiasm for, we are largely left to guess.

The Unrealized Film has always held an allure singular among the arts, cinema being unique in its vulnerability to whims that are not those of the artist. In lieu of a finished product, the obsessive cinephile must settle for the bittersweet pleasures of imagining, say, Dreyer's *Jesus*, Lynch's *Ronnie Rocket*, or Bresson's *Book of Genesis*, some even augmenting their fancies by sifting through what relics remain of these deferred dreams. To the company of these and other unmade masterpieces—for all films are masterpieces until they are made, just as all children are innocents in the delivery room—I submit *Trash: Part II*, *The House of Klang*, and the rest of the submerged iceberg of Morrissey's creative work, of which his completed films form only the tip.

MORRISSEY'S FIRST EXPERIENCES shooting "scripted" drama—following, that is, his would-be feature debut *Sleep Walk*, abandoned in 1964—came with the back-to-back productions of *Flesh for Frankenstein* (1973) and *Blood for Dracula* (1974) for producer Carlo Ponti, both starring Udo Kier, filmed in Rome and what was then Yugoslavia. (This was Morrissey's second foray into transatlantic production, following 1972's Paris-set *L'Amour*.) Even on these shoots, Morrissey's approach was highly unorthodox. Both films were, contrary to usual practice, shot in sequence. "I told the actors what to say in the morning," he informed the audience at a 1974 American Film Institute seminar. "They sort of memorized it during the lighting setup... And each day, I'd think of what further absurdity might logically follow." A producer in name alone (at least according to Morrissey), Warhol had no practical involvement with these films, which bear his imprimatur as "Presenter" in order to take advantage of brand-name recognition. If an additional authorial credit ought be given on Morrissey's monster movies, it should go to longtime Warhol collaborator Pat Hackett, whose transcriptions of his daily dictations were posthumously published as Warhol's *Diaries*, and who was standing by to take down Morrissey's off-the-cuff dialogues each day, contributing, as he would later recall, quite a bit of material of her own.

These two finished films, however, were predated by several treatments and more or less developed screenplays, which show Morrissey and collaborators attempting to launch projects that would similarly proceed according to something other than an entirely improvisation-based model. Following the niche success of 1968's *Flesh*—the first Warhol production to credit Morrissey as sole director—the Hollywood Dream Factory had begun to pay court to the Manhattan Sleaze Factory. It must have been clear to Morrissey that if he wanted to thrive inside the system, the ad-libbed style that had distinguished their output until that point would have to be adjusted to an industry that relied on careful scheduling and budgeting in pre-production.

In spring of 1969, Columbia Pictures flew out a small Factory coterie, including Morrissey and Warhol, to discuss whether the studio would underwrite a film tentatively titled ***The Truth Game***, loosely "adapted" from a collection, bearing the same name, of interviews with and profiles of celebrities (and would-be celebrities) by the writer John Hallowell, who would eventually appear as a gossip columnist in 1972's *Heat*. The extant 11-page treatment concerns an idealistic reporter on the entertainment news beat, to be played by Darling, who, over a series of encounters with subjects embodying various Tinseltown archetypes—an aging sex goddess, a fucked-up nepo baby, "flower child" prostitutes working Sunset Boulevard—grows disillusioned with show biz and the human wreckage that is its byproduct. The treatment finds Morrissey treading into docufiction terrain, possibly with the intention of locating a happy medium between the freewheeling extemporizing of the Factory films and the demands of some semblance of structure from a major studio backer, with the stated "intention of confusing the audience so as to make them wonder which part of the scene is real." Continues Morrissey:

> This tactic will be followed... as much as possible, with the performer creating their own dialogue and conversation from events in their own lives. However, the incidents and actions that these people perform will be imposed on them by this outline. The implication that words lie and that actions are real will be made. However, for the large part the stars' words will be the truth and their actions lies.

An April 24, 1969 "Scenes" column in *The Village Voice* reported on the progress of *The Truth Game*, teasing possible cameo appearances by Natalie Wood, Rita Hayworth, and Clint Eastwood, one of the few emerging stars of the period, outside of the Warhol stable, for whom Morrissey expressed unguarded enthusiasm. It was not to be. Though Columbia were in dire financial straits at the time, and evidently grasping at straws, they ultimately preferred to sell off their studios on Gower Street before letting Warhol, Morrissey, and their gang of miscreants on the lot.

Other relics of aborted undertakings from the early-to-mid '70s find Morrissey hewing closer to traditional screenplay format. The 46-page script for ***West***, dated c. 1971, is an oater very far from the Eastwood mold. Returning to the queer cowpoke terrain of Warhol/Morrissey's *Lonesome Cowboys* (1968), *West* imagines a frontier almost entirely barren of women, in which

"You'll never walk alone..." A household shrine, at the Paul Morrissey apartment, to some of his sustaining inspirations, including "Duke" Wayne and Candy Darling.

the sole saloon/brothel in the one-horse town where the film lays its scene is staffed entirely by female impersonators. "The idea," writes Morrissey in a brief statement of intent, "is that this was common practice in the Old West before women came—that men were used as women." In the same opening, it's noted that "the movie will at all times be in the serious style of other Westerns and never be played for comedy at all." Accordingly, one must imagine entirely deadpan readings of, for example, a green cowpoke's lament: "I've got no technique. Only what I learned from making love to the cows. You seem never to be sure if they like it from you or not." Or the following exchange, between protagonist Joe and one of the saloon gals:

> BELLE: Out here you're either a killer or a queer—by the way, what're you?
> JOE: I'm just passing through.

Any "Joe" appearing in scripts of the period we can safely presume to have been a part reserved for Morrissey muse Joe Dallesandro, and another surfaces in the c. 1972 screenplay for ***Animal***, for which Morrissey shares credit with the young soon-to-be Warhol studio manager Vincent Fremont. Dallesandro, who'd been street-cast by Morrissey and Warhol while they were shooting 1967's *Four Stars*, was a staple of Morrissey's work through the mid-'70s. In *Animal*, he would have been playing a "white savage" discovered and then trapped by a trio of American adventurers in the jungles of an anonymous Latin country—first sighted in flagrante delicto with a wild panther, no less. Somewhere between King Kong and Tarzan, the unspoiled Joe is favorably contrasted with his civilized captors, an echo of Morrissey's preference for untrained actors rather than those overburdened with technique. (As he put it in a 1970 interview: "College types tend to lose a lot of their interesting qualities. I don't know why. College does something to people.") The university-affiliated explorers' ostensibly scientific mission is compromised when one of their number scents a potential payday in exploiting such a magnificently feral specimen, ginning up a lucrative scheme for a "Name the Savage" contest while the Yanks and the caged Joe cool their heels at a sty-like hacienda presided over by oversexed land baroness "Holly"—most probably as in Woodlawn—and her degenerate progeny.

Another media-manipulating publicity scheme—a phenomenon largely born of the peculiarly American genius for ballyhoo, which plays a role in several 1930s screwball comedies (1937 alone produced *Nothing Sacred*, *Angel's Holiday* and *Waikiki Wedding*) so much admired by Morrissey—is at the center of ***Girl of the Year***, an early '70s script that shares its rather jaundiced view of the women's liberation movement with Morrissey's *Women in Revolt* (1971). The 33 pages, co-written by Morrissey and Richard Turley, a Wall Street lawyer who had recently drifted into Warhol's orbit, concerns an attempt by *Matriarch Magazine*, a fictional women's lifestyle magazine in the prim, staid tradition of *Ladies' Home Journal*, to keep up with the times by bringing on a militant feminist editor, whose propositions to drag the magazine into the modern world include the addition of a male nude centerfold and a nationwide search for a Girl of the Year: "a woman who has been exploited and victimized by male chauvinism without having let such treatment destroy her." The winner, North Dakota-born, Detroit-based go-go dancer Patty Miller, is brought to New York with her loutish biker boyfriend for a Gloria Steinem makeover,

Klang.

We should be getting all of this on video tape, — Only I'm not in the picture!

Ahmed

You should get some sleep too.

Klang.

With all that coke in me, forget it. Look at these magazines, (He goes to a filing cabinet and removes a thick folder of magazine pages). These are just some of the drug addict marketing strategies the others have used. (We see a series of pages that he is flipping through. Page after page show young models in different settings, - bathrooms, kitchens, hallways, vacation spots, - all looking either unconscious or dead, spread out on floors, rubber bands around their bruised arms. A caption on one of the pages reads - "Drunk, Suicidal, Dead? or all three?"

end p. 82

go back to Page 76

Klang -

Look at all these overdosed kids! Page after page! Just like at the disco

A page, in Paul Morrissey's hand, of the ultimately unrealized *The House of Klang*, a vituperous comedy set in the controversy chasing 1990s fashion industry, which occupied Morrissey's attention for the better part of a decade.

but the revolutionary reeducation fails to take. Not unlike Woodlawn's character in Morrissey's *Trash* (1970), dreaming from the depths of urban squalor of getting on welfare to become, in her own words, "respectable," Patty's aspirations are strictly suburban, going no further than "some wall-to-wall carpeting." Morrissey's underclass characters, in the main, don't want to remake the world; they'd settle for an American Express card, a station wagon, and a matching bedroom set.

Another Turley-related project kept Morrissey busy through the end of 1974: the ill-starred, Turley-and-Warhol-produced Broadway musical *Man on the Moon*, a "space opera" inspired by Neil Armstrong's moonwalk and written by John Phillips, formerly of the Mamas & the Papas. (Addled by cocaine and heroin abuse through the '70s, Phillips would later claim, apparently in earnest, that George Lucas had stolen the idea for 1977's *Star Wars* from him.) Hired as director and deep into rehearsals with the cast, which included Phillips's ex-bandmate Denny Doherty, Phillips's third wife, Genevieve Waite, and *Flesh for Frankenstein* actress Monique van Vooren, Morrissey was replaced—reportedly at Turley's behest—mere weeks before the show's January 29, 1975 opening, though his name remained attached. Given the brutal reception *Man on the Moon* was to receive, this was a matter of adding insult to injury.

At approximately the same time as Warhol's lone venture onto the Great White Way was being critically savaged, Morrissey turned out the 33-page treatment for ***Dead Chinaman***. An excursion into Sax Rohmer Yellow Peril territory, it concerns an ex-SFPD detective turned private dick's investigation into seemingly senseless killings at the home of a White House lawyer, which opens onto an ornate conspiracy involving pidgin-speaking Chinatown locals ("No savvy. Maybe closs stleet"), a Fu Manchu–esque crime boss given to ridiculously lapidary expressions of courtesy ("If the Terror of Evildoers will honor one of my deplorable chairs by resting his divine body in it, I can assure him the chair shall be burned afterward, so no lesser being may use it"), and the Third World Freedom Army, a group of campus radicals headed by an entity known as The Whistler. That name, The Whistler, recalling a 1942-1955 radio mystery program and its spinoff Columbia Pictures film series, conveys the pulpy, throwback spirit of *Dead Chinaman*, though Morrissey also introduces a touch of post-Watergate paranoia when our hero discovers that the chief executive of the United States has been receiving kickback payments from the CCP "in return for foreign aid grants that the president has given the Chinese Communist regime." Despite his iconoclastic sensibility, Morrissey was always sensitive to which way the winds were blowing in the business, and his scripts and treatments are scattered with references to cursorily similar recent successes. (A 2009 pitch for ***More Blood for Dracula*** cites Sam Raimi's *Drag Me to Hell*, released earlier that year, as an example of audience appetite for horror-comedy.) With this in mind, a certain 1974 film directed by uncredited *Blood for Dracula* actor Roman Polanski, a movie Morrissey publicly admired, seems to have been a possible inspiration for his excursion into Chinatown.

TALKING TO *HUSTLER* magazine in 1975, Morrissey can be found discussing his desire to produce the sort of fare represented by *Dead Chinaman*. "I'm looking to be commercial in more of the strict Hollywood fashion," he says. "I want to start making adventure films." In an AFI seminar the previous year, the man who'd established his name with the $5,000-budgeted *Flesh* was effusive on the subject of "spectacle films," telling his audience, "I've always wanted to do something about ancient Egypt—the pharaohs." The nearest he would come to his sword-and-sandals opus were a few drafts of a scenario from the late '80s called ***Ankhesen: Bride of Tutankhamun***, which he proposed returning to the Italian studio Cinecittà to shoot, hoping money could be scrounged up from the national broadcaster RAI or media mogul and prime minister-to-be Silvio Berlusconi.

Distinguished by its description of the 18th Dynasty king Tutankhamun as "an extraordinary man with large pendulous breasts," the project is one of a few instances discovered among Morrissey's papers of the sporadic flaring up of his frustrated DeMille-ian impulses. Others include a two-page "prologue" for a project, ***Torc***, dated c. 1976-77, the "story of Cucullen [sic], Ireland's epic hero, known from his time on as the 'Hound of Ulster'"—like Tutankhamun, a proto-monotheist, pitted against the priestly castes of his respective times and country—and, also from the late '80s, ***The Edge of the World***, about a 10-year-old "modern-day Robinson Crusoe," Jones, who lives in self-imposed isolation battling scrofulous child gangs in a near-future wasteland, pitched as "a combination of *Mad Max* and *Crocodile Dundee*." (An interest in George Miller's world of postapocalyptic trash scavengers shouldn't exactly be unexpected of a filmmaker specializing in the world of pre-apocalyptic trash scavengers.) These projects share certain affinities—both Cú Chulainn and Jones have the same superhuman coup de grâce move that wouldn't be out of place in a Shaw Brothers production, the ability to "leap through the air, suspend [themselves] above [their] victim[s], and finally descend for the kill"—as well as the fact that none proceeded past the barest preliminaries.

THE BIG STUDIOS were not eager to entrust Morrissey with the budget for a sprawling period piece. In fact, they were reluctant to give him any kind of budget at all. The seven years between the release of *Blood for Dracula*, his last film to carry the Warhol brand—whatever its demerits, undeniably useful as a fundraising tool—and his return to his roots in low-budget independent filmmaking with *Madame Wang's* (1981) were a time of professional frustration. After *Flesh* he had managed to finish features at a brisk, nearly annual clip, but only one film emerged in the abovementioned seven-year stretch, the 1978 Peter Cook/Dudley Moore–starring British comedy *The Hound of the Baskervilles*, a Sherlock Holmes farce primarily filmed in the environs of Berkshire's Bray Film Studios facilities, and a mangy cur of a movie that all parties involved would have reason to wish put down. His English misadventure aside, a litany of false starts, well represented in the archive, is all that remains of Morrissey's earnest attempt to make it on the West Coast, where he had set up headquarters by 1977. A 1980 *Wet Magazine* profile pays him a visit in an apartment on Crescent Heights Boulevard in Los Angeles, "literally a stone's throw from Schwab's drugstore." When the interviewer asks Morrissey why he's come to Southern California, he responds, "Oh, probably making a big mistake."

Fallow years, then, and years of labor in vain. There is an original script from 1975, ***Wipe Out***, co-written with one Kevin O'Neal—brother of actor Ryan and an actor himself, who two years earlier Morrissey had told the *New York Times* was helping him prepare a "Clint Eastwood-type Western done in my style" to be made for Alberto Grimaldi. (Could this have been *West*?

A question for future scholars...) A blackly comic thriller centered on a straitlaced couple whose supposedly idyllic Hawaiian vacation, won via game show appearance, *Wipe Out* ends in the duo's immersion with a pack of feral hippies, a gang rape, and a vengeful slaughter-by-speargun. Morrissey had seen and admired 1974's *Death Wish*, but was a sharper writer of mockeries than massacres, his script dripping with equal derision for reprobate back-to-earth types who've reverted to obeying the Law of the Jungle while living amidst unspoiled natural splendor and the "assembly line vacation" experience of aging, homely hula girls, sprinkler-dewed rainforests, inedible pig roasts, and "the Volcano Room of the Kahala Hilton."

The bulk of Morrissey's completed (and unproduced) screenplays in the years after his Ponti films, however, consists of scripts based on existing literary properties, something he'd first attempted—the highly unorthodox treatment of *The Truth Game* notwithstanding—in an 89-page script, completed in the early '70s, titled ***Lafacadio's Adventures***, an adaptation of André Gide's 1914 medieval farce *Les Caves du Vatican*, about a gang of fraudsters who circulate a rumor concerning the kidnapping of Pope Leo XIII, which was intended as a Warhol-produced vehicle for Mick Jagger. Other stalled projects in the same line from the latter half of the decade are ***Song of Iceland***, based on the journalist, screenwriter, and raconteur Ben Hecht's Hollywood-set 1944 comic novel *I Hate Actors!*, and, in close order, attempts at Kurt Vonnegut's 1973 postmodern satire, ***Breakfast of Champions***, and Dashiell Hammett's 1929 foundational text of hardboiled crime fiction, ***The Dain Curse*** (an effort by all evidence unrelated to the three-part telefilm that aired on CBS in 1978).

Morrissey's screenplay for ***Attack of the Fifty Foot Woman***, dating from approximately the same period, stands out as his lone attempt to "reboot" a preexisting film property, the 1958 Bernard Woolner-produced drive-in favorite of the same title. He kept the earlier film's basic premise—a wealthy housewife with a no-goodnik lothario husband grows to giant proportions after her encounter with an alien—while adding some signature Morrissey touches: the aforementioned husband, a real-estate con man (a recurrent bête noire of Morrissey's), makes his colossus of a wife the freakish centerpiece of his "Studio Forty-Five" discotheque, replete with sex couches, a cocaine concession, and cross-dressing trapeze artists. "In Hollywood, for a while, I wrote scripts for producers who then tried to sell them to the majors," Morrissey said in 1984, when summarizing his Tinseltown sojourn. "But I quickly understood that it was a dead end for me. All big companies have a bureaucratic mentality and they hate anything original or eccentric."

Morrissey learned through experience that Warhol's laissez-faire approach was far from prevalent in studio boardrooms. And though Morrissey could at times be as cutting towards his former partner as he was when criticizing corporatized cinema, his business relations with Warhol himself—including joint maintenance of Eothen, their oceanfront estate in Montauk—remained cordial up until the latter's sudden death in 1987. *Breakfast of Champions* was tentatively planned as a Warhol production, to be directed by Morrissey (as reflected in a non-executed legal agreement housed in the archive), and he testified to *Cinématographe* in 1982 that he was offered *Andy Warhol's Bad* (1977) before Jed Johnson, following Morrissey's pass, took the reins.

To Paul Morrissey's later chagrin, some of his best-known films—films that he, by all accounts, was the primary driving creative force on—would be marketed as "Andy Warhol" movies, both before and long after Warhol had shuffled off this mortal coil.

Warhol, too, appears to have had nothing but respect for his erstwhile partner: in his *Diaries*, he records a visit to the Waverly cinema to catch a screening of *Mixed Blood* in January of '86. "I just loved the movie," Warhol wrote. "It was everything he's done before, but it was photographed well and he seemed to know so much about the Lower East Side and the Alphabet—Avenues A, B, C, and D—for someone who hadn't been in New York for so long." In fact, the resentful tone at any mention of the Warhol name gradually crept into Morrissey's interviews only later, following a protracted struggle for the ownership of his films with the posthumously created Andy Warhol Foundation, and a mounting sense of being considered an obstacle in the construction and burnishing of the Warhol effigy.

BY THE END of the '70s, having failed to make a conspicuous hit as both a director of established talk show–circuit talent like Cook and Moore and as a hired-hand utility player in Hollywood, Morrissey was eyeing a return to New York to re-entrench himself in familiar creative territory, working and reworking the script for a proposed sequel to *Trash* that would have reunited Dallesandro and Woodlawn. ***Trash: Part II*** picks up with our proudly parasitic antiheroes, who, in the decade since last encountered, have amassed an impressive brood of children of various provenance, including a 10-year-old introduced helping his mother lift contraband steaks from the supermarket, a 13-year-old who has wasted no time getting herself pregnant, and a 15-year-old threatening to light off to Delaware to elope with his teacher. With the kids on the verge of leaving the nest and Joe having been exposed on television news for working an under-the-table gig at a pizza parlor—Dallesandro's actual pre-Superstardom gig—Holly must scramble to stave off threats to her hefty welfare sinecure.

You can almost hear Morrissey cackling to himself when writing such scenes as that of Joe and Holly crashing a PTA meeting at their children's school, where US history is learned from Spanish-dubbed videos and "an epidemic of V.D. [venereal disease] among children aged 9 to 14" is raging; that of Holly's visit to the "fancy" McDonald's on 95th Street and First Avenue ("Aren't we putting on airs?"); and the finale in which she quick-thinkingly orchestrates a staged auto accident involving one of the kids, with the resulting insurance settlement allowing for the family to relocate from slums to suburbs. "What do we do when this money runs out?" Joe asks as they're moving into their new digs. "We'll get back on welfare, like everyone else," replies Holly. "I was born on welfare and I'll fucking die on welfare, and I'd like to see those bastards stop me!"

To understand Morrissey's repeated returns to the subject of government-provided financial relief, it is worth remembering that in the '60s he had been employed as a field reporter for the City of New York Department of Welfare—an experience that seems to have left him with both a deep skepticism of the system's effectiveness in improving people's lives and a grudging admiration of those he perceived as resourceful scammers who manipulate it for their own ends. A handwritten note by Morrissey on a 1964 probationary period report from the department, found in the archive, reveals his real, engaged human interest in his "cases": "The most important consideration regarding any type of work with people," it reads, "should be the ability of the person to talk intelligently with people and attempt to understand their problems." If *Trash* is, and if *Trash: Part II* might have been, more than an angry screed against the perceived failures of Great Society liberalism, it's thanks to the fact that Morrissey never lost his basic sympathy for those on society's fringes. In the script for *Trash: Part II*, as in its predecessor, it is the smarmy bureaucrat envoys of government assistance programs, rather than the loafers who batten on it, who come closest to registering as villains.

The 59-page ***Flash***, written around the same time, is the story of one Eddie Sikes, an American musician with classical training from a Dutch conservatory school who demeans himself and his talent for fame as a dope-stupefied guitarist/keyboardist in the titular heavy metal act, a group that, with their face paint and "blatant, mocking" sexuality, seem very likely to have been inspired by KISS. Temporarily cleaned up after a hilariously botched blood replacement procedure, not unlike that undertaken by the Keith Richards of urban legend, Sikes is reunited with an old flame back in Amsterdam who's now making ends meet by performing in a live sex show. Their road to reconciliation is not without potholes of recidivist bad behavior, but *Flash* stands out somewhat among Morrissey's completed scripts in that it's the rare morality tale to conclude with the suggestion that its tarnished characters may manage to lift one another out of the pits of degradation they've dug for themselves.

Morrissey never tired of railing against rock 'n' roll's culture of license and excess in both interviews and screenplays. Yet, in another of the paradoxes that define Morrissey, he was often as enamored of rock stars as magnetic personalities as he was contemptuous of their music: in addition to hoping to enlist Jagger in *Lafacadio's Adventures*, he conceived of ***Tropicana***, an early iteration of *Heat*, as a vehicle for Creedence Clearwater Revival's John Fogerty, and Morrissey's list of proposed stars for *Torc* included Robert Plant and Marc Bolan.

The last intriguing original property to emerge in this fertile '79-'81 stretch, alternately titled ***Sleep, Doggie, Sleep*** and ***Stray Dog***, seems possibly to have stemmed from Morrissey's immersion in the history of 1920s California criminal life while writing *The Dain Curse*. Though the 27-page treatment, dated October 1980, and the various drafts of a complete screenplay, dated '92-'93—co-authored by Kurt Voss, director of the Brad Dourif-starring LA indie curio *Horseplayer* (1990)—are contemporary in setting, they are obviously inspired by events surrounding the Wineville Chicken Coop murders, a series of abductions and murders of young boys that occurred between 1926 and '28 in Los Angeles and Riverside County, specifically the strange case of nine-year-old Walter Collins.

Five months after Collins's disappearance the LAPD, facing increasing pressure from the press and the public to track down the perpetrators, "found" the boy in DeKalb, Illinois, and reunited him with his grieving single mother. When Christine Collins kicked up a fuss, insisting that the child the police had unloaded on her was not, in fact, her son, the ingrate was dutifully chucked into a psych ward, only released when her suspicions were vindicated. If this sounds somewhat familiar, it's perhaps because this same affair inspired 2008's *Changeling*, directed by Clint Eastwood from a J. Michael Straczynski script, a rather more "straight" telling of the Collins story than either of Morrissey's attempts—his first version involves a sadistic lesbian running a racket involving the cryogenic freezing of canine pets. Given Morrissey's known admiration for Eastwood and the parallels between certain scenes in the finished film and the two Morrissey scripts, might some iteration of *Sleep, Doggie, Sleep* have passed through Malpaso, Eastwood's production company, and been optioned for further development in other hands? What I do know, via filmmaker and *The Metrograph* contributor Owen Kline, is that Morrissey was still trying to get the project off the ground himself at various points in the '90s; Kline recalls that it was pitched to his mother, Phoebe Cates, as a vehicle for them to star in together.

The only film that Morrissey actually shot in SoCal during his sojourn there was *Madame Wang's*, a scabrous and hysterical look at (low)life in the slum districts of Long Beach. It was another broadside directed towards rock music, here the burgeoning LA punk scene—the title is a riff on Madame Wong's, the Chinese restaurant that provided a stage for otherwise unbookable hardcore acts like Black Flag and Fear—as well as a return to form for Morrissey, proving there was, in fact, Life After Warhol. The film's protagonist is an East German spy, Patrick Schoene's grimly stoic Lutz, who arrives stateside intending to rendezvous with comrade Jane Fonda but instead is adopted by a community of colorful wastrels, his mounting disgust with American decadence rivalling Morrissey's own. In the year of *Madame Wang's* release, another "Lutz," very possibly the same character—he's also an Ossi operating on the other side of the Wall, here paying for acts of anti-American agitation in cold, hard deutsche marks—pops up in a Morrissey script, revised several times by its author, ***Baby Street***, a film set in divided Berlin, described by Morrissey in a 1982 interview as "a sort of *Christiane F.* (1981), but a lot less heavy." Concerning the art-school-dropout daughter of a US Embassy attaché and the various misadventures that befall her while she tries unsuccessfully to sell her body on city streets overcrowded with underage trade, *Baby Street* had Annette von Klier and Fassbinder actor Dieter Schidor attached to it at one time or another—and an early draft of the screenplay, "adapted from a story by Paul Morrissey," was by Burkhard Driest, who'd appeared alongside Schidor in Fassbinder's *Querelle* (1982)—but was destined, finally, to remain but a twinkle in its father's eye. (Morrissey would, eventually, complete a very different film in the German-speaking world, 1985's *Beethoven's Nephew*, filmed in Vienna and co-written with actor Mathieu Carrière.)

MORRISSEY MADE HIS first and only film concerned with fresh-faced young hustlers after he'd set up shop in New York again, and it was back home that he encountered a figure who would arguably be as crucial to the second part of his career as Warhol had been to the first: California-born playwright Alan Bowne. Bowne was 26 when his first produced show, the two-act *Forty-Deuce*, opened at the Perry Street Theatre in Greenwich Village and closed less than a month later. Morrissey was agog over the play, and adapted *Forty-Deuce* for the screen in 1982, following Bowne's script quite faithfully and employing most of its original cast members, including a young Kevin Bacon, who won an Obie for his performance as the cool, cunning Ricky. Bowne would go on to be Morrissey's writing partner on his other two NYC-set features still to come, *Mixed Blood* and *Spike of Bensonhurst* (1988), and play the part of creatively reinvigorating kindred spirit.

Bowne's best-known play, *Beirut*, debuted in 1988, at the height of the AIDS crisis, which would take the playwright's life the following year. The show—later adapted into the 1993 TV movie *Daybreak*—is set in a crumbling downtown Manhattan where a community of lesion-afflicted "positives" have been packed into a Kraków ghetto-style quarantine and branded on the buttocks with an identifying "P." Such subject matter belies a greater interest in gay rights-related issues on the part of Bowne than Morrissey ever publicly espoused, but the men evidently bonded over a shared interest in unlettered roughneck urban primitives and their savory street patois.

Two short treatments submitted to Morrissey by Bowne in the mid-'80s also suggest simpatico senses of humor and penchants for provocation. The first, ***Death of an Urban Pioneer***, is a mystery-thriller imagined as a two-part TV movie, revolving around a conspiracy between organized crime and bought-and-paid-for city officials to transform burnt-out and gutted tenements into a destination for high-rollers ("They want to turn the LES into Las Vegas East"), that again takes aim at real-estate developers. The second, ***Commie Killer***, is proposed as "a film in the *Terminator* mode, a blend of sci-fi, revenge thriller, and horror movie." Bowne's tantalizing basic premise—an escapee from the Eastern Bloc now living in Western Europe is hypnotized into acting as an unstoppable killing machine by members of a clandestine anti-Communist underground—would be seized upon and spun by Morrissey into the 72-page screenplay ***Against the Wall*** in 1985. This is presumably the project he is touting in a 1986 *Time Out* interview ("I'm also going to do an anti-terrorism story; kill the commie filth!"), in which he takes time to enthuse over Arnold Schwarzenegger and Rae Dawn Chong's performances in *Commando* (1985).

In *Against the Wall*, Morrissey moves the action to a near-future 1994, when "the government in the East has fallen and been replaced in a Fascist Nazi takeover by Politburo members who are the spiritual heirs of those Russians who had once signed the Hitler-Stalin pact," while those in the West, "exhausted by years of liberty and freedom," turn envious eyes towards their totalitarian neighbors. ("People from the West hate the West," Morrissey proclaims in a 1982 interview. "There's a sort of nostalgia for authority.") The weak-willed, due-process leniency that the few remaining democracies show when confronted with threats to the safety of their citizens, along with a popular culture that blindly worships brutality—in a scene set at a punk-industrial performance the group's frontman "repeat[s] an actual speech of Adolf Hitler's to a kind of reggae-rap accompaniment"—seems to spell the imminent collapse of civilization. The resistance, however, can play dirty too, unleashing a brainwashed puppet to act as scourge of the Fascisto-Commies. The script disposes of Bowne's high-camp line, "Karl Marx was a fag," while Morrissey introduces a deliciously absurd twist in which our protagonist, after racking up scores of enemy kills, reveals that he has in fact been acting of his own free will the entire time, announcing: "I can't be hypnotized, I'm not the type." (Morrissey produced another vigilante justice-oriented treatment at the height of the '80s craze for action extravaganzas, ***East Side - West Side***, its depiction of young girls sold into "Arab harems" predicting 2008's *Taken*. This is not a compliment.)

After the release of *Spike of Bensonhurst*—a film whose opening, introducing a small-time club fighter who specializes in taking dives for pay, is presaged in an early '80s treatment by Morrissey and O'Neal, the Depression-set ***Sideshow***—Morrissey's main focus appears to have been a script titled ***Self-Help***, of which no less than five distinct complete drafts can be found in the archive. An actor who earns his bread and butter appearing in televised crime reenactments is roped into conducting a morally dubious hidden-camera exposé in Morrissey's take-no-prisoners satire, which takes potshots at health food faddism, personal empowerment gurus (a lifestyle coach preaching enlightenment through real-estate investment with bestselling books including *Real Estate, the Real You* and *You Are Where You Live* features prominently), and the ever-more ghoulish, rubbernecking tendencies on display nightly in prime-time programming, with thinly veiled references to *America's Most Wanted, Unsolved Mysteries*, and tabloid infotainment of the Maury Povich school. About the only organization that appears to earn Morrissey's approval is Curtis Sliwa's citizens-on-patrol Guardian Angels, foiled in intervening in a crime scene by the NYPD, with New York's Finest depicted, much as they were in *Spike*, as sawed-off do-nothing runts who turn a blind eye to the crime and chaos that swirls around them.

THE '90S WOULD pass without a Paul Morrissey feature, his only completed film of the decade 1993's *Changing Fashions*, a New York-set, 16-minute short shot without sync sound and paid for by *Details* magazine, in which gorgeous young riff-raff Anthony Kiedis and Sofia Coppola flee the nefarious influence of a haranguing Debbie Harry—finally, Morrissey had got his hands on some rock stars!—across an East Village not quite gentrified into a ghost of its former self, featuring a bevy of drag queens, sidewalk junk shops, and a closing shot of Kiedis being chased down the street in his boxers that homages Buster Keaton's *Seven Chances* (1925).

This dearth of completed projects does not, of course, mean that the boundlessly energetic Morrissey was resting on his laurels. In the archive one finds short treatments for family reconciliation stories (c. 1990's ***Quality Time*** and c. 1992's ***Underground Party***, whose slim scenarios suggest a forced sentimentality little evidenced in Morrissey's other work), as well as another with the promising title ***South Beach Skin Trade***, in which a DEA agent bearing the comically straitlaced name "Scott Smith" is ensnared by a crossdressing femme fatale. There are, intriguingly, also two embryonic ideas for contributing to the vast wasteland of broadcast television: a five-page proposal for a talk show, ***Instant Replay***, and an outline for 10 episodes of a workplace sitcom, c. 1991's ***Fast Food***—denouncing junk food was a staple of Morrissey diatribes against American junk culture—whose cast of characters is determined by his singular idea of DEI hiring ("Half the staff must be male and half female, and only half can be considered pretty"). Most bafflingly, two sets of notes attest to Morrissey attempting a polish on the script of *Redemption: Kickboxer 5*, the final entry in the martial arts franchise, released direct to video in 1995, which finds Mark Dacascos taking the wheel from Sasha Mitchell, the star of *Spike* and lead in the previous three installments. But none of these projects absorbed a fraction of the attention that Morrissey gave to a script that began its life with the title *Filthy Rags* and would soon become known as ***The House of Klang***.

All of the vitriol stored during the years that Morrissey spent observing—and stewing over—grunge, gangsta rap, ghoulish talk show spectacles, Chris Ofili's *The Holy Virgin Mary* scandal, and heroin chic would be violently disgorged in his utterly gonzo screenplay for *The House of Klang*, the earliest iteration of which was finished in 1995, and which he was still revising and revisiting as late as 2001. A full-throated jeremiad of a script, a work of epic demoralization, hands-thrown-in-the-air despair, and fatalistic glee, downright Rabelaisian in its scattershot scatological humor, which includes an in-demand dauber who decorates canvases with blasts of paint from his rectum, *Klang*, arguably inspired by Morrissey's then-recent dealings with *Details*, concerns the eponymous fashion designer Hugo Klang—character name obviously indebted to Helmut Lang—a third-rate couturier and conceptual-video-art collector who, in a make-or-break effort to distinguish himself from his competitors, masterminds a calculatedly transgressive campaign for a new line of underwear for teens while simultaneously launching himself into the public eye as a new media artist and notorious "bad boy" deviant. ("To enhance my reputation as a sexual predator, I've hired a Public Relations expert.") Cultivating contact with a wide range of professional pop nihilists, including a group who "do a Menudo style dancing in line as they sing about prostitution, getting high, [and] committing suicide," Klang justifies his blitzkrieg assault of shock tactics with the language of social justice, all while conveniently ignoring the exploitative chain of production that makes fast fashion profitable, churning out "things that cost only pennies for underage children to make in Third World countries." The defining "concept" of his first post-rebranding line is the ghoulish fetishization of down-and-outer Skid Row immiseration, which puts Klang ahead of both John Galliano's 2000 "Hobo Couture" collection for Christian Dior and its skewering as

I

Metrograph A–Z
I Is for *India Song*

Words by
Tacita Dean

I saw Marguerite Duras's film only once over 30 years ago, but I have never forgotten its elegant lassitude and utter forlornness. I remember nothing of the narrative that I'm now reading on Wikipedia, only the sparseness of Duras's style, and her cinematic minimalism. Apart from the elegiac presence of Delphine Seyrig and an exceptional ensemble cast, who drift and encounter each other inside a narrative that feels untethered from the film that is carrying it, Duras's principal tool is the soundtrack. It is the sound alone that persuades us that we're not on the dank outskirts of Paris (where it was filmed) but in monsoon overcast Calcutta. The story, if it be story, is delivered through voiceover, detached from the picture like the characters inhabiting the film. The imagined location is imposed on the scenes that present themselves, an elsewhere created with the barest of aural props. Did I see peacocks or merely hear them? But they are there, in my mind's eye. Which brings us to "India Song," the song. Carlos d'Alessio's music underwrites and haunts every minute of the film. Driving around France in the mid-1990s, I would listen to a cassette of Jeanne Moreau singing "India Song," seemingly dredging up the words from a bygone era of decadence, boredom, and desire where they once might have had resonance: *Chanson / De ma terre lointaine / Toi qui parleras d'elle / Maintenant disparue...* The tune repeats and repeats in the film until it stays with you forever. Believe me, you will never get it out of your head... *India Song* (1975) is radical cinema. More radical now, it occurs to me, than it was even then.

Derelicte the following year in Ben Stiller's *Zoolander*—by comparison a kid-gloves treatment of the industry.

Sometime in the course of writing and rewriting *Klang*, Morrissey had gotten wind of the Dogme 95 manifesto, and in its "vows of chastity" and mission to purge cinema of egregious directorial intervention—including the eschewal of prepared sets, non-diegetic or post-recorded sound, "special lighting," and directorial credit—he saw a back-to-basics spirit akin to that in which he and Warhol had begun working in the 1960s. A Morrissey-penned piece titled "The House of Klang as a Dogme Film," presumably written in an effort to raise funds, indicates his intent to make the picture according to Dogme rules—even down to the unusual for him employment of handheld camera—as does a 1999 piece in the *New York Observer* that reports Morrissey "working out the financing details" for his next feature. The part of Klang was intended for Kier who, decades after portraying Baron Frankenstein and Count Dracula, would be playing his most diabolical role for Morrissey: a "monster" created by the market for depravity. Manolo Blahnik was also pursued, which would have represented Morrissey's first bit of casting from the world of haute couture since Karl Lagerfeld's appearance in *L'Amour*. (Morrissey's interest in the milieu is further evinced by 2005's *Veruschka: A Life for the Camera*, a documentary about the Prussian aristocrat and supermodel that Morrissey co-directed with Bernd Böhm.)

Instead of the howl of scornful laughter that Klang might have been, Morrissey's swan song was 2010's *News from Nowhere*, a film, fitfully written and completed only after his near-fatal encounter with a moving van, that seemed to satisfy neither critics nor Morrissey. From that point on, the frenetic scriptwriting, the ceaseless struggle to launch new projects and target fresh absurdities for skewering, tapered off entirely. Morrissey's feelings about the proper usage of the twilight of one's life may perhaps be glimpsed decades earlier, in his 1987 treatment for a feature to be set in a senior citizens center in South Miami Beach, titled ***Urban Renewal***. The film, writes Morrissey, would depict

> the life of such an establishment wherein the old people, rather than settle down and accept the obvious fate of their declining years of simply watching the sun go down, invent absurd arguments and problems... Since they're not about to fall in love with anyone, they can still fall into bickering and petty hatreds so as to remind themselves they are still alive.

While Morrissey never lost his taste for bickering, insisting to anyone who might ask on his essential, undervalued, and deliberately obscured role in making "Warhol's" films, for one, he seems to have evinced no desire to spend his remaining years milling about hat-in-hand, raising funds and chasing dreams. His particular version of "watching the sun go down" involved a steady daily diet of TCM, Fox News, and select reality television: *Hardcore Pawn* and *Pawn Stars* were unsurprisingly favorites of the ardent antiquer, who in his films depicts time and again a landfill world populated by grubby gleaners. By all appearances he never reconciled himself to the man-made world, which he left behind in his 86th year, but the body of work he produced in his passage through it is a testament to the bemused tenderness he felt towards the human menagerie, and offers a lasting solace for all of us still muddling in the muck.

A sober and punctilious man surrounded by reprobates, speed freaks, and people who'd been told they were insane and therefore acted the part accordingly, Paul Morrissey was the "normal guy" in the Warhol circus—playing a straight man part that is, if contemplated at any length, almost surreally freaky. But here's the thing: he held on to everything.

THE METROGRAPH INTERVIEW #2

THE LATEST INSTALMENT IN OUR CENTERPIECE INTERVIEW SERIES

CHRISTIAN

PETZOLD

WRITTEN BY CHRISTINE SMALLWOOD

TRANSLATED BY JAMES LATTIMER

PHOTOGRAPH BY JULIA SELLMANN

Christian Petzold can plumb, like few other contemporary filmmakers, the infinite depths of a look of longing. His characters are memorable less for what they say than for what they don't. Most films are, in one way or another, detective stories, asking us to interpret motivations, connect a cast of characters, or piece together clues to make sense of events. But Petzold is notably drawn to characters who keep secrets, or can't tell the truth about who they are. Even when they stand to gain something from speaking, they often have difficulty getting the words out.

He was born in 1960 in Hilden, a small city in the far west of divided Germany, to parents who were refugees from the East. After fulfilling his mandatory civil service by running a film club, he came to Berlin to study literature; in Berlin, however, as he has said, "I really only went to the cinema." He became an auditor at the German Film and Television Academy (DFFB), taking classes with Hartmut Bitomsky, Dominik Graf, and Harun Farocki, and enrolled there in 1989, the year the Wall fell. Farocki would become a mentor, friend, and close collaborator, co-writing several of Petzold's films.

As a student, Petzold spent much of his time watching films, not making them. After graduating he wrote and directed a number of shorts and TV movies, and eventually released his first feature, *The State I Am In* (2000), when he was 40 years old. Since then, he has worked at a fast clip, averaging a new feature every two years—his 11th, *Miroirs No. 3*, premiered in the spring at Cannes.

Though an established player on the arthouse circuit, Petzold is known for drawing on the conventions of genres such as thriller, noir, and melodrama, not to create some kind of avant-garde pastiche, but to honor and, in his words, "reconstruct" the conventions of classical cinema. (He is very fond, as well, of American Westerns.) His work—and conversation—is peppered with filmic and literary references, but never feels pedantic or conceptual. Critics have often placed him, alongside DFFB alumni Angela Schanelec and Thomas Arslan, as a member of the first wave of the Berlin School, an informal group that uses certain techniques—unhurried pacing; long takes; austere, wide, or static framing—to make distilled, realistic, sometimes cryptic dramas about everyday life. He has had a special interest in post-reunification Germany. Having been a firsthand witness to *Die Wende* and its socioeconomic fallout, he is unusually attentive to struggles around work, money, and jobs; many of his stories involve financial necessity colliding with the sudden irruption of romantic desire.

Whereas some of his New German Cinema forebears, like Wim Wenders and Werner Herzog, sought exotic foreign landscapes and Hollywood financiers, Petzold has seemed content to shoot largely in Germany, filming often in Berlin (where he still lives) and other northern cities and towns. Perhaps because he has continued to work with modest, government-subsidized budgets, averaging somewhere between two to three million euros per film, little is overtly flashy or attention-getting about Petzold's visual style. Literature has been as profound an influence on him as cinema, or perhaps more; he has credited Simenon and Chekhov with first inspiring him to make a feature film. Still, the meaning of a film hangs on an image, and Petzold is most interested in the human subjects of his images; all of his choices, from mise en scène to editing, are in the service of creating and capturing intimate moments between people, especially between male and female romantic interests. Petzold speaks often about ghosts and "transit spaces"—places where a transformation of some kind is possible. But his films remain resolutely grounded in bodies.

Working repeatedly with the same actors—Barbara Auer, Paula Beer, Matthias Brandt, Benno Fürmann, Nina Hoss, Julia Hummer, Franz Rogowski—Petzold elicits loose, naturalistic performances that, at their best, haunt the viewer for some time. When discussing Rogowski, Petzold notes that he "exudes a sense of loneliness." But many of his troupe do, from Fürmann driving in *Jerichow* (2008) to Hoss, wide-eyed and afraid in *Yella* (2007), to Auer imploring Beer to play the piano in *Miroirs No. 3*. Even the way Petzold stages car crashes, which he does in a number of films, is lonely; when his cars flip, veer off the road, careen off cliffs, or burn, they do so alone. An automobile resting on its side in an empty field, rather than a multicar pileup on a busy road, is how he signifies disaster.

Though people in Petzold's emotionally precise, historically specific thrillers are under intense pressure, and often driven to desperate actions, there is a slow burn to their structure. Three early films comprise his so-called "Ghosts" trilogy. The first, *The State I Am In*, is about a couple living in exile who once committed an unspecified act of left-wing terrorism, and whose daughter, pulled by the pangs of adolescence, unwittingly compromises their safety. In *Ghosts* (2005), a teenage orphan meets and falls in love with another girl, a sophisticated drifter. The movie reaches its climax when a woman whose toddler was abducted from a supermarket years earlier claims that our heroine is her missing daughter. In *Yella*, a loose remake of the eerie *Carnival of Souls* (1962) about a woman who doesn't know that she is dead, Hoss plays a woman being stalked by her bankrupt ex-husband, who falls into work as an accountant for a shady investor. A mounting sense of dread and unease characterizes all of these films, as past events inevitably catch up with the present.

Three of Petzold's later films, the so-called "Love in Times of Oppressive Systems" trilogy, approach politics more explicitly. In *Barbara* (2012), arguably Petzold's most celebrated work, an East German doctor, played again by Hoss, must choose between defecting to the West to join her lover and remaining in the backwater where the authorities have sent her—a place where, to her surprise, she finds not only intriguing romantic possibility but, perhaps more importantly, meaningful work. Hoss's Barbara is distrustful, even resentful, but she is revealed to be highly principled; run down but ultimately in command of an inner freedom. In *Phoenix* (2014), Hoss plays a cabaret singer who escapes Auschwitz, gets facial reconstruction surgery, and tracks down her ex-husband, who, failing to recognize her, enlists her in a plot to steal her own money. It's Petzold's least characteristic and perhaps most daring project: a horror movie that lives by Hoss's huge eyes and damaged vulnerability. She trembles her way through the film, at once profoundly suffering and magnificently

Christian Petzold consults with his frequent collaborator Franz Rogowski in Marseille on the set of *Transit* (2018), in which Rogowski portrays a German political refugee who assumes the identity of a deceased writer in his flight from a fascist state. Photograph by Marco Krüger.

possessed. *Transit* (2018), a canny update of an Anna Seghers novel from 1944, stars Rogowski as a man who steals a dead writer's identity in order to flee a fascist state; it feels more prophetic with every passing day. Farocki died several years before the film was finished, but Petzold had initially developed the story with him—Farocki had given him the book decades earlier, and, Petzold once said, "It always served as the number one reference for all [our] screenplays."

If Petzold's characters are keeping secrets, perhaps it is no surprise that they are led to betray one another. In *Wolfsburg* (2003), Fürmann commits a hit-and-run and then, instead of confessing, becomes romantically involved with the mother of the child he killed. In *Jerichow*, inspired by the several iterations of the noir classic *The Postman Always Rings Twice*, Fürmann plays a veteran of the War in Afghanistan who becomes a driver for a local businessman, a Turkish immigrant, and then begins an affair with that man's wife, which culminates in a murder plot. In interview after interview, Petzold has claimed that he is not a "political" filmmaker, which I take to mean that he isn't using his films to prove a thesis or argue an idea. But his characters live in the mess of a present day that is clearly a product of political and economic forces—of failed systems. His films investigate what it feels like to get up, go to work, and fall in love when the world is on fire, when history itself seems to have crashed like an automobile on some highway to nowhere.

His most recent films, all starring Beer, are exercises in intimacy, foregrounding the banal miracle, and tragic consequences, of connection. In the spellbinding romance *Undine* (2020), she plays a historian of Berlin's urban development who turns out to be a mythological water nymph. Beer does so much to establish the emotional reality of her heartbreak, rage, and desire that the plausibility of the scenario is never in question. (It's also a film about work; Undine's love interest is an industrial diver, and the film is rigorously attentive to the mechanics of gear, featuring extended and hypnotic underwater sequences, in which words are replaced by evocative looks.) In the charming, chatty, and ultimately terrifying *Afire* (2023), a writer's summer vacation by the Baltic Sea is threatened by an encroaching forest fire. Again, Beer lends a casual glamour and stability to the scene, acting as a force that steers events (though ultimately her power is nothing compared to the power of the elements). And in *Miroirs No. 3*, Beer plays a pianist who, following a tragic car accident, becomes attached to a grieving family.

To say that Petzold's subjects are secrets and betrayal is perhaps another way of saying that his subject is love. No matter how inappropriate the situation, or inopportune the moment, his characters can't help but be waylaid by desire—with desire comes attachments, commitments, entanglements, complications. They are pushed into the future by these flickers of passion, which are also flickers of hope.

CHRISTINE SMALLWOOD: Over the last five days I've watched all of your feature films, so I feel like... am I in your dreams? It's a little surreal to actually see you on the other side of the screen. I want to start deep in the past. I read that the first film you ever saw was *The Jungle Book* (1967). What memories of that do you have?

CHRISTIAN PETZOLD: I was eight or nine years old, and an older neighbor took me to what was the last cinema in our village. I always remember two things about that day. One is that this film hooked me. I didn't want to leave the cinema at all; I wanted to see the film again right away. There's such a physicality to how Mowgli floats down the water on top of the bear's belly. I thought to myself: that is freedom. It was a sense of physicality, of corporeality, that I'd never experienced before.

But the second thing is that the projectionist made a crazy mistake. He showed a trailer before *The Jungle Book* for *Liane, das Mädchen aus dem Urwald* (Liane, Jungle Goddess, 1956), which is an adult picture. In the film you see an almost naked, blonde German model in a cage about to be roasted over an open fire by cannibals. She screams for help. For a moment you see her bare breasts. This combination of *The Jungle Book* and *Liane* was, I think, a formative experience.

CS: What other movies in your childhood or adolescence left a mark on you?

CP: When my two children were around seven, eight, nine years old, we watched *SpongeBob SquarePants* a lot. There's an episode ["Graveyard Shift" from Season 2 -Ed.] where SpongeBob suddenly gets scared in the dark. And for a second, an image from F.W. Murnau's *Nosferatu: A Symphony of Horror* (1922) is spliced in: Max Schreck on the ship. My children screamed! Because of Nosferatu, because of this picture, because of this image of Count Orlok. This crazy fear that my children had, it reminded me that *Nosferatu* was the other big film from my childhood that made an incredible impression on me. It was shown on television at all hours. I remember so many things about it, but two sequences left the biggest mark. The first is of the coach going over the bridge and the intertitle: "And when he crossed the bridge, the phantoms came to meet him." That's key for me. The second is later in the film: a shot of a cemetery on the Baltic Sea, where many crucifixes are stuck in the sand dunes. Later, when I saw the John Ford Westerns with cemeteries on the outskirts of small towns, I thought that they looked just like the graveyard in *Nosferatu*.

CS: We could have a whole conversation just about ghosts and spirits. Do you think something about film as a medium makes it especially well-suited to ghost stories?

CP: Cinema and the spirit world have always had something to do with each other. Spirit photography was one of the first types of photography, just as ghost films using double exposures and things like that was one of the first types of cinema. I also believe that the characters that cinema is most interested in are those who are about to become ghosts: people who have lost their jobs; people who have lost someone they love, or their parents, or their homes; people who are on the run, who drift, who are afraid of disappearing, and whose basic longing is to take material form again—to find a home, to find a job, to find an identity.

Count Orlok is someone like this: a ghost who wants to love again and get a body. The moment he loves, he has to die. The moment he stays behind and the sun hits him, he has to die. You could also say that almost all such characters find themselves in spaces of transit or transition. They don't know where they are going. Cinema loves these characters because cinema itself is a transit space.

CS: One of the things that I find amazing about your films is how you work with actors. And an actor is a real body that, through the technology of cinema, becomes light.

CP: In Germany, most actors come from theater schools. For actors, the theater is a place where they are not ghosts. They are more like masks. But when these actors move into a filmic space—cinema captures the space between people, the energy that arises there. I don't want to overdo it with the metaphor, but that is the space where ghosts also feel comfortable.

CS: You've often spoken about how you approach shooting and production: you introduce your actors to the locations, do a lot of rehearsals, and then prefer to shoot only one or two takes. I wonder if you have an anecdote to share about your most recent shoot, for *Miroirs No. 3*? Did anything happen on set that surprised you?

CP: Sometimes you don't even have to rehearse with the actors; you just give them material. When we shot *Transit* in Marseille, we had an open-air cinema built on top of our hotel, and we always waited until 10pm, when it was dark, to watch films with the actors. The first one we watched together was *The Graduate* (1967) by Mike Nichols. Because *Transit* is about the refugees who fled from National Socialism and ended up in Marseille, the actors asked: "What does this have to do with *Transit*?" I said to them, "Mike Nichols was born in Berlin in 1931. He had to leave Germany with his family in 1939 during the pogroms, and went to America and directed plays on Broadway and then made two fantastic films, *Who's Afraid of Virginia Woolf?* (1966) and *The Graduate*. In these films we see bodies. In these films we see certain kinds of movement. There is a certain physicality. We see a completely new form of montage, a desire for the world and an open form that we no longer have in Germany, that we have lost."

The German writer Anna Seghers, who wrote the novel *Transit* and lived in Marseille for a year, en route to Mexico, read Raymond Chandler, Dashiell Hammett, Ernest Hemingway, and F. Scott Fitzgerald when she was on the run from the Nazis. She read modern American literature; her novel *Transit* is infected with it. It is infected with something new. And at the same time, it is so insanely horrible and tragic that Germany lost this kind of art. For the actors, it was crazy. [Watching *The Graduate*] they understood the transit space—what their characters had lost in their escape and what they dreamt of and what they desired from where they wanted to get to. That was better than any form of rehearsal, just watching a movie together and talking about it.

For *Miroirs No. 3*, we built a house on the outskirts of Berlin, in nature. It is very beautiful. In the film, a young woman [played by Beer] comes to this house and meets a family that has experienced a tragedy, though they don't talk about it. On the day of rehearsal, the actors simply walked through the house and thought about how this family lived here.

What kind of traces they left behind. I just sat on a chair and left the actors alone in the house for an hour or two. I saw how they moved through the space, how they had a drink in the kitchen, how they sat down in an armchair, how they looked at the garden. I think that was one of the best rehearsals I've ever had, because the actors occupied this place as architecture but also as a dream space.

When I was a film student, we had a seminar with Hartmut Bitomsky, in which we watched a film and then, more carefully, watched a sequence from the film again. We had to write down, in this sequence, where is the kitchen, where is the bathroom, where is the hallway? We had to reconstruct the space.

I think that cinema has something to do with architecture. You have to be able to feel the space. We have to know where we are. That's something I talk about a lot with the actors; we build a space in which the audience can also orient themselves. In the seminar, we watched the sequence from *Blue Velvet* (1986) where Kyle MacLachlan's character hides in the closet and has to watch Frank Booth rape Dorothy Vallens. We have to know: where is the closet? Where does the rape take place? Where is the bathroom where she could hide? Suspense arises out of the configuration of space.

To return to the idea of ghosts, I have been feeling very sad about the death of David Lynch. For many, many days now. I rewatched *INLAND EMPIRE* (2006), which is a masterpiece. I watched an interview with him on YouTube, where he's asked, like always, about his movies being "Kafkaesque," or like nightmares. And he says, "No, no, my movies are daydreams." He says he loves to sleep in the afternoon. When you sleep in the afternoon, you're both there and somewhere else. And in the cinema itself, as a moviegoer, you're there and gone at the same time. Between dreams and reality, that's the space in which the cinema should linger.

CS: What you're saying about daydreams reminds me of something I read recently. I can't remember who said it, but it's a quote from an artist or a writer, someone from the past, who liked to take naps. His friend had said to him, "I don't want to sleep, I'll sleep when I'm dead," and he replied, "But you can't dream when you're dead."

CP: To return for a minute to the idea of daydreaming, one of my favorite films is *La Notte* (1961) by Antonioni. In *La Notte*, Marcello Mastroianni lies down on a sofa in the middle of the afternoon, and you can see the curtain blowing behind him. While he's ostensibly sleeping, Jeanne Moreau, who plays his wife, walks the streets outside. At that moment, the whole film is like a daydream. He is someone who has betrayed his ideas and sold his soul to industry. And she is moving through the urban spaces that were once their home, which are also the spaces of neorealism. That's what I mean by transit spaces: places at once very realistic and very dreamlike.

CS: I want to ask you more about architecture. How does what

ON LOCATION WITH CHRISTIAN

Written by
Paula Beer

The nice thing about preparing a movie with Christian is that he invites you into his universe. He talks about books that he admires, screens movies that he likes. I always have the feeling that I am slowly being immersed into the atmosphere of the movie. My character development is anchored in this process.

Transit was our first collaboration. I remember meeting him in the casting director Simone Bär's studio. We drank coffee and talked about God and the world for at least an hour. Then, Christian told me the story of the movie, and asked if I would play the character Marie. That was the most relaxed "casting" that I have ever had.

Preparing and shooting *Undine* was very different. I had never made two films in a row with the same director before. The trust that we built up during the first helped immensely. Because we didn't have to get to know each other, we could concentrate on other things. The most unusual part of the preparation was definitely the diving lessons. Franz Rogowski and I spent the first days of filming completely underwater. A large water tank was set up in Babelsberg. It was just as enchanting as it appears in the movie. When we were underwater, Christian could only communicate with us via a loudspeaker, and we could only answer him with a few hand signals via the water camera. Starting the shoot this way made an indescribable impact on the rest of the film. Our next project, *Afire*, had a completely new dynamic. It was accompanied by an incredible lightness. We had only two locations, so we spent an incredibly hot summer either on a lonely peninsula on the Baltic Sea or in the forest outside Berlin.

Taking actors to the exact locations where the film will be shot is part of Christian's rituals. As he once said, the sets are not yet sets, but places free of the hustle and bustle of the many people who will eventually arrive when the shoot starts. This tradition has helped me build personal feelings for these spaces, which I incorporate into my preparation. It also brings the actors closer together. It's a bit like going on a school trip. Everything that can grow, in terms of trust, helps later once filming starts.

Our latest project, *Miroirs No. 3*, is associated with the light and the vastness of the fields of the Uckermark, in northeast Germany. Since we shot (almost) entirely at one house, we were outside the whole summer. I saw farmers harvesting and plowing the fields, deer walking in the twilight, and, towards the end of the shoot, migratory birds gathering in huge flocks, then flying south.

By now Christian and I know each other very well. We respect and trust each other—and we don't take ourselves too seriously. Perhaps the biggest difference between working with him and with other directors is that he simplifies moments in order to create the greatest possible freedom. The way a scene is set up alone determines how it is shot. And Christian always manages to have enough time for every scene, no matter how small, and to, in that time, create something that you could never plan on paper.

Top: Nina Hoss, who has appeared in six of Christian Petzold's films, cycles across the East German countryside in *Barbara* (2012), one of several such clandestine trips that she will make to visit her lover, Jörg (Mark Waschke), and plan to join him in the West.

Bottom: Franz Rogowski in *Transit* (2018). Christian Petzold once declared the Freiburg-born actor, who also stars in his 2020 *Undine*, his "muse." "In this film," Petzold said of *Transit*, "this city [Marseille] is a prison for... these people."

you think about space, and knowing where we are in space, influence your approach to rehearsals, and to framing or composing a shot?

CP: For the last 10 films, it's been like this: during the shoot, I get up in the morning (not very early) and meet with the actors in costume. Together, we rehearse the entire day's work—without a camera, without sound—just us rehearsing. The actors have a lot of freedom. We take all the time we need. Once we have figured out the scene that we're rehearsing, only then do the DP and the sound person come and take a look. Then the actors go to makeup. And only then do I think about the framing. I have to see the rehearsal first. I can always recognize films where the framing has been decided before the rehearsal, and they drive me crazy.

CS: This confirms something that I think viewers feel intuitively about your films, which is that they're grounded in character and the situation. Even when there are big ideas, those ideas feel like they have germinated out of something more organic.

CP: There are a few things that I always need to know ahead of time. Is the movie more water? Is it more air? Who is telling the story, whose perspective is it? These are decisions I make beforehand, but I don't decide about framing or camera movements. All that happens after the rehearsals. For example, in the film I've just made, which is about a house and a family, I know the windows, the light, the curtains, the passageways, the garden; I know that fresh air will blow through these stagnant relationships and create something new. That was already determined beforehand. But the mise en scène is only decided upon once rehearsals have taken place.

Last night, I rewatched *Midsommar* (2019) by Ari Aster. What I like so much about this movie is that it's a horror film that establishes the identity of its characters right from the beginning. There's a young woman who loses her family; there is a group of guys, her friends, who don't like to talk about feelings, so you already have conflict from the start. At the beginning of horror films, you usually just have people that you don't care about. They're carbon copies of existing characters who gain an identity only by becoming victims. With Aster it's different, and I'd say that's how it is in my films as well. From the opening, the characters carry some sort of weight around with them—in terms of their biography, their conflicts, their problems, their loneliness. Then, through the story—whether it's horror, a crime story, or a drama—they are freed from this baggage and given a new existence.

CS: Many films are about someone keeping a secret. But your films seem to put a special emphasis on people who are unable to speak: there's Nelly in *Phoenix*, of course, but information is withheld in *The State I Am In*, *Wolfsburg*, *Yella*, *Jerichow*, *Transit*, *Undine*. And it's not just withheld; one could say that all of your characters are suffering over something they can't say out loud. What's at stake for you in that inability to say something that must be said?

CP: The moment television infected and took over the movies, dialogue reappeared. Television series are mostly pure dialogue; there's a belief that a proper conversation can solve all problems. That's the case in many American films, too—we just have to talk about it and we'll sort everything out. But if we're being honest, most of the time talk leads to disaster. I like it

Christian Petzold on set of his latest film, *Miroirs No. 3* (2025), which was shot in the countryside outside of Berlin. Petzold spends a great deal of time rehearsing in the spaces where he will shoot, so cast and crew know the terrain intimately by the time the camera is rolling. Photograph by Marco Krüger.

Top: Paula Beer plays an urban historian who is revealed to be more than she at first seems in *Undine* (2020) after she falls madly in love with an industrial diver, played by Franz Rogowksi. Christian Petzold's oneiric fairy tale is a spiritual heir to the trio's previous outing *Transit*.

Bottom: Paula Beer confronts her former lover played by Jacob Matschenz, who also starred in Christian Petzold's genre-bending 2011 film *Dreileben: Beats Being Dead*, one third of a television feature alongside contributions from fellow German directors Dominik Graf and Christoph Hochhäusler.

when people lose their language to find a new one. That transition interests me—not when you believe in language to such an extent that everything can be expressed in words. Because movies are a different kind of expression.

Film loves producing something, loves the act of becoming, of something being in motion. And two people who haven't yet found a shared language but are still developing one are interesting. But two people who already have a shared language and use it are uninteresting. In Kenneth Lonergan's *Manchester by the Sea* (2016), Casey Affleck can hardly speak after his trauma. There's a boy who has lost his father and Affleck, who has lost his family, and they have to find a way to speak to each other. That is the event. Cinema is not just "death at work" [as defined by Jean Cocteau —Ed.]; it is people who are trying to speak.

CS: It seems to me that over your career, the kind of female protagonist that you write has changed. In the earlier films with Nina Hoss, such as *Jerichow* or *Phoenix*, they tended to be very traumatized, even abused. Whereas the last few films with Paula Beer, those characters are a bit bolder, freer, they're more able to move. Do you have any thoughts about what this evolution might be about?

CP: This is an interesting question. I'll have to think about it. Nina has always struck me as someone who lives in exile, like a tsar's daughter, someone who is forced to live somewhere but doesn't actually belong to that world. I could never imagine Nina as a mother in a movie, let alone some sort of soccer mom or something like that. With Paula, I always have the feeling that she doesn't live in exile but that she comes from Germany, that she's had an education, that she can write books, or be a saleswoman. She's grounded in a different way, and that has brought forth different stories.

CS: Although I do think that Nina Hoss is incredible as the mother in *Wolfsburg*. Especially the last shot: the ending of that film combines the passionate revenge of her son with an act of care that's also an act of revenge. It's an amazing portrait of motherhood.

CP: That's interesting, because with *Wolfsburg*, I wrote the script for another actress, before I knew Nina. And then I met Nina and I wanted to make it with her. But I had to change the whole script because of her. In the first draft, there were scenes of mother and son. In the movie, you never see mother and son together. Just one shot at the hospital. But you never see an ordinary scene. It's something to do with—even as a mother, she's in exile.

CS: I would be remiss if we didn't speak a bit about politics or history. I've read some critics who say, "Oh, his early films were not political. And then history entered, with *Barbara*, *Phoenix*, and *Transit*." Then other critics say, "Oh, the early films are all about German reunification and the politics of German identity." It's interesting to watch people try to decide if you're "political" or not, or in what way.

CP: There's such a strong tradition of political cinema in Germany that it's very hard not to be infected or even poisoned by the idea of "political film." Maybe it's some sort of reaction to the propaganda made by the Nazis. According to that specific conception of political film, film doesn't stand for itself, but is only a medium to transport ideas. And that seemed so terrible to me when I first started making films. I thought I would never want to do anything like that. That's why the first films are just small films. *Wolfsburg*, for example, isn't political in that sense. Then my friend Harun Farocki and I were going on a lot of walks, and at some point I said, "Let's tackle those historical period pictures from Germany—let's attack them head on." We did three projects—*Barbara*, *Phoenix*, and *Transit*—where we told one story during the war, one in the postwar period, and one in the dying GDR. Making those films was such fun. It was Rainer Werner Fassbinder's films that taught me that you can narrate German history like a trashy novel, with an insane construction like in *Phoenix*, and that it could be much more political than the political films that are shot directly with the classroom in mind.

CS: When making *Afire* you talked a lot about Éric Rohmer. With *Miroirs No. 3*, was there another director who was important to you, somebody who was really on your mind?

CP: I didn't tell the actors this, but Claude Chabrol was the key filmmaker for this one. He once made a not-altogether-successful movie called *Alice or the Last Escapade* (1977) that is basically an *Alice in Wonderland* story. I still really like the way he did it. It's about a woman who has a car accident and ends up in a strange world. We know nothing about her, but in this world, through the way she behaves there, she becomes someone. That's often the case in the work of Chabrol: there's some accident, a very small narrative, an instance of corruption, and that's how the actual story starts. That's what I set out to do.

With the actors, I only watched Nanni Moretti's *The Son's Room* (2001). There weren't so many cinema references for this film. For the next one, there are many, many films I'm thinking about.

CS: Christian, I'm sure you read many interviews with directors and filmmakers, so I want to ask you, what question would you want to ask? Is there a question that you always wish your favorite filmmakers were asked? And can we ask you to answer that question?

CP: [Laughs] I would be too shy. When I was at the Telluride Film Festival, there were so many fantastic people who I love so much. Actors, directors. And it's not only because of my poor English! I saw them and I... I couldn't speak. But the only thing that I'd want to say to them is not a question, I'd want to say, "Thank you. You opened my eyes."

CS: What have you been watching or reading lately?

CP: I was on the train two days ago, and I finished *Three Days in June* by Anne Tyler. I love this book. I love all these women writers from the States who are now over 60 years old—Elizabeth Strout, Anne Tyler. And then in cinema, I have to see all these Academy movies. I love this movie by Ti West, *MaXXXine* (2024). I love the whole trilogy. I want to see *Den of Thieves 2: Pantera* (2005), I think it will come out soon in Germany. I love the Sean Baker movie *Anora* (2024). Also the new Clint Eastwood movie, *Juror No. 2* (2024)—the final scene is great. There's so many. But I have to write two new scripts now, so I can't watch too much.

Next year I want to make a movie based on the communist movie *Kuhle Wampe or Who Owns the World?* (1932), written by Bertolt Brecht. Kuhle Wampe was a garden colony near Müggelsee in Berlin where, at the beginning of the 1930s, a number of young communists, resisting fascism, lived and worked together, with the hope of changing the world. But they lost. I want to make a movie there set in the present day that explores what is happening to these ideas.

CS: I can't believe how quickly you work.

CP: I have so much time! Twenty-four hours a day! [Laughs] I like to sit down at the table and write down stories, and then—because it's very, very lonely writing a script—I love meeting all these actors, DPs, and people behind the camera. This collective work, I like it so much. Therefore, I'm writing. Therefore, the loneliness is okay.

J

Metrograph A–Z

J Is for Jazz

Words by

Jonathan Rosenbaum

1. Distinguishing between being alone and being part of a group or audience, a major theme of both Count Basie and Jacques Rivette, is also a fundamental part of the experience of both jazz and cinema, whether you're a player/filmmaker or a listener/spectator.

2. Sometimes the best jazz films are those we assemble inside our own heads, whenever we're listening to our favorite tracks and spontaneously and semiconsciously create visual tracks in sync with their vibe. Whereas the worst jazz films are usually the kind seen in the real world, committee efforts that often stoop to adding gratuitous voiceovers out of fear that we might actually get lost in the music (i.e., listen to it).

3. When I turned 70, a fellow film and jazz buff then living in Mashhad, Iran, Ehsan Khoshbakht, kindly celebrated that event by posting a few items on his website, Take the 'A' Train. One item was a list of my favorite jazz recordings. But now that a dozen years have passed and Ehsan, a programmer at Bologna's Il Cinema Ritrovato Festival, has reproduced that list as an appendix to his new book-length interview with me, I start to fret about certain gaps in my selections. Why no big band pieces apart from "Boplicity"? And why, especially, nothing by Duke Ellington?

Trying to pick my favorite Ellington cut, I eventually settle not on the 1940 classic "Harlem Air-Shaft" but on the more unkempt "Diminuendo and Crescendo in Blue," featured on a 1956 Columbia LP, *Duke Ellington at Newport*, where Paul Gonsalves's rousing 27 choruses on tenor sax—ripe bluesy meat sandwiched between lush orchestral slices the way a buckle holds a belt together—turn the restive late-night Newport crowd into a clapping, dancing, orgasmic maelstrom that helped land Ellington on the cover of *Time* the following month. You might even say it recharged his career.

Unlike critic G.E. Lambert, who describes Gonsalves's solo as "a very exciting performance ... spoilt by the noise of the audience," I think the crowd deserves some credit for the excitement. Live jazz combines individual creation with collective response, making audience and fellow band members co-auteurs. In short, I cherish this number for the movie it projects in my brain, a communal lovefest inviting me to join in its swing.

35. (CONTINUED)

I thought you were the one who

REV. June 10, 1971

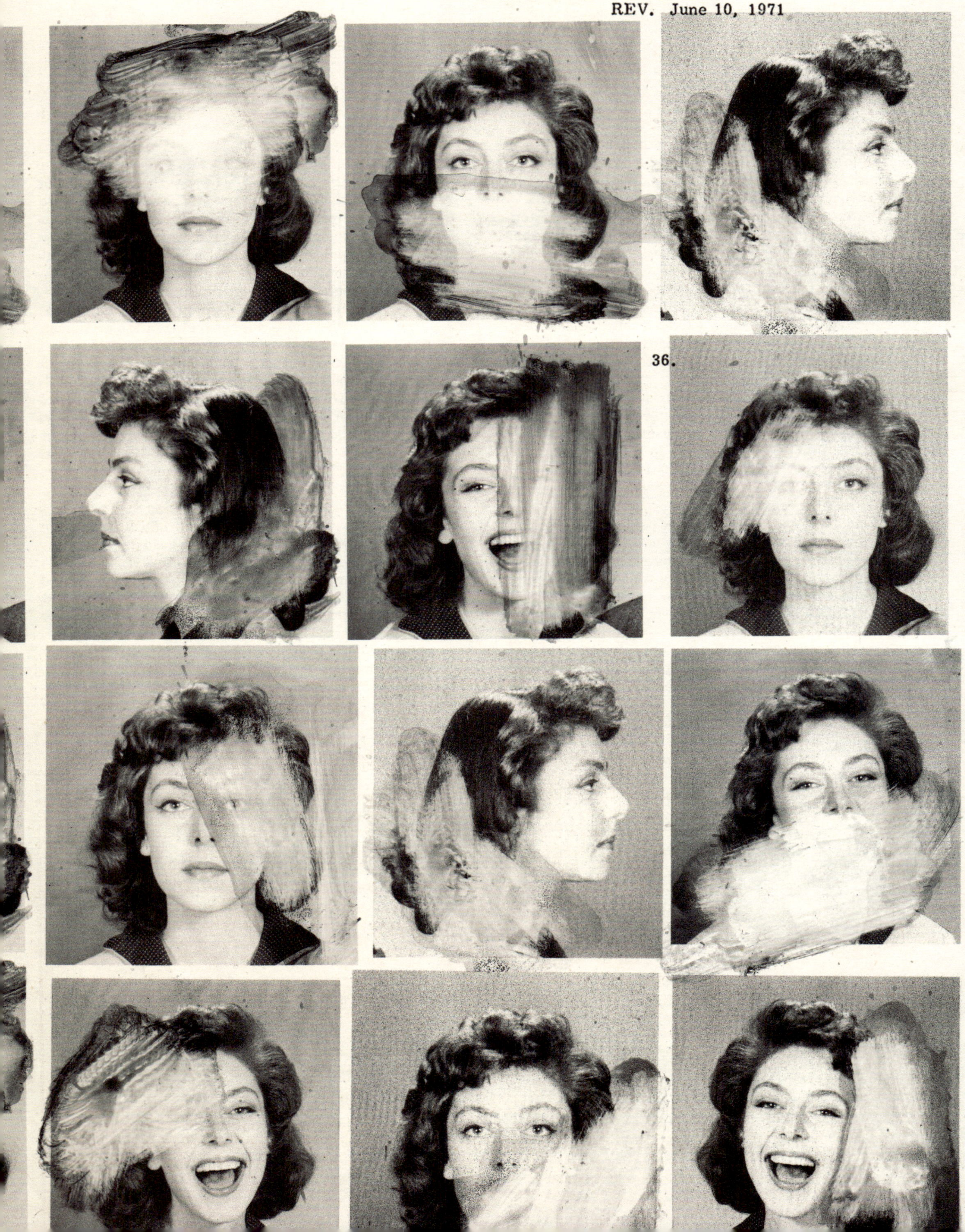

ELAINE MAY SPEAKS

AN ELAINE MAY PORTFOLIO

ILLUSTRATION BY VANESSA SABA

SPEAKING OF ELAINE MAY

Last December, Elaine May came to the Metrograph theater for a rare public appearance to discuss *Mikey and Nicky* (1976), her third feature as a director, with editors Phillip Schopper, ACE, and Jeffrey Wolf, ACE. Long ago reclaimed by May's ever-growing army of admirers, the film saw its initial release clouded by the studio battles that had waged throughout and following its production, which ran significantly over budget. Paramount ultimately revoked May's "final cut" privilege, leading to two reels disappearing—a gutsy if perhaps not entirely legal measure to protect the film, the details of which remain somewhat shrouded in mystery today. Her director's cut would not be presented publicly until 1978. Always a little coy with her audience—as is explored in the later pages of our May portfolio—she answers some questions below, and leaves others dangling in the wind.

PHILLIP SCHOPPER: You rarely do interviews, so we really appreciate this.

ELAINE MAY: Ask me anything.

PS: Let's jump right in: where did the story for *Mikey and Nicky* come from? Is it something from your life?

EM: I was thinking, "For what movie can I be sued by a studio?" [Laughs] I knew if I did a comedy, they would like it. So that's how it came to me; I thought, "What is a movie that has no laughs?"

PS: This movie has a lot of laughs!

EM: It does, but not the cheery kind.

PS: What about the genesis of the story? Are these two characters, Mikey and Nicky, people you know?

EM: They were actually our neighbors when I was a little girl. Well, one of them was our neighbor, and the other was his brother—and they were gangsters. My mother told me this story. It could be totally untrue because she always made things up as she went along, but this is what she told me: when he was younger, this chubby guy, our neighbor, and his rather good-looking younger brother worked for a famous gangster who put a hit out on the younger brother. The mother of both guys received a telephone call one night to get the younger brother to come down; the mother knew that it was in order to kill him—such a terrible story—but then the mother sent down the older brother because she loved the younger brother more.

PS: She was essentially given a *Sophie's Choice* (1982) situation?

EM: The interesting thing about gangsters in Chicago was that it was like a Greek tragedy. If you stole, you didn't go to trial or anything—they killed you. So nobody really stole much. And nobody who knew they had done something and that there was a hit out on them ever left town. It was as though it was their fate. They stayed, and they always called their best friend, because they needed a best friend. But the best friend turned them in, always. That's what happened, time and again.

PS: Because of your background in improvisation, probably in most people's minds here—

EM: No.

PS: You know what I'm going to ask, right?

EM: Yes, you're going to ask if there was any improvisation. It's impossible to improvise a movie like this. Something's going to have to happen to these guys at the end, and the fun of the movie is all about setting that up. You can improvise a loose comedy but not something that is so plotted.

PS: Yet, John Cassavetes, one of your two main actors, is famous for making movies that are largely improvised. Did he want to improvise in this?

EM: No. Nobody wanted to improvise. They were both very good. John and Peter [Falk] were both Method actors. They were only interested in who they were as characters.

JEFFREY WOLF: How did you come to cast them?

EM: We were all friends, and they just seemed right. Peter seemed right and John seemed right.

PS: Did you have them in mind as you wrote?

EM: No, I wrote this when I was still improvising in Second City [comedy club] in Chicago. I wrote it as a one-act play—because I never forgot the story; it was such a terrible tale, that the mother had sent the older one. Then when I started to do movies, I wrote it as a movie. I knew Peter and John, and I mean really, they were absolutely perfect. I didn't have to look.

JW: Is that also true of the other actors, did you cast them because they were friends?

EM: Carol Grace [Nellie, Nicky's mistress], was Walter Matthau's wife. I'd done *A New Leaf* (1971) with Walter, and she had come to set, and we became friends. She [makes voice airy] spoke like that, she was wonderful. So I cast her.

PS: And Joyce Van Patten [Nicky's wife]?

EM: I only vaguely knew Joyce, but she's a wonderful actress. Still is... Actually, one part of the movie was improvised. You want to know which? The scene on the bus where they're driving to the place where Nicky's supposed to be shot because Mikey has set him up. John and Peter were sitting in front of an extra who was from a class of mine. I thought they had nothing to do on this bus drive, so I said to her, "Make up a line and do it"—just to throw them. They were smoking, so she said, "No smoking on the bus." They didn't know I'd told her to do that so they were insane with rage. [Imitating a garbled exclamation] "Cut!" She said, "Was it wrong?" I said, "No, do it again!" So she tapped [tsk tsk] on their shoulder—they were doing this dramatic-thinking scene—and again said, "No smoking on the bus." They said, "Goddammit!" John realized that I had done it, but Peter didn't; he was incensed that this extra kept annoying him. Then the third time that she did it, John knew [and he ran with it]: the two of them had this little fight, but it was nice; it broke it up for John. It was the one improvised thing in the movie—and you didn't know! [Laughs]

PS: In terms of the writing, the movie is extremely economical. I've heard you say that when you write, no scene can ever be about just one thing. Take the scene with Ned Beatty, the hitman, for example: he's in the hotel room looking at a map; we know he's on the phone to somebody, getting details about a murder, setting up Nicky to be killed; we can discern all of this, without even an establishing shot. When this hitman finishes talking on the phone, you cut to Mikey hanging up the phone in the bar. In a single cut, the movie turns on a dime. We were thinking this guy is Nicky's oldest friend, that he's going to help, but now we know the hitman was talking to Mikey, that Nicky's being set up.

EM: Did you wonder, even before that? I've always wondered when the audience would guess Mikey was setting Nicky up. You only knew when they cut away, huh?

JW: Well, we believe Nicky's suspicious all the time. But Mikey has that great line: "I got your towel." You were talking about the humor being dark but there are so many funny moments. For instance, when Nicky says, "Ma, if anything happens to me, Mikey did it."

EM: Well, that was their joke—"Mom, if anything happens to me, [my brother] did it." Here's an interesting thing: during the movie, Peter occasionally asked, "Does he know?"—meaning John. I said, "Well, he read the script, of course he knows." He said, "I mean, in the movie, does Nicky know?" I said, "I have no idea if he knows or when he knows, I really don't." But Peter was so interested, he was so involved in it. He was even nervous about it. He had such belief in the movie, in what he was playing, that he didn't want Nicky to know. They were very good friends in life, so it worked well. But Peter genuinely wondered. I really had no idea.

It is a good actor's question, in a funny way. More interesting than I thought. But in this world, when you know a hit is out on you, you also know that the guy they're going to call to set you up is your best friend, because he's the only guy you'll trust: "Guess who'll kill me? My best friend." So I guess he kind of knew. It no longer exists, this kind of gangster tradition. Now it's all in politics. [Laughs]

JW: When you look back at some of the things you've written, do you now see them in different ways?

EM: Well, I wrote this early, as I said, as a play. When I left Chicago, when I left that particular life, I thought about it more. It really interested me in another way than it did when I was living it, or when it was being lived around me. I don't think I could ever write anything like it now because I'm so far away from it and the people and their humor... That's not true, I could write it now. [Laughs]

PS: With Cassavetes's portrayal, we see that this character, Mikey, purposely messes around with things: in the Black bar, with his wife, and the bus driver.

EM: I think that's what they said the younger brother was like: he was the kind of guy who was stupidly mischievous, in a funny way. But I want to say this about John, because people often ask if he improvised: he was the most Method actor ever. He had to know everything, he had to know every word. As did Peter. They were wonderful actors, they really were, and they sound improvised because they sound like they were really saying it. When I said "Cut," John would say to Peter, "She hated it." And Peter said, "She just said cut!"—but John was always right. Years later, I figured out why he was always right; it's because he hated it, and he knew if he didn't like it, then I wouldn't like it.

JW: I was in the editing room and there was a lot of footage—a million and a half feet of footage!

EM: Well, the movie was in trouble from the beginning, because originally I had stupidly cast the president of Paramount, Frank Yablans, as the killer. Yablans was a tough guy. I said, "Just do it as you would any contract that you're actually making to the studio." And he did, he was wonderful. But we were in rehearsal in San Francisco, in the middle of a scene, when the phone rang. We heard a loud voice as he answered it, and the moment Yablans hung up, he said, "I quit," and he left. The guy who was calling was the owner of Paramount [Charles Bluhdorn], who didn't know Yablans had taken the part of the killer. He was really displeased, because Yablans had never told him he was appearing in the film. I said to John, "Well, it's not going to bother us." He said, "Yes, it is, because we saw [the president] humiliated, and he's going to get us." And he got us. He made it miserable for us. He would not send money on time, and it was very difficult to edit [the film] afterwards, because the sound was off. Everything was off, because there was no money. So that's another thing I learned: don't humiliate the head of the studio.

PS: I don't know if you want to get into this, but there were troubles at the end of the film.

EM: Yes. I was sued.

PS: Eventually it came to a point where they wanted to take the movie away from you.

EM: Paramount fired Yablans and brought in Barry Diller, but he didn't understand the movie. He thought it was a comedy and it wasn't. They didn't like it, and they didn't like Yablans, and they sued me. They sued me for almost a year.

PS: And at some point they tried to physically remove you from the picture.

EM: Well, they couldn't remove me from the picture; they tried to remove the picture from me. I told my lawyer that I had received a strange call from a Paramount executive. My lawyer said, "Here's what I want you to do: leave the door unlocked, put the film where it can be seen, and get out of there and take your editor with you—and do it tonight." And I thought, "This is so like a movie." So I did it, and the next day when I came back, the movie was gone. And I hadn't taken it! I really hadn't. It was gone and they sued me to get it back but I had no idea where it was. No fuckin' idea where it was.

Mario Puzo, the guy who wrote *The Godfather* (1972), called me and said, "I'll hide your movie for you." I said, "What?" Because it was already known that the movie was gone and there was a lawsuit. He said, "I'll hide your movie for you." I didn't know, but he was also a client of Peter's lawyer. I said, "Thank you very much, but I don't know where it is." He said, "I understand." But I really didn't know.

Finally, after about a year, Paramount met with me and said, "We spoke to a judge in New York"—where the film was shot—"and he said that if it had been taken over state lines, well, she can go to jail." One of the men in the room who had been silent said, "Do we really want to be the only studio that has ever jailed a director for going over-schedule?" And my lawyer, who was very smart, said, "You wouldn't do this if she wasn't a woman"—which is probably not true—but anyway. They got really nervous that I would be jailed, and they said, "We're stopping the lawsuit," but I still didn't know where the movie was. I asked my lawyer. He said, "I don't know, but I can narrow it down." It turned out that my husband, who was a doctor, had driven over, taken the movie, and given it to a surgeon who was living somewhere in the Hills, out of town. The surgeon had no idea what my husband had given him. He'd said, "Just keep this." And so the surgeon gave it back to my husband, he gave it to me, and I gave it to Paramount, and we settled it.

Fortunately, a vice-president at Paramount, Julian Schlossberg, liked the movie. He left Paramount, started a distribution company, and called me and said, "I would like to represent the movie." I said, "It's on a shelf in my kitchen. I have no idea what to do with it." And he has represented it for over 45 years.

THE FILMS OF ELAINE MAY

Perhaps one explanation for Elaine May's reluctance to speak publicly about her directorial work can be found in the way that she and it were treated in the course of her career. The first film she directed, *A New Leaf* (1971), was recut without her consent, causing May to (unsuccessfully) attempt to remove her own credit from the film, her version of which remains lost forever. Even on the comparatively easy shoot of *The Heartbreak Kid* (1972), she was contending with a contract that gave screenwriter Neil Simon the power to approve or turn down any changes, even a single line, to his script. And, as May describes in the preceding pages, the production of *Mikey and Nicky* was hardly a walk in the park. There would be an 11-year hiatus between *Mikey and Nicky* and her next and to-date most recent narrative feature as director, *Ishtar* (1987), which was savaged by the entertainment press before it was even released for running excessively over budget. May kept herself busy and gainfully employed, before and after *Ishtar,* as a screenwriter and script doctor, usually working under a self-imposed veil of anonymity, and lending her singular talent to countless—that is, due to her secrecy, literally uncountable—Hollywood productions. Now, with most of the studio executives who hampered her directing career gone the way of the dodo and her corpus having been reclaimed by a new generation of admirers, Metrograph turns our attention to what has endured—May's films. To wit: four artists respond to the four films that Elaine May definitely, absolutely, positively, directed.

A New Leaf (1971, dir. Elaine May)
By Aubrey Plaza

A New Leaf is one of the movies that made me want to become an actor. May is someone that I don't think people know enough about, especially this younger generation. She was a prolific figure in the comedy scene in the '60s. She was a brilliant writer and a brilliant filmmaker. She herself is just inspiring to me and is one of my all-time heroes. And I love this movie. She's incredible in it. I think knowing that she's behind the camera directing this film, making something that was so good and so funny, and then acting in it, and having her hands all over it and just being the badass that she was, she's been an inspiration for me every step of the way. So, I have to give it up to her.

The Heartbreak Kid (1972, dir. Elaine May)
By Radu Jude

"Detail, details, that's what counts the most," said Jean Renoir, and I guess this idea fits what I enjoy so much about *The Heartbreak Kid*. Not only the story (great!), not only the actors (amazing!), not only the style (so rough for a mainstream film!), but this richness of details that one finds also in Cassavetes, but in a slightly different way, although they're often compared. If in Cassavetes's movies there is a deep humanism at the end of the line, a love for humanity, I have the feeling that in this film all things, all details (the dialogue, the gestures, the costumes, the movements, the objects), all go in only one direction: to prove a huge stupidity, an overall stupidity, a metaphysical stupidity. And in finding this deep stupidity of human beings May is much less Cassavetes and much more Flaubert.

Mikey and Nicky (1976, dir. Elaine May)
By Athina Rachel Tsangari

In May 1973, one of the most untamed, uncompromising, underappreciated mavericks in American cinema began shooting one of the most legendary, and yet barely released films three years later: a magnificent buddy comedy neo-noir crime drama about cracked masculinity. Starring John Cassavetes and Peter Falk in electric turns as two low-level mobsters having a nervous breakdown, May's *Mikey and Nicky* patiently follows the wreckage of an old friendship during one long night of affection, reckoning and, inevitably, betrayal. In a rare interview, she says: "The [two men] have a code. God knows what it is 'cause it's constantly broken, but they live by it—and they break it." And so did May—in every step of her trailblazing advance. She broke every code and barrier in a male-dominated industry, and she was punished for it. Long live Elaine May, New Hollywood unapologist and my own personal saint of "women's lane" defiance.

Ishtar (1987, dir. Elaine May)
By Luc Moullet

Elaine May is one of the best American directors. She was often misappreciated, the complete opposite of Francis Ford Coppola, who is very overrated. I am a fan of *A New Leaf* and *The Heartbreak Kid*, soft and magnificent studies of the human heart. Her masterpiece, though, is *Ishtar*, a terrific commercial flop, but also a wonderful funny and paradoxical adventure. It is very amusing to see Warren Beatty, generally considered as a Don Juan, playing a poor loser when he tries to conquer women.

SPEAKING OF ELAINE MAY

An interview with screenwriter Larry Karaszewski.

To learn for the first time of the existence of script doctors and their secretive world is to never again take the "Screenplay By" credit—at least on an American studio film—at face value. Since the days of Old Hollywood, when multiple "polishes" of a script were routine business and Ben Hecht was the industry's bootblack extraordinaire, studios have leaned upon external consultants to shore up weak spots in screenplays or add a little something extra to them (sometimes for credit, sometimes not).

Among the most in-demand and credit-shy of her time was Elaine May, who quietly lent her comic sensibility and gift for fine-tooled characterization to an unknown number of productions. (At one point, she formed a collective company with Joan Didion, among other writers, to be able to work even more anonymously.) Taking on total rebuilds, finesse punch-up gigs, and offers to just hang around on set in case her particular brilliance was suddenly needed, May turned incognito screenwriting into an under-the-radar second career.

To better explore this aspect of May's professional life, we spoke to Larry Karaszewski, who, along with his writing partner, Scott Alexander, has for many decades complemented his acclaimed screenwriting output for directors such as Miloš Forman and Tim Burton by occasionally moonlighting as a script doctor par excellence, lending a hand to many, many, many, many films. Karaszewski told us about the difference between rewriting and doctoring, May's aesthetic ethos, and his unrealized '90s remake of May's *A New Leaf* (1971).

LARRY KARASZEWSKI: It's funny, Elaine May is famous for rewriting other people. Scott and I might be the only people who rewrote Elaine May. Producer Cary Woods, and director Barry Sonnenfeld—right after *Men in Black* (1996)—approached us with the idea of remaking *A New Leaf*. We all worshipped that film. I'd seen it many times on its first run, when I was 10 years old. Cary pitched the remake as like a revival of a play: take what works about the film and make it sing for today. It was very respectful. We knew May was disappointed with how much material had been lost in the editing room, so we got a copy of her original screenplay—and indeed there was a lot cut. And it is much darker. The Walter Matthau character actually commits several murders.

There are the twin legends you hear about May: one, that she's open to improv and changing things... and that's why her shoots go forever and she has a million feet of film in the editing room; two, that she's out to protect her vision and knows exactly what she wants. But when you watch *A New Leaf* having read the script, you can follow along on the page. Even though May is a famous improviser, the script definitely reads like the movie, the final film version is faithful to her screenplay. But then, fresh gems pop out—May was looking for perfection, but she was also trying to find a spark of life. When Scott and I were rewriting *A New Leaf*, we thought, "What if we return to May's initial, darker approach and try bring it justice?" But when our script went to the head of the studio, it met the same resistance that May had: "We're not going to make a movie where the guy's just trying to kill his wife for 120 pages!" Twenty-five years later, it was the same problems.

Usually script rewriting occurs when a project is in development, the original writer has used up all their steps or decided to go a different way, and someone new is hired to rewrite the whole thing. Whereas script doctoring—I mean, the word "doctor" implies an emergency room situation. Say you have an actor attached who has a three-month window in which a movie has to be shot, but it's now a month away and the script isn't up to snuff. If anything, it's probably messier because it's had multiple voices added over time. The writer who invented that cop subplot was replaced by another who didn't care about it, so it doesn't pay off at the end, but sets might've already been built, locations locked, an actor hired to play the cop. It's hard to come in and say, "Get rid of the cop." You can, but it's triage at that point.

It's funny—the projects that tend to have the most writers are the ones you'd be like, "Really? That?" For a week or two, we worked on *Stuart Little* (1999), from the original M. Night Shyamalan script. The cover page listed everyone who'd contributed, and it was a litany of ridiculously huge writers, Academy Award winners, 12 or 15 people. The studio was throwing money around to make it work. But at the end of the day it was still *Stuart Little*.

When May came in later on a script, she saw herself as a relief pitcher, I think. She was probably doing what Scott and I do, working in service of a project, trying to keep it on track to get made. Working on structure and dialogue and distilling the scenes. I think of screenwriting almost like haiku: you have to fit the ideas into this compact thing. You say, "Here's a four-page scene, but the only thing we're getting out of it is that a car gets stolen. Can it be two pages? What if instead of giving a speech they do it with just a look?"

Often this sort of script doctoring is done to give the studio confidence to greenlight the film. Or sometimes it's to give a director or an actor confidence—if, say, Julia Roberts wants someone to come in and give the script a female voice. May had the confidence of certain people, like Warren Beatty; he liked having her around so that he could ask, "What else can happen in this scene? This is not landing as funny as it should." When you're a director—and particularly if you're directing yourself, like Warren was—it's a gift to have someone you can look to and say, "If Elaine feels we can move on, we can move on."

Scott and I tend to contact the original writer... And May did, too. She made a point of reaching out to say, "I'm not out to steal your credit, I'm here to try to make the movie better." In fact, she wouldn't do a project if they didn't give her permission—and then she often refused any kind of credit anyway.

Sometimes a credit can get leaked to the press, as was the case with May and *Such Good Friends* (1971). Often it happens before the Writers Guild has made their decision about who should get credit. Scott and I tend to go along with whatever the Guild says; I could name a bunch of movies a lot of our stuff is in, but like May, we don't feel like taking anybody's credit away. The one project we worked on briefly that has been made public is *Mars Attacks!* (1996), because Tim Burton did that right after we made *Ed Wood* (1994). People seem to know about our involvement because we came up with the Martian language. In the original screenplay, the Martians' speech was not specifically spelled out: it would just say, "And the Martian commander yells." Scott felt you couldn't get a sense of a scene because you didn't know if the Martians were talking for a long time or asking a question, etc., so as a placeholder he typed: "Ack, ack, ack." Sometimes this would be followed by a question mark, sometimes there'd be 30 "acks" in a row, like the Martian was mad and really yelling at someone. But we never remotely thought the Martians would specifically say "ack, ack, ack" in the film. It wasn't until Tim showed us a rough cut that we found out the language had stuck!

Sometimes it's the small details—the stuff May was so good at—that can really make a movie come alive.

THE FILMS OF ELAINE MAY?

Searching for telltale signs of the "May Touch" on projects where she definitely, absolutely, positively did something...

Such Good Friends (1971, dir. Otto Preminger)
By Keva York

After the legal hoo-ha of *A New Leaf*, May sought refuge in a gun-for-hire gig doctoring an already much-passed-around script, only to have Preminger betray her pseudonym, Esther Dale, in a bid to boost ticket sales. Adapted from Lois Gould's pulp-feminist bestseller, *Such Good Friends* relates the cruel awakening of Manhattan housewife Julie Messinger (Dyan Cannon) to the utter hollowness of her marriage, all while her husband lies comatose in hospital following a minor procedure gone awry. The scenes of Julie negotiating the vagaries of the health system—as the medical and marital complications build to a tragicomic pile-up—play like spinoffs from Nichols and May's comedy album, *Examine Doctors*. "What happens when you come here to be operated on for something serious, do you develop a mole?" quips Julie. "Mrs. Messinger, please try not to be too bitter," one doctor counsels. "You'll have plenty of time for that later."

Heaven Can Wait (1978, dir. Warren Beatty)
By Nathan Silver

May's writing always affectionately gravitated toward characters in desperate and often downright disreputable situations, wringing gag after gag from people's folly and foibles. So, it's not Beatty's dull caught-in-Limbo football player protagonist who stands out in *Heaven Can Wait*—which is mostly faithful to May's original script—but rather the couple trying to kill him after he inhabits the body of a wealthy industrialist. Played by May favorites Charles Grodin and Dyan Cannon, the duo is slapstick gold. Look no further than the scene where they discover their murder plans have faltered. They find themselves in a hedge maze, Grodin's hand covering Cannon's mouth, lest she scream. He whispers loudly (in a very Grodin way): "Listen, there is nothing to be frightened of. There's plenty to be worried about, but there is nothing to be frightened of. Dearest, are you all right? Can I trust you?" This is pure May.

Reds (1981, dir. Warren Beatty)
By J. Hoberman

Insiders have long known that *Reds* was extensively rewritten by an uncredited May. That she blacklisted herself attests to her own coming of age during the McCarthy era. Professing not to get the movie's politics, May surely understood that she had written Hollywood's most comsymp production since *Song of Russia* (1944). Nostalgic for the '60s, left-lib critics loved it while right-wingers had to find a way in. John Simon praised *Reds* as a "screwball comedy of battling, wisecracking lovers"—Beatty and real-life gf Diane Keaton—who, per John Podhoretz, "spoke to each other as though they were at an Esalen retreat." He was satirizing what was already satire. *Reds* may have been Beatty's psychodrama. (An apocryphal story has the star asserting that he was not playing Jack Reed, Jack Reed was playing him.) But it is also a monumental skit: think Mike Nichols playing Reed playing Beatty, with May feeding Keaton her lines.

Tootsie (1982, dir. Sydney Pollack)
By Haley Mlotek

May was the fifth screenwriter invited to rewrite *Tootsie*, a strange, silly comedy of sexual errors that was something of a vanity project for Dustin Hoffman, who retained full creative control throughout. Her celebrated (though per her request, uncredited) fixes include introducing the Bill Murray roommate character and a love interest, written for Teri Garr. Upon rewatching, though, May's influence seems to be everywhere. There are her signature deceptions and shenanigans, of course, but perhaps it is the deconstruction and delusional reinvention of a self that most makes *Tootsie* a work in her canon. Hoffman's character's earnest attempts at beauty, inside and out, are the rom-com version of May's abiding themes: how to get away with murder—or a slightly milder scheme, like impersonating an actress? Where lies the line between comedy and cruelty? And above all, why are men so drawn to women they can't understand?

Labyrinth (1986, dir. Jim Henson)
By Aimee Knight

In 1984, when Monty Python alumnus Terry Jones sat down to write the screenplay for *Labyrinth*, did he, I wonder, ask himself, "What if we made *The Wizard of Oz* gross?" That would explain why, in early drafts, teen heroine Sarah ends up at a Venetian ball-turned-orgy. Naturally, Henson—that family-friendly pastor of Muppets—had concerns. He asked a small army of trusted collaborators (including Frank Oz, George Lucas, and his talent agent) for their two cents. Perhaps deciding that middle-aged men were not best placed to explore the interiority of a pubescent girl, Henson eventually called May. She helped "humanize" the, I'll say it, deeply irritating characters, transforming Sarah from entitled airhead to an acceptable annoyance. That is May's specialty, after all. She filed her rewrites, a Hail Mary pass, four days before cameras rolled. Her name does not appear in the final film, but neither does the orgy.

Scrooged (1988, dir. Richard Donner)
By Medaya Ocher

Frank, a successful New York TV executive played charismatically, if a little loudly, by Bill Murray, has shouted his way to the top. He's putting on a live production of *A Christmas Carol* on Christmas Eve, but wouldn't you know it, he's a Scrooge: mean, cynical, and stingy; most of his Christmas presents are towels. When he is then visited by the three enlightening ghosts of Christmas—one, played by the inimitable Carol Kane—he finally learns his lesson, exclaiming: "The Jews taught me this great word: schmuck. I was a schmuck, and now I'm not a schmuck!" This is the most succinct summary of *A Christmas Carol* ever. It also feels like a nudge from behind the camera. May's name doesn't appear on this film, but don't be a smuck [sic]—the credit is in the dialogue: Frank admits that the word is borrowed, and it's not from Dickens.

Working Girl (1988, dir. Mike Nichols)
By Amalia Ulman

It has long been rumored that May was brought in to punch up the script for *Working Girl*, though this has never been confirmed. It makes sense when you remember that the working-class revenge fantasies here are classic May, not to mention the hilarious one-liners Joan Cusack gets to deliver as Melanie Griffith's buddy from Staten Island: "Six thousand dollars? It's not even leather!" My mother has a very intense relationship with this film. She wouldn't like to admit it, since in her opinion the film is very mainstream and uncool, but something must have resonated with her when she first saw it: alone, in a remote town in Argentina, a year before I was born, when she still dreamed of moving to the big city to become an independent working girl herself. I asked her why she likes it so much. She shrugged and said that it is *redondo*, as we say in Spanish, round, a perfect film.

In the Spirit (1990, dir. Sandra Seacat)
By Sean Price Williams

A few Christmases ago, I had Covid and no one wanted to be in the room with me, so I threw on *In the Spirit*; I had all the laughs and little conversations during and after this New Age satire buddy movie alone. First, I was struck by the ladies. Marlo Thomas is a total babe. Olympia Dukakis is family. I remembered that I can happily watch May's face say or do anything. She is the greatest living comedian. Her daughter, Jeannie, who also co-wrote this, is so fun. Throw in a little Melanie Griffith and it all makes sense. But the key to understanding the why and how of the film is Peter Falk. I'm not sure if he read the whole script or if he was even asked to. It feels like that rare movie made by friends for the damn fun of it. No matter how you spin it, making movies is work, but I'm convinced this was genuinely a hoot. Some people say May secretly directed this, but who knows?

Wolf (1994, dir. Mike Nichols)
By Elissa Suh

After Jack Nicholson suffers a lupine attack but before his full transformation from long-suffering book editor into an alpha male begins, he gets a rabies shot. His doctor, played by Ron Rifkin, delivers a hilariously flat monologue about snakebites and the inevitability of brain damage—a phrase he repeats, each time sounding less reassuring. It's a small moment, but one that crackles with May's signature touch: the clinical professional rendered absurd, much like the tax attorney in *A New Leaf* or the hotel clerk in *The Heartbreak Kid*. These minor characters, with their dry detachment, become strange little gems in her world. And in *Wolf*, this humor—which I attribute to May's uncredited touch—helps to soften Nichols's otherwise high-gloss, adult horror-romance. *Wolf* was always going to be a little strange, and May's script polish lets us feel like we're at least in on the joke.

The Birdcage (1996, dir. Mike Nichols)
By Michael Koresky

There's a gag in *The Birdcage*—one of the few films that May wrote with credit—that so demonstrates her ability to push a joke past comfort level that it justifies an American remake of *La Cage aux Folles*. As part of preparations to meet their ultra-conservative in-laws-to-be, Robin Williams's Armand instructs his limp-wristed long-time lover, Nathan Lane's Albert, to "walk like a man"—a tired spectacle right out of *Tea and Sympathy* (1956). To thwart Albert's swishiness, Armand suggests Albert imitate John Wayne. The moment appears in the 1978 original, though Ugo Tognazzi buttons up the joke by flatly taunting Michel Serrault's hapless attempt: "That's John Wayne's daughter." May, however, eternally poking holes in American machismo, dared to push a sacred cow right off its saddle. After Lane lurches across the café like a mincing zombie cowboy, Williams retorts, astonished: "It's perfect. I just never realized John Wayne walked like that."

Primary Colors (1998, dir. Mike Nichols)
By David Sims

Just two months before *Primary Colors* was released, the Lewinsky scandal broke, destabilizing Bill Clinton's second term and stealing the film's thunder as real life eclipsed art. In hindsight, though, Nichols and May's final official screen collaboration is perhaps most valuable for the way it clocks the dream of Third Way neoliberalism, then pours acid all over it. Any adaptation of Joe Klein's poison-pen roman à clef about Clinton's 1992 presidential campaign would show some healthy skepticism, but May's script is more concerned with asking why Americans would ever take at face value anyone seeking power. May's clearest analogue is fiery gay political operative Libby Holden (Kathy Bates), a sharp-elbowed true believer who comes to realize the man she works for is as gutless as the rest. "I will destroy this village in order to save it," Bates tells her boss, her tragic last words. For May, idealism goes hand in hand with brutality.

3

DEPARTMENT HEADS

Contents

I'VE CREATED A MONSTER!

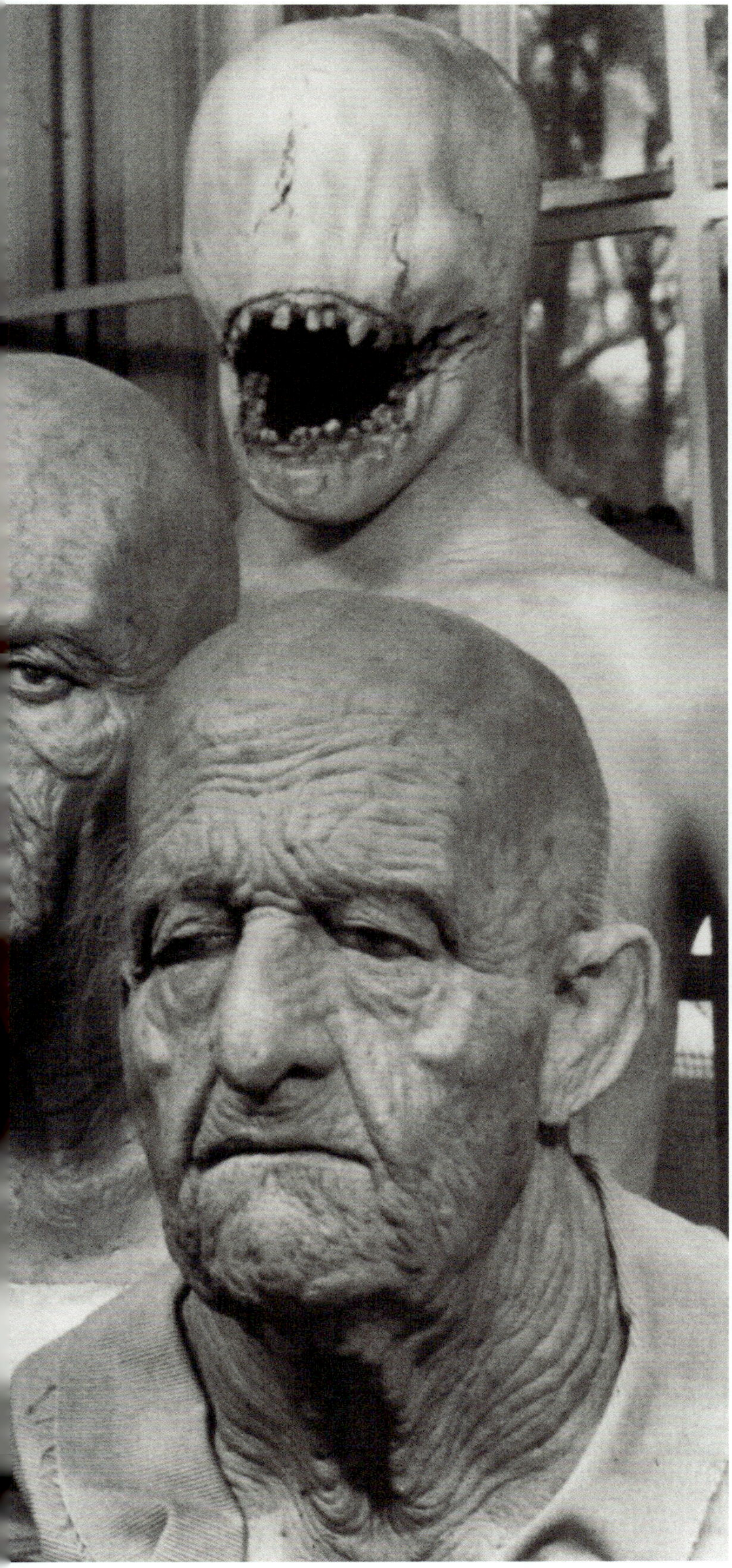

An introduction to the weird, wonderful world of special-effects makeup and creature design.

Left: Makeup artist Dick Smith, photographed with some of his aged and alien creations, 1973.

Behind every indelible movie monster, space invader, or any of the other fierce and fantastic creatures that exist only in the world of cinema, there are enough byproduct *objets d'art* to fill a sizable gallery—ancillary artifacts including concept drawings, maquettes in a variety of scales, and hand-carved busts that are works of extraordinary craftsmanship unto themselves.

To take one example: in the time that passed between Steve Johnson and visual effects company Boss Film Studios first receiving the assignment to create the galaxy-hopping big-game hunter of *Predator* (1987) and the arrival at the finished product—the iconic mechanical mask with servo-driven cable-actuated mandibles, ultimately designed by Stan Winston, and worn by Kevin Peter Hall in the sweltering rainforests of Chiapas—a whole menagerie of alternate would-be Predators of various shapes and sizes had come and gone, with only the sketches and sculptures left behind as testament to their brief lives. (These products of trial and error may even, at times, be the lone physical evidence of films that never saw the light of day, as with the array of models and drawings of impish, nefarious extraterrestrials produced by Rick Baker and Ron Cobb for Steven Spielberg and Tobe Hooper's unproduced sci-fi horror *Night Skies*.)

Crafting pre-production concept sculptures is integral to the practice of special-effects makeup artists. It is used by both those working with prosthetic FX—that is, those in which the human face becomes a template to build upon, like Dick Smith and Paul LeBlanc on Miloš Forman's *Amadeus* (1984)—and by those creating full-face masks, like that of Baker's American werewolf, which netted him the first-ever Academy Award for Best Makeup in 1982. In the case of the former, this often involves using, as a "canvas," a lifecast of the actor who'll eventually be sitting in the makeup chair; in the case of the latter, depending on whether the headpiece will ever actually house a living person or simply be a blueprint for digital modelling, such accommodations to the dimensions and necessities of the human form may be minimal to nil.

Is all of the trimming, molding, finishing, and other assorted fuss that goes into good old-fashioned concept sculpture outmoded in the age of the 3D printer and other such modern wonders? The argument can be made—but cinema's great makeup artists, its great freakmakers, have all learned their craft through an intimate knowledge of anatomy that can only be attained via the painstaking process of working with and learning through their hands. Their final creations are bestowed with a certain quality that is the result of careful consideration and getting one's fingernails dirty, and which translates into incredibly detailed and deeply expressive character design.

How are human faces altered beyond all recognition? How are physiognomies never before seen on this Earth summoned out of thin air? Where does one even start? Our host, the New York-based special-effects makeup artist Emily Schubert, pulls back the curtain.

BEHIND THE MASK: TUTORIAL WITH EMILY SCHUBERT

Photograph by
Tom Scanlan

The world of creature design for film and theater is a small one, and hidden away within that, the world of professional mask makers is even smaller. Far from the big special effects studios, there are solo practitioners, known mainly to an inner circle of specialists and movie producers. They are like magicians who perform tricks before an audience that does not even know they exist—let alone understand the training and science behind the magic.

As a mask maker and special-effects makeup artist myself, I admire the masters of the discipline who have shown at the highest level what it is we do, like Dick Smith, Tom Savini, Ve Neill, and Stan Winston. Sharing their knowledge now feels important, when technological advances could increasingly take the place of the human hand.

In the next pages, you'll find a tutorial that compiles ideas and techniques from Jordu Schell, another influential veteran of this elusive art. Schell's monsters, fantastical aliens, and freaky appendages have appeared in movies like *Edward Scissorhands* (1990), *Men in Black* (1997), *Galaxy Quest* (1999), *Planet of the Apes* (2001), *Dawn of the Dead* (2004), *Hellboy* (2004), *300* (2006), *Avatar* (2009), and *Batman v Superman: Dawn of Justice* (2016).

I learned some of Schell's secrets while at his studio in Chatsworth, in Los Angeles's San Fernando Valley, where he showed me his curio cabinets and some of his collections that inspire his work—of bugs, bones, books, masks, and more. We spoke about masks and what makes them effective: the psychology of the forehead, the technical aspects of the pronounced chin, the persuasiveness of wet eyes, and *Maskenfreiheit*—a German word that means the freedom afforded to you while wearing a mask. And over three days, we recreated the first ever mask that Schell made 40 years ago when he was 16 years old. I might call it a pouty humanoid bullfrog; Schell used the phrase "swamp alien." Its name is UL.

A guide to making your very own latex monster mask with Hollywood special-effects makeup artist Jordu Schell.

Written by
Emily Schubert

Photographs by
Michael Schmelling

01

WED clay is the perfect medium to sculpt in: it softens with water, but also builds up and dries quickly. This lets you impress fine details as you move toward your final sculpt.

02.

First, create an appropriate work surface. Score a particle board, either with a box cutter or by drilling holes into the board. The idea is to establish a grip for the clay to lock into. Spray the board with water and work your clay into the grooves. WED clay is heavy, but scoring enables the clay to attach, even in thick, heavy amounts. Schell is using a board screwed to an easel, which rests on a lazy Susan. The easel is hinged, so the sculpt can be flipped upside down and worked on from a different perspective.

03.

Build your clay into the rough shape of a head. Decide how far down on the wearer you would like the final mask to sit. Here, we're creating a mask that extends to the collar.

04.

Now it's time to define the anatomy of the species. "At its basis, design comes down to geometry," Schell tells me. "Finding new, eye-catching ways to rearrange basic geometries is how you come up with a good design." But new and eye-catching does not necessarily mean wholly made up: "One thing missing from most modern creature designs is real attention being paid to nature," he says. "Because nature is really quite simple in its design. Form follows function, and nature doesn't gild the lily. Designers are always trying to have little things here and there, which might be cool, but doesn't necessarily make sense."

05.

When establishing the underlying bone structure, consider the undulating shape of the skull around the temples, the projection of the chin and forehead, the jaw (overbite or underbite). Some notes on chins: decide if you want the chin to be weak or lead the silhouette. A weak chin is goofy, comical; a strong chin makes the creature dominant, aggressive. "There's a million ways to convey in a sculpture what a character's like, how they might sound or move," says Schell. "Are they clumsy? Are they cunning? Are they brilliant? For a character that's supposed to be dumb, the mouth might hang open; the eyelids could be half-mast. Whereas something cunning is going to look poised and kind of effete. Cosmopolitan. Focused."

06.

When placing orbital bones, consider whether you're creating predator or prey. Prey animals typically have eyes farther apart, giving them a wider field of vision for staying on the lookout. Predator animals have close-set eyes for increased depth perception. Schell adds that personality can be reflected in the size and position of the eyes: small and close together register as stupid; big and close together are anatomically unlikely, so look jokey and ridiculous; large and far apart seem intelligent; small and far apart seem sinister.

09.

Create differences in planes of the face with an even finer-toothed rake. Taper the jowls. With a wooden sculpting tool, define "the wattle" (the excess skin and fat on the neck) to suggest age and movement. To create crepey skin, etch small ravines into the clay with a loop tool. When it comes to the forehead, adds Schell, "Humans who have a lot of facial movement are generally considered more intelligent." A lack of forehead movement suggests someone is "kind of dumb."

10.

To make the lips round and solid, define the upper lip with bubbles of clay, then blend with a loop tool. Think about the way your creature's mouth moves while communicating and consider how the gums attach to the jaw. Renowned special-effects makeup artist Tom Savini has said that a sculpture can be broken down into many little sculptures.

07.

Starting with hard, perfect spheres of clay is crucial for sculpting eyes. Look down from above to make sure both eyes are set in at the same depth. Then carefully add clay on the orbital bone, above and below the spheres, to form eyelids. This is a good opportunity to indicate the age of your creature. The goal is to make it feel like it's lived a life, like there is real history in the face.

08.

Use a steel scraper to clean up and refine your primary form. Smooth out your sculpture's planes, smearing and cutting as you move. Rake further with another tool, a wide-toothed scraper, to create areas of rest. This is one way, Schell says, to be true to the natural world in character design. "Most creatures have an area with little detail," he says. "For example, insects: their back, their carapace, is often totally smooth."

11.

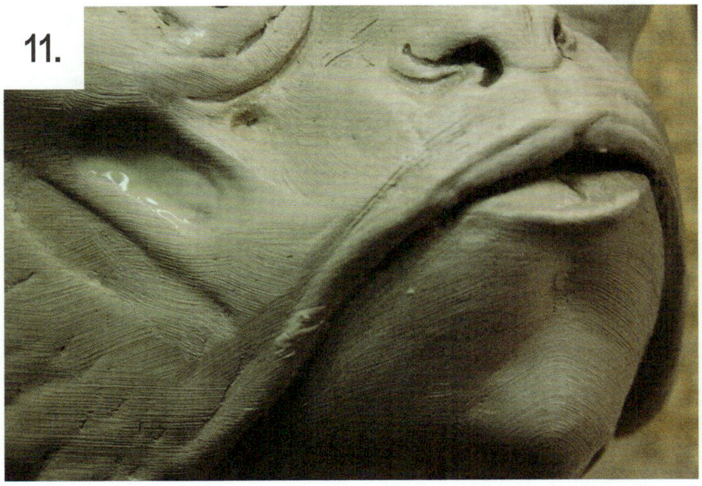

With the facial structure in place, smooth the surface in order to "bake in" the features. Spray the sculpt with water, then make a series of swiping motions with a superfine sponge to lightly coat the entire face. WED clay is water-based, so work quickly—the water makes the surface very soft. There is a balance here: watch your pressure. After swiping, stamp your superfine sponge onto the clay. This will imprint your creature with apparent skin pores.

12.

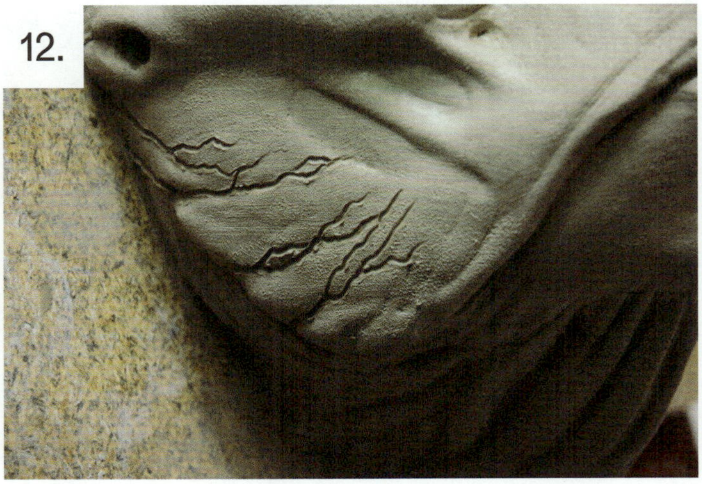

Now that the basic sculpture is complete, add more details. Using a fine carving arrow, etch into the jowls and under the eyes to create more ravines and wrinkles. Exaggerate the details, then use a soft wet brush to temper them, so they appear more natural. With a circular buffing motion, use the sponge again, going both with and then against the grain. To finish the eyes, use a wet brush to buff bits of "slip" (clay that is more liquid than solid) into any gaps or holes. This is a good time for another round of smoothing to recess your details.

13.

Hit the sculpt with a blow-dryer set on cool so that the clay sets slightly, then douse it in cornstarch-based baby powder before blowing off any excess.

14.

Use a texture stamp to press a final look into the flesh, adding more powder as needed to keep the stamp from sticking to the clay. This guarantees a cleaner read from the texture stamp. Blow-dry the sculpt again. Here, Schell is using a mold by special-effects makeup artist Rick Baker for a scaly skin texture. If you don't have a mold, Schell mentioned another technique for making texture stamps: sponge layers of liquid latex onto a dead or sleeping iguana or snake, then peel it off.

17.

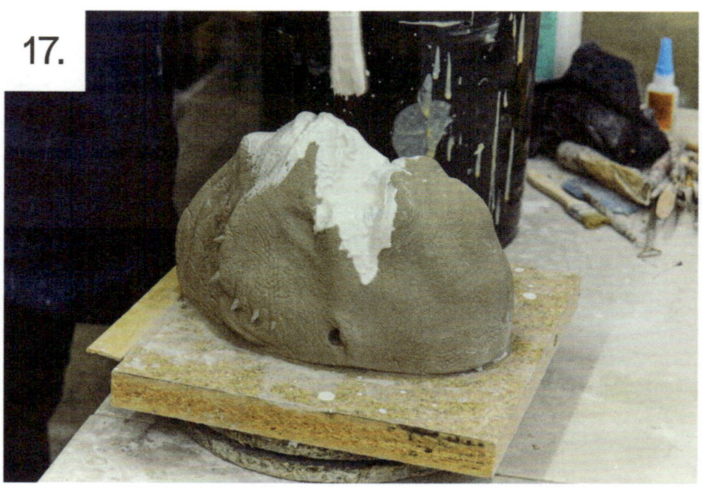

Now it's time to start the mold-making process by introducing plaster. Here, we're using a white gypsum cement called Hydrocal. Fill a bucket with water, then slowly add Hydrocal. Keep sprinkling until plaster forms a mountain whose peak sits above the water line. It should take up about 50% of the surface area. Mix the plaster by hand, feeling for lumps. When the solution is smooth, you're ready to cover your sculpt. Begin by painting a thin layer of plaster onto the form while using a blow-dryer, set on cool, to direct plaster into every crease and crevice. This will prevent dangerous air bubbles.

18.

Add a second layer of plaster, building up the thickness. The goal is to no longer touch the surface of the sculpture, just the painted-on plaster. Hydrocal is fast-setting, so you must move quickly, but this also makes it easier to build up. Lay it on by hand until you achieve a uniform thickness.

15.

Add protection to the fleshy areas—here, we added spikes. Take into account the sensitive parts of your creature and what protection they might need to survive.

16.

When finished, lay down your sculpture flat on its back. Review the top of the head, which has likely been neglected. Consider once more how the creature moves. This creature's neck needs to account for up-and-down movements, so a horizontal wrinkling scheme has been etched in.

19.

Refine the mold using a rubber kidney. The cleaner the mold, the easier it is to handle and store. Be warned: spiky molds can cause injuries! Cover your hands with water and rub the mold to smooth it down.

20.

Clean around the perimeter of the mold with a scraper tool. (Optionally, inscribe it with the contents of the mold and the date. UL is the name of this creature, which Schell first made in 1983.) The plaster will heat as it dries. Once the mold has hardened—it will be hot to the touch—remove it from the board using the scraper. Be patient, or you risk cracking the mold.

21.

Remove clay from the inside of the mold. (The layers that were closest to the board can be reused so long as they don't contain plaster.) Use your spray bottle of water and a chip brush to clean the mold and dislodge any clay. Use a rasp tool to file back the sharp edges of the mold for easier handling.

22.

Make sure you fully dry out the mold at this stage. Residual moisture trying to escape from the plaster can result in air bubbles, so set your mold in front of a fan overnight.

25.

Set the piece in front of a fan until it is dry to the touch. In this case, we turned the rubber mask into a display. To do this, we used FlexFoam, an expanding flexible foam, to fill the rubber mask. After pouring in the foam, place cardboard on top, creating back pressure to prevent air bubbles. Setting times depend on which product you use.

26.

Pull out your mask by folding it in around the sides until it releases—a satisfying moment. Trim the excess around the perimeter of your latex mask using a pair of scissors. Then trim any air pockets on the surface with superfine nippers or cuticle cutters. To smooth the area further, use a soldering iron. Naphtha—a kerosene-like liquid—can be applied with a brush or Q-tip to clean and smooth any burned areas.

23.

When the mold has dried, pour liquid latex inside and brush it into the hollows—especially, in this case, into the spikes. Anything that has a lot of detail (teeth, for example) is prone to air bubbles. Hydrocal is especially suited to this step in the process because it is so highly absorbent that it soaks up water and ammonia from the poured latex.

24.

Fill the mold to the brim with liquid latex. In fact, let the liquid latex spill over the lip of the mold a bit, so that you have something to grip when you remove the latex. The temperature and moisture level in your environment determines how long it takes for the latex to "set up." Keep track of how the material is behaving is by filling a plastic cup with the liquid latex at the same time as you paint your mold, and check the wall thickness periodically. When you have achieved the desired thickness, pour the unused latex back into a bucket.

27.

Mount the foam onto the same easel as before using hot glue. Use PAX paint for the base, as it is one part acrylic, one part Pros-Aide, a medical adhesive. Start out with a darker color than what you'd like to end up with. (If you create your own PAX, use a very opaque acrylic—pigments for mural-painting have the appropriate density. Thin it out with water as needed.) Cover the piece entirely with paint.

28.

Next, add some white to the base color. Use a milk frother to mix colors for the best blend. You can also add a red or blue tint if you'd like your piece to be warmer or cooler in tone. In this case, we added blue. Lightly brush the new shade across the top of the piece to bring out the sculpting details. This is called "dry brushing." Work in multiple directions to avoid an overly brushed look.

29.

Airbrushing helps diffuse color across the sculpt and thereby make it look more natural. I like to do this manually, by trimming a chip brush and flicking its bristles to create a cloud of pigment. Schell uses an Iwata electric airbrush. To follow his technique, take your dry brushing color and blend it with denatured alcohol in a one-to-one ratio. Strain your colors through a coffee filter before putting them in the airbrush to prevent clogs. Mist over the entire sculpt, focusing on areas that you'd like to stand out.

30.

"Base out" your sculpt by painting your intended patterns with the previously mixed lighter color. Now select a darker color for contrast—we chose a muted purple-gray to complement the cool tones of the highlight and contrast with the green. The contrast color goes around the perimeter of the highlighted areas and into the depths of the sculpt. Begin the contour process using a light hand, then move in closer with a heavier hand to achieve clear outlines. This will give the edges more depth.

31.

Airbrush the color of your mucous membrane—the areas of skin at body openings—into the nose, eyes, and ears, and around the mouth. We chose an orange tone, but typically any warm hue works. Thin veining can be added around the entire sculpt to break up any solid or heavy areas. You can remove the tip of the airbrush to create a freckled or spattered appearance.

32.

Paint the eyes with a base color. We used white. Use a secondary tone on the inner and outer corners and along the perimeter of the eyes. Generally speaking, it's best if the eyes contrast with the face color. You can paint tiny blood capillaries here as well. For the finishing touches, do a pass with an iridescent powder or pearl paint (Schell's preference). Here we used an opalescent blue. We painted the mini-horns with a white base color similar to the eyes, then worked in dark green at the root to create depth and a gradient.

33.

Being alive means sweating, secreting, pulsing, breathing. All that is liquid, wet. Finish up with a clear, five-minute epoxy to simulate wetness. We used some in the eyes, around the nose, and in the mouth. Welcome to the world, UL.

PHANTOM THREAD: ZELDA WYNN VALDES

Tracing the work of the visionary designer behind countless stars.

Written by
Kelli Weston

Singer Joyce Bryant wearing one of Zelda Wynn Valdes's signature mermaid silhouette designs. In preparation to open for another Wynn Valdes client, Josephine Baker, Bryant dyed her hair silver with radiator paint and applied sweet almond oil to her skin, giving her a porcelain appearance. She varnished her inch-long nails with silver polish to curate an all-silver look from head to toe.

Real stars are made, not born. The would-be luminaries of mid-century Hollywood needed to be in possession of that sacred, ineffable something that comes alive on celluloid, but talent alone was not always enough. They, or those well-placed around them, had to command a robust fluency (women more so than men) in the image, a grasp of industrial cultural production: an intuitive business to be sure, but a skill that has routinely established our most recognizable idols. Mythology remains crucial to the equation. Which is to say, cinema owes a debt to the modeling agency that advised auburn-haired Norma Jean to transform into the platinum blonde who'd become Marilyn Monroe. And to Audrey Hepburn, for testing then-dominant bounds of gender with the pixie cut that catapulted her to sudden fame in *Roman Holiday* (1953). A year later she convinced Hubert de Givenchy to design some of her costumes for *Sabrina*, among them the gowns perhaps most wed to her iconography, securing herself a treasured place in the Old Hollywood pantheon. Glamour was central to the machinery that shaped stardom, a feat of storytelling, fabricated or otherwise.

Take, for another instance, Ella Fitzgerald: in March of 1955, the 37-year-old jazz artist, laurelled by her peers and critics alike, had just wrapped a brief singing cameo in the Warner Bros. musical *Pete Kelly's Blues*. That spring, she was preparing to make what would become a career-changing first outing at the Mocambo, its fabled walls, adorned with painted plaster figures and glass aviaries containing live cockatoos, macaws, and parrots . The green neon lights of the Sunset Strip celebrity haunt—which unofficially passing as the social capital of Hollywood's elite—routinely lured the likes of Lana Turner, Louis B. Mayer, Carole Lombard, Barbara Stanwyck, Hedy Lamarr, Cary Grant, Henry Fonda, et al. Playing here promised Fitzgerald previously unmatched visibility.

Nightclubs marked some of the earliest places where Black artists could perform, even when they could not gain entry otherwise. As popularly told today, the apocryphal story of Fitzgerald's appointment at the Mocambo credits Monroe, the singer's friend, with persuading the club's proprietor, Charlie Morrison, supposedly reluctant to book a Black performer. It's certainly true that Monroe was an early supporter of Fitzgerald (the photograph of the pair often used as evidence of her intercession was taken not at the Mocambo, as sometimes believed, but at the Los Angeles Tiffany Club in 1954). However, biographers have challenged this narrative, not least because by 1955 the Mocambo was already integrated. Fitzgerald was preceded as a headliner by other notable Black actresses who straddled the stage and screen: Lena Horne performed there in 1942; Dorothy Dandridge made her debut in 1951; Eartha Kitt's

run in 1953 compelled the owners to expand to three shows a night (shattering a 13-year policy) to accommodate the high volume of reservations; and just a month earlier, a then ascendant Joyce Bryant—better known as "the Belter"—garnered glowing notices for her sensational two-week engagement. What seems to have troubled Morrison was Fitzgerald's "look" (such as he perceived it); by most available accounts, he did not believe her glamorous enough for the crowd the Mocambo courted.

With her polished, youthful soprano and bright, beaming visage, Fitzgerald had always felt most at home in the spotlight. She had weathered a turbulent girlhood, and offstage was known to be a shy, self-conscious woman. Promotional and event photos from the period often capture her dressed modestly, in voluminous garments inclined to drape over her shoulders and chest. Even swaddled in the furs and minks she was so fond of, the curvaceous Fitzgerald embodies a certain, if decidedly elegant, reserve. But as her outing at the Mocambo approached, she knew this moment required something different of her. So she turned to the much sought-after designer Zelda Wynn Valdes, by then established as an architect of glittering, high feminine frocks, a supreme diviner who conjured women anew in her bespoke gowns, often specially designed for nightclub appearances. True to her reputation, Wynn Valdes promptly dispatched four gowns in five days, just in time for Fitzgerald's opening.

In its April issue, *Jet* magazine reported that her debut drew a parade of Hollywood dignitaries: among them Frank Sinatra, Judy Garland, and Kitt, who gifted Fitzgerald with a bouquet of roses at the show's end (Monroe was notably absent). In *Jet*'s coverage, the singer wears a fitted black dress, tucked at the waist, with sheer, embellished sleeves and a perilously low (as the designer was wont) V-neck, a shimmering broach nestled at her bustline. She was a certified triumph.

Wynn Valdes has long gone unnamed in retellings of this widely misrepresented episode. But she was, in fact, the Pygmalion behind countless Black icons of the era, including Dandridge and Kitt. The couturier put it this way herself in a 1994 interview with *The New York Times*: "I just had a God-given talent for making people beautiful." Seamstress, stylist, dressmaker to the stars, the very name Zelda Wynn

Lively hostesses in their trademark bunny suits "ornament" the wall of the new Playboy Club in New York City, December 1, 1962.

Valdes smacks of a loftiness all its own, although regrettably—much like her similarly accomplished predecessors (Elizabeth Keckley, Ann Lowe)—she cannot quite claim widespread recognition today. Her career sprawled some 60 years, but there exists no archive dedicated to her designs. The story that must be told, then—her story—necessarily corrals the scattered images left behind of the stars she dressed.

HER BIOGRAPHY READS like a steady accrual of achievement. She was born June 28—likely 1905—in Chambersburg, Pennsylvania, about 25 miles outside of Gettysburg. Her mother and grandmother taught her how to sew. (We might reasonably assume that this grandmother survived the Confederate burning of Chambersburg 41 years before Wynn Valdes's birth.) Otherwise, training as a classical pianist at the Catholic Conservatory of Music occupied much of her girlhood—an early hint of her precocity and discipline. After graduating high school, she took a job in White Plains, New York, altering clothes at her uncle's tailoring shop, which served an affluent, white clientele.

Around this time, Wynn Valdes began cultivating her own private roster of customers. In 1935, she opened her first shop in White Plains, advertising herself, historian Nancy Diehl records in *The Hidden History of American Fashion*, as a stylist and "Colored Designer of Fashions for Women and Misses." A series of regional fashion shows for social clubs and local charities raised her profile among Black socialites who keenly embraced reprieve from the humiliation of shopping at white stores. She was flush enough by 1948 to found her own boutique, Chez Zelda, on what is now Broadway and West 158th Street in Washington Heights, when the neighborhood was still principally home to Irish, Jewish, and Greek immigrants, and starkly divided along ethnic lines. (Her dressmaking studio is generally considered the first Black-owned business to have operated there.)

Over the years, her work would inspire a revealing loyalty. Tanisha C. Ford writes in Wynn Valdes's belated *New York Times* obituary that she used "only the finest textiles... she turned silk organza, crepe, hammered satin, and Italian knit jersey into slinky, curve-hugging evening gowns, with intricate hand beading and sequins." She boasted exquisite taste and, crucially in her business, the gift of sight: she saw plainly what others did not. For example, Ford notes that Wynn Valdes could estimate with striking precision, from just a tabloid photograph, any changes in the measurements of the famously nomadic Fitzgerald, who spent much of her life on tour.

The year 1948 brought one more crowning feat: Wynn Valdes dressed the bridal party of Maria Ellington and trailblazing balladist Nat King Cole (right as his celebrity crescendoed, "All for You" and "The Christmas Song" already behind him). For Harlem, it was a century-defining affair, attended by the congressman Adam Clayton Powell Jr., who officiated, his wife, the superstar Trinidadian jazz singer Hazel Scott, and tap-dancing actor Bill "Bojangles" Robinson, alongside other Black luminaries. Maria Cole's $700 ice-blue satin gown, spiral embroidery carving a serpentine loop from its off-the-shoulder lapel to the skirt's train, heralded the artistry that would later earn Wynn Valdes the abiding devotion of stars like Dandridge, Kitt, Josephine Baker, Marlene Dietrich, Diahann Carroll, Mae West, and countless others.

Today, Wynn Valdes is best remembered for an altogether different satin outfit. In the winter of 1962, at 5 East 59th Street in Manhattan, Hugh Hefner opened the first of his exclusive men's clubs in New York. Stationed on Midtown's retail corridor, the Playboy Club required the ownership of a key to enter. Inside, amid the leather sofas and stairways cloaked in velvet, waitresses patrolled the floor in glossy corset bodysuits replete with bunny ears, a fur tail, and a bowtie. Wynn Valdes has long been credited as the author of this original, now notorious uniform, but the truth is less sexy, her victory more complicated.

Diehl reveals that the designer never claimed to have "invented" the costume and indeed, Playboy's maiden Club had launched in Chicago two years earlier. The originator, such that one existed, is still a matter of dispute, but Wynn Valdes likely contributed to its formative iterations, and we know that Hefner commissioned her to produce a set of them herself. Certainly the "suit" intersects with some of her signature design elements: the revealing neckline, the tight fit, the precise tailoring. We also know that the Playboy Club, and its Bunny corps (Black women were sometimes dubbed "Bronze Bunnies") was racially integrated when New York nightlife generally was not, and that Hefner offered Wynn Valdes space to stage a series of fashion shows at the Midtown location, events that became known as "Zelda at the Playboy." While Elsa Schiaparelli and Christian Dior presented their collections at Saks or Sorbonne's Grand Amphithéâtre, this was probably the only venue that would have offered Wynn Valdes comparable visibility in the fashion world.

The broad facts announce a woman possessed of powerful drive. In the nominally integrated North, she was enterprising enough to establish herself, a blue-collar girl with no formal training, among not just the Black (and white) moneyed classes, but the ranks of celebrity. She worked with such resolve that she would frequently fall asleep on a large table in her studio. The finer details of her personal life are sparse. She married twice, and may or may not have had children. Joyce Bryant's biographer, Jim Byers, who interviewed Wynn Valdes in 1999 before she retired, describes her as a "small woman" who embodied a "wry impishness." One oft-recycled black-and-white photo attests: chin cradled in her hand, Wynn Valdes smiles, almost winkingly, into the camera.

Deft enough to summon a visual grammar nearly approaching hagiography, Wynn Valdes had already proven her natural literacy in image-making some years before Fitzgerald's tenure at the Mocambo.

Dorothy Dandridge, 1953, promotes one off her nightclub appearances, wearing a strapless pearl dress designed by Zelda Wynn Valdes. Dandridge was one of the stylist's most faithful customers throughout her career.

She first met Bryant during the summer of 1951, when the singer made her premiere professional showcase on the East Coast at Bill Miller's cliffside nightclub, The Riviera. Perched on the Hudson River Palisades, The Riviera resembled, from the outside, an ocean liner peeking through the verdure. The main room accommodated an Art Deco bar, a revolving stage (so that one act could transition to another without pause), floor-to-ceiling windows, and seated a thousand diners who could dance in the moonlight under a retractable orb-shaped roof. (There was, too, a hidden casino upstairs for high-stakes gambling.) Distinguished patrons, including Joan Crawford and Sugar Ray Robinson—whose wife Edna Mae was also a Wynn Valdes client—enjoyed there a coterie of superlative entertainers: Sinatra, Pearl Bailey, Dean Martin, etc. Bryant would later say that no other club she had ever performed in had made her feel more like a star.

On stage she brandished a prodigious four-and-a-half octave range, which, for all its vigor, poured out of her smooth as the finest velvet. The singer, who hailed from a pious family of Seventh-day Adventists, was not yet the pearl-haired siren that those who know of her might recognize, but a demure vision in ruffled chiffon, almost certainly off the rack, with a girlish halo of dark curls. It apparently struck Wynn Valdes that Bryant's magisterial vibrato did not quite match the otherwise modest ingenue she saw before her. The next day, Byers recounts, she gifted Bryant three gowns from her boutique. A partnership was born.

From that moment on, the singer dressed exclusively in Wynn Valdes's designs. Something special characterized this alliance, fostered by the natural gifts of both parties: a sleek marriage of the costumer's meticulous dexterity and the singer's innate presence and delivery. Bryant remains the most exemplary display of the dressmaker's impeccable craft. In one portrait, shot by writer and artist Carl Van Vechten, Bryant wears a gold, pleated, strapless gown that clings so snugly to her figure it could nearly pass for a second layer of skin. Wynn Valdes had perfected the strapless, backless fit—her gowns were some of the earliest in this style—and by the time she started working with Bryant, she had mastered how to use boning to keep her tubular dresses upright without slippage. In the article "Defying Gravity," Byers observes that, while strapless gowns usually sit high on the back, Bryant's gowns would plunge toward the small of her back. Wynn Valdes had produced a silhouette immaculately suited to Bryant's body, tailored to her elongated bustline, so that the bodice fell at her cleavage. The effect was nothing short of extraordinary.

Their collaboration helped transform Bryant into the woman soon crowned "The Bronze Blonde Bombshell." Already she had achieved some distinction as a dark-skinned Black woman who wore her sensuality with ease and magnetic dignity. A 1955 *Ebony* spread named her, alongside fellow Wynn Valdes clients Dandridge and Kitt, among the "Five Most Beautiful Negro Women." Lena Horne and Hilda Simms rounded out the quintet, making Bryant the only dark-complexioned performer included.

Under better conditions, she, too, might have carved out a film career for herself. (She was reportedly considered for the titular role that ultimately went to Dandridge in the 1954 musical *Carmen Jones*.) Certainly, few Black actresses working in the '50s could expect to stay professionally afloat on film roles alone. Many of them were relegated to standalone live musical sequences (which narratively twinned their lounge acts), easily excised for distribution in the South. Like Fitzgerald, Horne, and Dandridge before her, Bryant had filmed live singing interludes for at least two films: *Mr. Ace* (1946) and *The Girl Next Door* (1953). In the former, her scene takes place in a swanky bar so shrouded in darkness that she appears as little more than a shadow onstage. The footage from the latter film was cut and discarded, likely to satisfy Jim Crow censorship laws that would not countenance even the pretense of racial integration on-screen, much less the bold sexuality of a woman like Bryant (at least two of her songs had been banned from the airwaves for their "provocative" lyrics).

Left: Actress Mae West was one of Zelda Wynn Valdes's most high-profile clients. The designer is believed to have popularized the mermaid silhouette, seen here on West in a sheer floor-length gown, worn in the Henry Hathaway screwball comedy *Go West, Young Man* (1936).

Right: Zelda Wynn Valdes during a fitting for her client Eartha Kitt, photographed by Gordon Parks for *LIFE* in 1952.

IN THOSE WYNN VALDES-DESIGNED bandeau pieces, with their delicate, fastidious creasing, and so often flared at the knees, Bryant recalls a mermaid. A 1953 photoshoot for *LIFE* magazine features Dandridge clad in a similar coral dress, fitted from the thigh up, the bodice traced by rows of wispy pleats charting a textured, diagonal path toward her calves, where the fabric swells into a cascade of exquisitely draped ruffles.

Wynn Valdes clearly favored this mermaid silhouette—which she helped popularize through her prominent customers—rivaling the dominance of Christian Dior's "New Look" with its signature wide shoulders, cinched waists, and full skirts. This opposition is instructive upon closer inspection: the New Look was born out of years of Nazi occupation and scarcity. Dior, born the same year as Wynn Valdes, departed from the more shapeless, unstructured styles that prevailed in previous years. Instead, his corseted A-line model borrowed openly from the late 19th century, France's Belle Époque, a "golden age" of peace, cultural innovation, and economic prosperity (to say nothing of ravenous colonial expansion). Carmel Snow, then editor-in-chief of *Harper's Bazaar*, famously hailed the New Look as revolutionary, but Dior had simply turned to the past. The clothes conveyed his own nostalgic impulses as the nation emerged from the horrors of war for the second time in his life. In other words, the shape itself took precedence over the distinct contours of a woman's frame, which was, for Wynn Valdes, not merely scaffolding but the very province of her craft.

Wynn Valdes did not have the benefit of such a clean timeline; she operated during the violent zeniths of America's regime of racial terrorism—its denials, rejections, humiliations, pogroms—which alchemized into a thinly veiled volatility by the '80s and '90s. Diehl contends that "the most important aspect of [her] career is its alignment with the Civil Rights Movement." Long civic-minded, Wynn Valdes was not indifferent to these matters: she was president of the New York chapter of the National Association of Fashion and Accessory Designers, a coalition of Black designers sponsored by Mary McLeod Bethune's National Council of Negro Women. She directed workshops for the Harlem Youth Opportunities Unlimited and Associated Teams. She continually invested in community for the rest of her life, and never abandoned her working-class origins.

Clothing label inside a bird bedecked dress, designed by Zelda Wynn Valdes and worn by Eartha Kitt, housed in the Smithsonian National Museum of African American History and Culture.

She may have learned certain valuable lessons, apart from skill, in her childhood: namely, defiance. She often spoke of the very first dress she made at just 11 years old, for her grandmother. In *The New York Times*, Wynn Valdes recalled, "She said, 'Daughter, you can't sew for me... I'm too tall and too big.'" When she completed the dress, her grandmother was so pleased with the result that she was buried in it. Years later, *The Pittsburgh Courier* wrote that Bryant's gowns were "so form-fitting that the singer cannot sit down in them." In her obituary, *The Telegraph* reported that "she had to be carried on and off stage." Two things strike me about these descriptions: Bryant's dresses were not necessarily designed for movement, despite the performance aspect, and thus reflected—they could not possibly hide—the body of their wearer.

If the female form, which Wynn Valdes sought tirelessly to mimic, proved the defining force of her aesthetic, she also demonstrated a sophisticated grasp of the aesthetic ecosystem her clients found themselves obliged to translate through a Black femme body. In her 1978 book *Black Macho and the Myth of the Superwoman*, scholar Michele Wallace writes of an antiquated image of Black women that stubbornly persists: she is "a woman of inordinate strength," for she "does not have the same fears, weaknesses, and insecurities as other women, but believes herself to be and is, in fact, stronger emotionally than most men." It is no wonder, then, that Wynn Valdes's gowns were so audaciously feminine and sensual, characterized by plummeting necklines, an archly precise fit, and soft materials. Perhaps the Mocambo owner's reservations about Fitzgerald were not openly racist, but the limits of his imagination cannot be extricated from her race; nor can the body Wynn Valdes hoped to honor, to emulate in her dresses. It is noticeable that her project was not to disguise or distort the body imago that so troubled the American consciousness, but enshrine it.

If we understand stardom—those Black women who have acquired it being no exception—as the body-turned-commodity, we can see how Hollywood provisionally corralled Horne, Dandridge, and Kitt (all thin and fair-skinned) as its principal representatives of the integration period. They were icons insofar as they could promote consumption, selling a respectable portrait of Black bourgeoisie living. That said, each of the aforementioned women, and far too many more, saw their careers wither when their dignity rightly intervened. Horne early on grew tired of filming abbreviated musical sequences and was later blacklisted for alleged communist affiliations. Kitt, too, was notoriously shut out of Hollywood after offending the fragile sensibilities of Lady Bird Johnson by daring to denounce the Vietnam War. Certainly Otto Preminger dispensed poor counsel when he urged Dandridge to accept only starring roles after her Oscar-nominated turn as Carmen Jones; but after years of playing tragic, tortured, racially ambiguous bit parts, how must she have felt to be offered the role of Burmese servant girl Tuptim (which ultimately went to Rita Moreno) in the 1956 film *The King and I* so shortly after her historic nomination?

All told, Wynn Valdes herself enjoyed a formidable tenure that stretched well into the '90s. In 1969, choreographer Arthur Mitchell, founder of the Dance Theatre of Harlem, appointed her the company's principal costumer. For over 80 productions, she would design its costumes—in yet another stroke of brilliance, she began dyeing each dancer's tights to match their skin tone, a major breakthrough in the world of ballet—and worked nearly up until her death in 2001.

Despite her prolific output, very few of her dresses have been preserved for the public. At least two are in the collection of the Smithsonian National Museum of African American History and Culture. One, belonging to Fitzgerald, is a black sequined floor-length gown with a scoop neck in front that dips, characteristically, into a V at the back. The other, designed for Kitt, is a crème, bias-cut silk gown, embellished with dainty, brightly colored birds and a high slit. In the fall of 2023, the Met's exhibition about female fashion designers, "Women Dressing Women," spotlighted Wynn Valdes with a James J. Kriegsmann photograph of Bryant wearing a textured white gown in the designer's signature mermaid silhouette. Indeed, some of the most popular celebrities today, wittingly or otherwise, still reference the couturier and her influential garments. Byers soundly observes that Wynn Valdes "is part of this story of the greatest entertainers who ever were." In the glaring chasm left by the archive, legend remains.

In these photos of Joyce Bryant, taken by writer and photographer Carl Van Vechten, we can see a number of Zelda Wynn Valdes's signature elements: the flared skirt, plunging neckline, and intricate, "feminine" detailing.

SOUND THINKING: BEN BURTT & DEAN HURLEY

A conversation between two adventurers into undiscovered countries of cinematic sound.

Ben Burtt on the Ewok village set in *Star Wars: Episode VI: Return of the Jedi* (1983), playing a tape of the Ewok language between scenes.

Doing sound for films is an endlessly complex practice whose power often goes undetected. George Lucas famously once said, “Sound is 50% of the movie.” According to Dean Hurley, David Lynch’s right-hand sound man, Lynch liked to offer his own twist: “Sound is 50% of the movie, sometimes even more.”

These two visionary filmmakers who so highly esteemed the role of sound were assisted throughout their careers by equally obsessive and pioneering sound artists. For Lynch, there was composer Angelo Badalamenti and sound designer Hurley, following on from Alan Splet, who passed away in 1994. For Lucas, there was Ben Burtt, a legend in the film industry and the creator of canonical sounds such as the hum of a lightsaber through to the voice of WALL-E. Speaking from their relative homes in Virginia and Northern California, the two swapped stories, advice, and unpacked the heritage of their craft.

BEN BURTT: Hello, Dean.

DEAN HURLEY: Hi, Ben. Thank you so much for taking the time to do this. It’s an honor. One of the things I so like about your work is that, as you’ve marched through your career, you always seem to have one foot in history, looking backward and drawing from the past. I love that you came to sound through special effects, and I think the full understanding that you have of the medium—as a director and an editor and a sound practitioner—gives you really unique insight.

BB: A small topic. [Laughs] Well, I’ve always been interested in the craft and history of moviemaking. Creatively, I’ve always loved to build on the past. You can’t discover something new unless you know where you are.

DH: What did you listen to with young ears that informed your later work, in terms of your sense of how movies should sound?

BB: I grew up in the 1950s and ’60s—in, I suppose, the first generation with television. Plus I loved acting out little plays to music. My mother tells me that if she put on a record, I would act out a story right then and there—from a young age, I found music in particular to be very stimulating to my imagination. It brought forth images of adventure and exploration, being a spaceman or a cowboy. As a kid, I then discovered movies. In those days, you entered a dark room with a big curtain that opened and there was a color movie on a giant screen, way beyond anything that television offered.

DH: What were some of the films?

BB: Oh, boy. I remember being scared to death in *When Worlds Collide*, the early disaster film, and *Flying Leathernecks* (both 1951), in which John Wayne is fighting in the South Pacific—we were cheering as the enemy ships blew up. I enjoyed Abbott and Costello films, and the cartoons, Saturday matinee fare. My parents took me to see the MGM musicals—*Brigadoon* (1954), *Gigi* (1958)—and I remember, when I was a little older, being overwhelmed by *Jason and the Argonauts* (1963). I was 13 or 14, coming home on the bus, having just been transported to a magical land. My enjoyment led to a curiosity about how movies were made.

But years before that when I was in first grade, I had encephalitis. I was hospitalized, and then I came home to regain my strength and was out of school for a few weeks. Knowing I was lying in bed, bored, my father brought home a reel-to-reel tape recorder. At the time, that was futuristic technology. It was technology nobody in my neighborhood had: the ability to record something and play it back. My father taught me how to use it. I could use a microphone and record myself, make funny sounds, play them at half speed, things like that. I was brought into the world of sound recording.

DH: This is so interesting, because you always seem to be at the forefront of these explosions, or seismic shifts, in technology. Later, especially when you were working at Lucasfilm (from 1975 onwards), you had access to all kinds of technology other people didn’t. Do you ever look back and say, “Holy mackerel, I was really working in a very interesting time!”

BB: Definitely. When I started my first sound design job [on 1975’s Roger Corman-produced *Death Race 2000*], the original generation of Hollywood sound people—individuals who had, in some sense, pioneered the first decades of movie sound—were retiring. And they weren’t really being replaced; there was a lack of new people coming into sound. At the time, motion pictures were still released with an optical soundtrack that was of inferior quality—it was not stereo, it was not multitrack. It was limited in its spectrum, in terms of low and high frequencies. And it wasn’t spatial: you couldn’t do things within the movie space other than monaural. But there were young folks like myself who knew better recording techniques were out there because of the advances the music industry had made. Music was the force pushing sound technology forward—movies were lagging way behind.

But right from the beginning, George Lucas and Gary Kurtz, the producers of the first *Star Wars* film, said, “Let’s do this in multi-channel stereo. We’ll combine forces with Dolby and have higher-fidelity motion pictures.”[1] Lucasfilm was supporting research. We had a small department that worked year-round, and Lucas encouraged us to record original, customized sound effects. I was there to build the library and to think things through. Between working on the sound editing of the movie, I was out recording and experimenting in the backroom. So, about a year before postproduction began, much earlier than sound people would normally start, I was hired to take my Nagra tape recorder and my portable stereo recorder and go out and find things, and to build a Lucasfilm library for *Star Wars*.

DH: You have always built fantastic libraries for your projects, but you also have an affinity for digging back in time and recognizing, for example, a certain sound of an arrow being shot used in *The Adventures of Robin Hood* (1938).

BB: My interest in sound effects libraries started when I was a child, recording things off television with my reel-to-reel recorder. If a science fiction or Laurel and Hardy movie were playing, I would record it, and then I could listen back anytime I wanted. That was very unusual—remember, there were no DVRs, no streaming. I built up a shelf full of tapes that I would listen to with headphones. The sounds brought back images in my head; I could enjoy the movies over and over again. I began to recognize certain sounds I really loved more than others. I also began to recognize repeats of sound effects. Each studio had their own distinctive collection that they reused, that gave them an audio brand. I was curious about their origins. I kept notes and enjoyed charting where they went, examining the provenance of, like you mentioned, the *Robin Hood* arrow. It started out in Warner Brothers' *The Adventures of Robin Hood*. Decades later, it was still showing up in movies: I'd go to the theater to see a Western, and I'd hear those same bows and arrows.

DH: The Western tropes especially hung on for so long, like the ricochets and specific recordings of gunshots. I've always thought of some of these sound effects like little packets of energy: they have certain characteristics that lend themselves to use again and again, but something interesting happens with the language, the sort of vernacular of how they are used. Have you ever thought about, for instance, hearing a red-tailed hawk usage for a desert expanse, or "castle thunder"[2] when a moody locale is revealed? What percentage of its impact is attributable to the sound effect itself, and what is just mere reuse from precedent?

BB: Absolutely, a language of sound effects was established by Golden Age Hollywood. If people heard an earthquake, or a dogfight between airplanes—those were not sounds that people heard in actual experience, but they experienced them in the movies. The choices that sound people made established an association between the listener and the specific sounds being used and reused. The studios were, in a sense, lazy—once they had a thunderclap that they liked in some film in 1933, they just kept it. There was no sense in sending anybody out to get another. The audience now understood that that was the language; those sounds were accepted as, like you said, the tropes. And I enjoyed recognizing that.

Ben Burtt's celebrated sound work on the *Star Wars* franchise includes crafting the hum of a lightsaber (recordings of an old film projector that he remembered from his student days, combined with interference from a TV set), Darth Vader's mechanical breathing (Burtt's own breath, filtered through a scuba mask), and the voices of R2-D2 (child-like noises, made by Burtt, fed through an ARP 2600 synthesizer), and Jabba the Hut (the voice of linguistics professor Larry Ward, mimicking the Peruvian-Inca dialect Quechua, manipulated, pitched lower, and then augmented with the sounds of Burtt handling his wife's cheese casserole and smooshing it between his fingers).

Later, I would go to drive-in movies—as you know, there were speakers you'd put in your car. I would disassemble the speaker, clip onto it with alligator clips, record onto my reel-to-reel recorder, and get a clean copy of *Goldfinger* (1964) or *Lawrence of Arabia* (1962). If a sound was clean, isolated, I could extract it and add it to my library. I collected as many sounds as I could; one friend called my collection "the veritable infinitude of sound." Some people collect baseball cards; I was interested in collecting vintage sounds. I went to a lot of effort, but it was a hobby. I never considered it as a career path, never considered being part of moviemaking professionally.

DH: I think that's important. As you've said, movie sounds are a sort of caricature of real-life sounds, and, unbeknownst to yourself, you were indoctrinating yourself into this language. It reminds me of the simple, distilled way that you often describe things, like how a good cinematic gunshot is a multi-syllable thing; it has components. It makes you think: what is it that makes a sound interesting onscreen? What makes it really do the business, in terms of giving it that power and storytelling capability?

BB: Yes, I was learning the language of Hollywood motion pictures. Later, when it seemed I might be headed toward a career, I thought, "Wow, if I ever get to Hollywood, I'll be able to have all my questions answered by somebody, because there must be experts there who know the origins of all these sounds. I'll be amongst people who share my interest." That never happened; as it turns out, not that many people were really interested. [Laughs]

DH: Yeah, you're that person now. [Laughs]

BB: I mean, I came across a handful of interested friends, but there wasn't this fraternity of sound people in Hollywood that shared my passion. You see, I was much more excited about the aesthetics of sound. Like, why do you pick a certain sound? Or if you're asked to design something—create a storm, create a space battle—where do you start? What's going to be effective? I wanted

1. 1977's *Star Wars: Episode IV – A New Hope* used the Dolby Stereo four-channel system, combining left, right, center, and surround channels; the film's massive success was pivotal in encouraging theaters around the world to upgrade and install stereo equipment.

2. "Castle thunder" is a sound effect that consists of a loud thunderclap during a rainstorm, first used in 1931's *Frankenstein*.

to take advantage of the fact that the audience has become educated and understands certain sounds in a shorthand fashion, but I didn't want to just repeat the old sounds. I wanted to build on them. Right from the first *Star Wars* movie, I was thinking, "What was done before? Knowing what I know about the provenance of a sound, can I design a new sound incorporating what is familiar to people but then surprise them with a variation on it, an expansion of it?" That was my approach for many films. The older libraries were still in full usage up to and through the '90s, before they were finally extinguished and lost, destroyed, thrown away. But I was still operating on the principle of: "What are the roots of these sounds?" I did not find that this approach was shared, though, by many other sound editors, who were perfectly good, creative people, but were less interested in the history. It's a difference in style.

DH: I relate so hard to this. It's something I've been trying to figure out recently, too.

BB: I mean, you were connected with David Lynch, who obviously passed away recently. I met him once at Skywalker [Sound]. He was here for some reason...

DH: Randy Thom mixed *Wild at Heart* (1990).

BB: Maybe that was it. I knew Alan Splet better because he used to have an editing room near me back on the first *Star Wars*. Richard L. Anderson, Alan, and I all rented rooms at an independent sound facility called Gomillion Studios. Alan was one of the few guys I could talk to about Hollywood gunshots... We didn't work on the same projects, but we shared a respect for the history of sound. He was one of the few people who appreciated it, and actually knew and recognized a lot of the tropes.

DH: Yeah. I've listened to all the original *Eraserhead* (1977) sound rolls. In listening to them, there was stuff that Alan and David did themselves, and then dubs of library stuff. I don't know where Alan was getting them—some of it I recognized, some I didn't—but it was fascinating to hear it all out of context. Like you, he was collecting a lot of exotic birds, bizarre animal sounds. And the other anecdote is that David had half of Alan's ashes and had put them underneath the console, so the entire time I was working at David's studio, I was literally working over Alan's ashes.

BB: Oh my gosh, okay! That is bizarre. But also very David Lynch-esque.

DH: Yeah. It also spoke to his endearing side. David loved Alan. They had a real partnership. They met doing the early short films, and I think when you meet somebody early on in their career, when someone believes in you and helps you realize a vision, that is ripe ground for a special bond, because it's about human connection. And they went through the wringer together. I mean, *Eraserhead* took so long to make, and it was such

In Philip Kaufman's 1978 remake of Don Siegel's 1956 *Invasion of the Body Snatchers*, one original element that sets Kaufman's film apart is the blood-curdling cry that is heard issuing from the extraterrestrial pod people when alerting their fellow invaders to the presence of a human who is yet to have their body appropriated. To create this sound effect, Ben Burtt mixed and manipulated recordings of pig squeals, resulting in the deeply effective, deeply unsettling klaxon scream.

a slow, methodical process. And the gathering! They were like Boy Scouts trying to get sounds. I would always be saying to David, "Tell me more stories about Alan." I can't do that anymore.

Going back to soundtracks, you mentioned earlier analyzing why something works—I have a theory about this. I feel there was this magical time in film sound technology around the mid-'80s when, because of the process you were going through—recording on Nagra, dubbing to mag stock,[3] taking that mag stock and mixing onto fullcoat mag, then that being used to create an optical element for the final answer print—so much layered harmonic saturation was occurring that, if you listen back to some of these printmasters now, the sounds have such oomph. They're like Motown drums, you know? They're distorted, but they have punch and clarity. Have you thought about this? Do you miss this in modern soundtracks?

BB: All that you've just said is true to the experience I've had. In the optical era there were limitations to the dynamic range of what could be recorded. If you went to record, for example, a gun or a thunderclap, the optical medium would place a lot of volume limitation on the recording. The optical track itself couldn't handle the range of volume and so on, so you had to compress it to have a less dynamic range. This created a unique form of distortion: if something was too loud, it came across as a smooth kind of rumble, a beefy sound. Even on the Nagras, with tape saturation, you ended up with a certain characteristic that is specific to mag.

But I also had some preamps built for the Nagra by our lead engineer Tomlinson Holman that could simulate some of the sonic characteristics of optical recording onto tape. You might call it a soft clipper.[4] These were never available to the public, only three or four were ever made.

DH: Wow.

BB: They're still on two of our Nagras, now retired and sitting in a cabinet. I'd asked Tom a lot about

3. Mag stock, also known as mag track, is film stock coated with a layer of magnetic oxide emulsion used to record sound. It comes in stripe or fullcoat, the latter which fully covers one side and can be used to record several tracks.

4. An audio processing tool that gently rounds off the peaks of an audio signal, avoiding harsh distortion.

why, even at modest levels, the optical sound effects seemed to be articulate and clear. At one point in the early '80s, I was even sending so me of our recordings out and having optical copies made—

DH: No way!

BB: I'd get an optical track back from the lab—you could make that in those days. I could listen and say, "Tom, this is kind of what I'm looking for. I don't want the hiss, and I want a greater range of highs and lows, a spectrum, but I want this characteristic." We had a couple of preamps that we used when we recorded sharp impacts, rocket launches, weapons of any kind—whacking things together, things with very high transients—in an effort to simulate the results of optical recording.

DH: This blows my mind. This is worth the interview, right here, just this piece of knowledge. I do the same thing today with tape, because I'm trying to get tape characteristics into printmasters or mixes. Hearing that you were obsessed with that optical sound because you grew up with it—"I like that characteristic, how do we get that?"—that's fascinating.

BB: And also, in those days, you still had a limit. You had a dynamic range that was much greater than optical, but even on mag there were limits. So when CDs first came out, suddenly the orchestra could come in incredibly loud, and then you could have quiet moments, and people were surprised. That was all great, but it doesn't work in a movie track. The theater just turns down the playback volume based on the loudest moment, and everything else is lost. So using a more limited dynamic range, that's a good thing. It's good to have limits.

DH: I mean, honestly, as we race through time and everything is getting remastered and spread out and given more dynamic range, it's becoming harder to find examples of what moviegoers actually listened to in the past. There is stuff on YouTube, including old trailers that have been transferred from optical. When I first heard this stuff, it was like a rush of early learning, of how my ears perceived things: "Wow, this sounds so comfortable. This sounds so familiar and good." I started analyzing the tracks: they are very limited, but they don't sound like it. You only figure that out if you look at the waveform; things are chopped off but it sounds impactful, present, and lively.

BB: When I was a projectionist in my years at the University of Southern California, when I was getting indoctrinated into early sound techniques, I often used to just sit in the booth. We'd run lots of old movies, optical prints from the '30s and '40s, and I would watch the VU meter[5] on the amps to see what was happening. In a war movie, there'd be dialogue and then there'd be a battle scene, and it was really six decibels—but I kept looking back and saying, "My gosh, they get such dramatic value." Those mediums forced you to be selective. You couldn't load up a track with every possible thing you might think of because the ear would never figure it out. Older films were sparse in many ways—yet they worked because you heard the right sounds at the right time, and it was an artform.

DH: In my experience, the more effective mixes are the efficient ones. It is very difficult to resist looking back and waxing poetic about simpler times.

BB: I'm in my mid-seventies so I tend to be a cranky old man. It comes with age. You look back and say, "They just don't do it the way we used to."

DH: More than any film department, sound guys seem to get the reputation for being the most cranky, I think.

BB: Oh, just a second, that's the telephone. (I'm on a call right now, I'll call you back.) That was a guy from Florida who records thunder every day. He calls at all hours to report the latest audio highlights. Anyway, what was I saying? I was talking about limitations. We sound people often think, "This kind of works—now I'm going to put something on top." It's an additive approach. Our digital medium allows you to just pile stuff on. But sometimes you need to think of a subtractive approach—what don't you need?—and start taking things away until you discover a moment where you're getting all the dramatic value you want and not necessarily hearing everything. Someone might ask, "Why can't we hear that car in the distance?" and you say, "Well, we don't need it, you shouldn't be paying attention to that."

DH: Without me even asking, you've answered the question of what is being lost today. In the piling on and dense layering of the modern film soundtrack, there is often a lack of focal emphasis, or importance... sometimes begging the question, "Hey, what are we even supposed to focus on?"

BB: Exactly. Of course there are films with good sound, scattered here and there, but a lot of films are just a wall of constant-density sound: today

Ben Burtt created the unforgettable accoustic vocabulary of the *Indiana Jones* world. Particularly memorable examples include the gurgling creak in 1981's *Raiders of the Lost Ark* of the coveted Ark being opened by the Nazis (Burtt's recording of sliding the toilet tank cover off of the toilet in his home)—an act that then releases swooping hordes of vengeful shrieking wraiths (animal and human screams mixed with dolphin and sea lion cries, run through a vocoder to become otherworldly)—and, in 1989's *Indiana Jones and The Last Crusade*, the repulsive swarms of rats that have infested the Venetian catacombs (a recording of a brood of harried clucking chickens, fed through a keyboard and played at high pitch, required because the 2,000 disease-free "movie rats" bred for the scene were silent on set).

5. Volume unit meter, a device used to measure the level of sound intensity on audio equipment.

it's all music, it's all sound effects, it's all yelling and dialogue, and it's the same from beginning to end. The loudness never really stops, and it's generic in many ways. You don't hear anything concise. You don't have moments where the sound is delivering a specific emotion, or creating an ambience that is part of the feelings in the movie. In the past, we always were limited. We did films like *Return of the Jedi* (1983) and *Indiana Jones and the Last Crusade* (1989), which is my favorite mix, with a 32-channel board. That's it. We were forced to be concise in our choices.

DH: Wow.

BB: And you'd plan everything. Of course, premixing would get things down so that you didn't use up all 32 channels. You'd leave a couple open for a sweetener or two, but you'd have to decide, structurally, what you were going to be held to, which layers were important. Back then you also couldn't do lots of things surgically: you couldn't go into one track, pick out one little thing, and change it. You had to make commitments in premixes, combining the right things and then sticking with them.

DH: Perhaps what has now happened, too, is the establishment of the idea of coming to a mix prepared with a multitude of options for every possible direction. "Hey, this is the final mix, here's 182,000 colors, which one do you want?"

BB: Yeah, it's tough, as I'm sure you experience, because you're working in the modern age. Final mixes now, most of them are just sorting things out. And it shouldn't be that way. When we had real control in the '70s, '80s, and '90s at Skywalker, we would do a lot of temp mixing and we would play premixes for people making decisions. They would come to the dialogue premix and pick out the ADR lines[6] they wanted. And we'd put those in. Then they'd listen to the sound effects pre-dub to give a reaction, and they'd say, "Oh I like that," "I have a different idea," or whatever. By the time we'd get to the final mix, we'd have made lots of decisions and pre-sorted possibilities. That's what drives me crazy about more modern mix approaches. Because the digital process permits endless procrastination, the films coming to the final aren't done yet–they're still writing them, maybe they're doing reshoots, the studio has one editor doing a version, a second editor doing a version... It's chaos. I think that's one of the other reasons you end up with generic sounds these days–you've re-cut the movie so much that the music doesn't fit any longer. Also nowadays, you

Ben Burtt created the voice of Elliott's alien friend by recording a sixtysomething California woman, Pat Welsh, whom he overheard in a photography store making a purchase at the counter. He was charmed by the particularly deep, low pitch, and somewhat genderless quality of her voice, partly the result of her religiously smoking two packs of Kool menthol cigarettes a day.

6. ADR, or automatic dialogue replacement, is the process of re-recording dialogue in a post-production setting to improve audio quality, fix errors, or adjust for script changes.

Metrograph A–Z
K Is for Kissing

Words by
Audrey Wollen

The world's first film studio was built by Thomas Edison in West Orange, New Jersey. The Black Maria was a cramped, boxy structure covered in tar paper, with a roof that hinged open to let in a flood of light. The entire building sat on a rotating turntable, to follow the sun. It was named after the local slang for a police wagon, as if working inside the studio felt like being hauled off somewhere unknown, a lurching gloom crowded with outlaws. It was these inauspicious surroundings that, in 1896, produced cinema's first kiss.

Directed by William Heise, the 12-second sequence is a peculiar, laughing smush of chins; disarmingly chatty, she—May Irwin—never stops talking, even while their lips pucker and search. (It reminds me of the Hays-defiant kissing scene in *Notorious* a half century later, where, to get around the three-second limit enforced by the Code, Ingrid Bergman and Cary Grant speak continuously, their mouths making glancing contact between every other phrase, drawing the kiss out for nearly three minutes.) After much coy nuzzling of cheeks, he—John Rice—steps back, tweaks his moustache, and lightly presses his lips against hers.

The Kiss was so scandalously popular that it provoked many imitations and adaptations. One, 1899's *The Kiss in the Tunnel*, splices a furtive peck into the then-fashionable genre of phantom rides: a train, shot from the front of the engine, rushes into a tunnel, creating the effect that the audience itself is hurtling forward, too. In the tenebrous enclosure of the cinema, the real world and the projection match for a quick, black second, like the screen has eaten the room, or vice versa. In the obscurity of the tunnel, sex grabs its fleeting chance, then departs.

The distribution company sold only the shot of the kiss, telling theaters to simply jam it into any spare train footage they already had. Some believe this intervention was the beginning of continuity editing as we understand it. Two unrelated visual situations, lined up in a specific order—a train plunges into shadow, a kiss occurs, a train re-emerges into the light—well, what do y'know, it tells a story. Both the kiss and the train are changed, by virtue of their proximity. A flash of eroticism becomes literally subterranean; desiring bodies are sent happily into the underworld. And the room, the real room, in real darkness, and all those inside it—changed, too, by their nearness, mouths blindly discovering mouths, brief stories blooming like moonflowers in the night.

get picture editors cutting a lot of sound just because they can, and that can often get things going in the wrong direction by jumping too quickly to a full-up track and short-circuiting a more measured approach.

DH: Yes. Honestly, out of every practitioner, I think picture editors today have probably the most control over what we end up digesting.

BB: Yes. When I entered the business, it was technically difficult for a picture editor to cut any sound. Most editing machines were set up to cut just one audio track with a Moviola or a flatbed, and you just left the sound editing for later. Now, because the technology is so flexible, you can attach many audio tracks to picture as you cut. I occasionally see an editor immediately start taking cues off a CD or Spotify or something, start laying them in, and cut the scene with the music... I don't think that's a good idea. You need to see what the visual material and production dialogue creates first, even if you know sound effects and music can be added later.

DH: When I was working with Duwayne Dunham on *Twin Peaks: The Return*, he was cutting without any music. It was amazing to me to see how, left without that stuff, the editor focuses on the inherent rhythm of performance alone. Sometimes we would put in some of Angelo [Badalamenti]'s music later, and it would just line up and fit because there was a naturally found rhythm to the assembly... there was an undulation to how it was formulated with just the cuts. It was eye-opening. Nowadays, people are starting with the music, instead of finding the musicality inherent in the edit itself.

BB: Yeah, there's a danger there. Even when I was cutting the *Star Wars* prequels in that era, the first time we screened it in a rough assembly, maybe even the first cut, we would do it without sound. We knew those things would have a big influence soon, but we wanted to evaluate the strengths and weaknesses based on a visual rhythm, what was captured in the dialogue, what was captured in its raw state. You want to develop confidence in what you've got in terms of visual cinematic language first, and not jump the gun by putting things in that would steer it before you've had a chance to explore those possibilities, to submit yourself to it. Then you start shading things in simply—not to press too hard, but to let it grow. I would deliberately hold off, and once we'd gotten a certain amount of work done, I'd go back and shade in some ambiences. I wouldn't treat it with every detail, or go after any foley or anything, but I'd begin to make the environments come alive, working from background to middle ground to foreground, over a period of time.

DH: What was the last film you did on a high-speed dubber before doing nonlinear stuff, where you were working fully on film?

For 2008's Pixar animation *WALL-E*, Ben Burtt created 2,400 distinct sound files, capturing every nuance of the robot's vocabulary of bleeps and bloops as well as each movement. For WALL-E's slowest movements, Burtt used a sample of an old Army generator being cranked by hand from a Western film—a common point of inspiration for Burtt—in this case, 1953's *Island in the Sky*, starring John Wayne.

BB: I believe it would have been the *Star Wars* "Special Edition" in the late '90s. Let's see... we'd be going through the *Young Indy* series, and that was kind of a hybrid between film and digital because it was using the EditDroid.[7] We had one foot in either camp. I might be wrong, because I was spending time between these films going off and directing. I'd disappear for a year, then I'd be back and everybody would have learned something new that I didn't know.

DH: By the way, I was showing my eight-year-old daughter one of the IMAX films that you did, *Blue Planet* (1990), and she was frightened by it. She was asking about the Earth and what was being shown onscreen, and said, "This doesn't happen in real life, right?" I was like, "Yes, honey, it most certainly does." She said, "I don't feel good, I'd like you to turn this off."

BB: Really? That's interesting. And that was one of the very first films that was gently talking about global warming. It got criticism from some activists who said we weren't strong enough, that we weren't pounding our hand on the table so to speak, but...

DH: It made a mark on my eight-year-old, that's for sure.

BB: It was a tactful, diplomatic sort of gentle message, because it was being done by the National Air and Space Museum, and they didn't want to scare anybody. They didn't want families to walk out depressed. The conservation message was not overemphasized.

DH: It's interesting to see how young minds and ears without a lot of precedent can pick up on stuff at a subtle level like that, and especially with sound. I mean, she did it with *E.T.* (1982). There's the overture that plays with no image at the beginning, and she said, "This is going to be a spooky movie." Without any language of cinematic history, she picked up on it.

BB: We are inherently sensitive to many kinds of sounds that stimulate strong emotion. Obviously, music is very effective. If I played any kind of

7. EditDroid was an early tape- and disc-based picture editing system that represented an intermediary between analog and digital editing, developed by LucasFilm in 1984. Never a commercial success, it was sold off to Avid Technology in 1993.

a minor chord to my children when they were young, or if I put on a movie that sounded something like that, they were immediately terrified, without knowing the content of the movie. The music just had a natural negative effect.

DH: Yeah, and that stuff is wired into us. This is the thing I think about all the time, the physiology of how sound works, how loud and distorted stuff is speaking directly to our primordial senses of hearing a distorted scream in the distance and sensing danger. It's fascinating.

BB: The fun thing about sound, as I'm sure you know, is to try to get a control of those natural reactions and see if you can capitalize on or exploit them, if you want the same desired effect.

DH: And that's your special effect. And that's what you achieve so well. Many, many times. It's been incredible to listen throughout the years.

BB: Well, I've had good opportunities. Fortunately, I was under the authority of people who gave my team the license to do that, and a generous amount of extra time to do things once in a while. I mean, Lucas did, of course. And Andrew Stanton, the creator of *WALL-E* (2008), was very interested in experimenting and working ahead of time. Those were fun opportunities. But especially in the '80s, there was a good relationship between the sound and the picture editing teams at Lucasfilm and Skywalker Sound. They were in the same building, so we could interact all the time. Discussions could take place about something working or not working. The whole idea was to probe, to experiment, to see what our options were... I was spoiled!

DH: Yeah. I was spoiled in a way, too. It's sad when you realize you're almost like a scientist, in that you can only do your work with large amounts of government funding.

BB: That's also the fun thing about the job. This is a medium that is fun to work in, but it needs the right vision behind it and time given for development. I am rarely given that opportunity nowadays.

DH: Well, it could be that your legacy is so daunting—the approachability factor. Maybe people have been scared off from asking you to do something!

BB: Some people say that. Another thing I have realized is that because of whatever legacy I represent, sometimes a client will think I'm such a magician that all they have to do is say, "Here's our film, make the sound iconic. Come up with something for X, Y, and Z." And they expect it instantly.

DH: Yeah. I hate that. I hate that.

BB: I'm thinking, "Okay, this again." Anything that's going to be iconic, it's not born iconic. It's something that—over time, over 10 years or something—maybe it'll reach some point where you can say, "This is now iconic, it's become a standard. A signpost." I've failed in certain projects because they expected something "iconic" within 48 hours.

DH: It's like earlier, when we were talking about hearing certain sounds over and over. For example, if you hadn't made the "Wilhelm scream"[8] famous through your repeated use of it, the tongue-in-cheek Trojan Horse over decades, then imagine somebody putting a mic in front of someone and saying, "Give me an iconic, multi-syllable death fall." You know? It's not going to strike anyone's ears the first time they hear it as being the thing. It's only after it's snowballed over time.

BB: Absolutely. That's been one issue I've faced. Clients who wanted a voice for a voice assistant robot or something, who have said, "We love R2-D2, it's got to be just like that, but not at all the same." You give them something different, and they say, "That doesn't work at all." But if I edge in a little bit of R2, they say, "Oh, I love it." Pretty soon I'm right back where I was: I've once again just repeated R2. They don't understand that things take development time: you plant an audio seed, then nurture it into something. It takes time and patience, and it is a process of discovery that can have very exciting, dramatic results.

8. A stock sound effect, originating in 1951 that was frequently reused by Warner Bros. for films of the era, often in scenarios when someone is shot, falls from a great height, or is thrown from an explosion. The effect was used by Ben Burtt in *Star Wars* (1977) to accompany a stormtrooper falling off a ledge, and then again in many of the films he worked on over the next decades, gaining the attention of other sound designers. To date, it features in over 400 films.

BORROWING THE SOUNDS OF BEN BURTT

Written by
Apichatpong Weerasethakul

I grew up far away, but the sounds Ben Burtt created reached me. His work shaped the films that became part of my childhood. I didn't know his name back then, but I knew what a lightsaber sounded like, what unknown creatures sounded like. Looking up at the stars from my small town in northeastern Thailand, I must have borrowed his sounds to build other worlds in my head.

There was a pond where my friends and I often went. We watched frogs and tadpoles move, and listened to the sound of water between our palms. The reflections, the waves of light, sound, and water dancing together—it was my first realization of "waves," of "being." Later, I realized that film, too, is the weaving of waves. As kids, everything felt real, and cinema guided us into that boundless world. It was the most precious thing.

Over time, my ears, like my eyes, adjusted to new technology. I watched sound evolve from simple stereo to multi-channel systems. When I started making films, I realized how much work goes into sound design, and it made me appreciate childhood even more. I never stopped admiring the play behind those early sounds—a play with something you could shape with your hands—analog cassettes, splices, magnetic reels. The path Ben continues to pave and evolve, celebrating that childlike anticipation, is a gift to us all.

OMINOUS WHOOSH

David Lynch's sound and music supervisor Dean Hurley breaks down one scene from *Twin Peaks*.

As told to
Matthew Folden and Annabel Brady-Brown

If one had never seen a film by David Lynch, the parade of encomiums that followed news of his death in January might have suggested a seemingly universally beloved figure who traded in the sort of reassuring entertainment that Americans, in particular, have always shown a bottomless appetite for. The uninitiated would be in for a shock encountering the actual films themselves—anxiety-fraught oneiric experiences seething with images of desire and disgust, trawled from the darkest depths of the id. No small part of the pervasive impact of Lynch's vision, by turns beautiful and terrible, comes down to what is not seen but rather heard: the richly detailed soundscapes that he crafted together with a number of key collaborators, which add depth and dimension to his uncanny and ineffable art, and proved hugely influential around the world. In the words of one such vital partner, Dean Hurley, "David ushered the whole landscape of cinema into a realm where we even have an interest to ask about sounds."

Initially trained in the visual arts, Hurley is a self-taught sound artist and sharp-eared engineer and musician, with a profound fascination for how sound functions on harmonic, physiological, and even mystical levels. He worked closely with Lynch, operating and managing his Los Angeles sound studio, Asymmetrical. Following the production of Lynch's *Lost Highway* (1997), the studio was built inside of the Hollywood Hills property that appears in the film: "In the movie, Fred and Renee's bedroom, that's where they dug into the wall and tunneled back to make an elongated studio," Hurley explained. "That is where Angelo Badalamenti conducted and recorded the score for *The Straight Story* (1999). Ron Eng mixed *Mulholland Drive* (2001) in the same room. Then in 2005, I came in."

Hurley worked on Lynch's last theatrical feature, *INLAND EMPIRE* (2006), as well as on all 18 episodes of 2017's *Twin Peaks: A Limited Event Series*, popularly known as *Twin Peaks: The Return*, some of the material for which can be heard on the first volume of his library-style Anthology Resource series. Alongside the film work, Hurley and Lynch wrote and recorded music together—one of their first collaborations was "Ghost of Love," the de facto theme used in *INLAND EMPIRE*—and over their 20-year collaboration, Hurley co-wrote and produced four full-length LPs with Lynch. In his memoir, *Room to Dream*, he describes Hurley as "solid gold."

To better understand the process behind their joint praxis, Hurley gave us a privileged look, outlining his role as sound supervisor, re-recording mixer, and composer for *Twin Peaks: A Limited Event Series* via a breakdown of one scene. Hurley chose the opening of Part 16.

SCENE SYNOPSIS: Attempts to summarize events that take place within the *Twin Peaks* universe are generally insufficient, as the work registers on levels perhaps too transcendent to belittle with words.

The mix stage crew from *Twin Peaks: A Limited Event Series*, in David Lynch's LA studio. Left to right: Ron Eng (re-recording mixer, who also collaborated with Lynch on 2001's *Mulholland Drive*), Luke Gibleon (sound editor), Dean Hurley (re-recording mixer), Xiao'ou Olivia Zhang (apprentice sound editor).

A rare insight into the mixing process, at David Lynch's LA studio. Resting on the console, Dean Hurley's notebook contains his detailed jottings on each scene.

Nonetheless, in the crudest terms, what passes in the eight minutes that make up this scene is as follows: an escapee from the Black Lodge, the evil doppelgänger of FBI Special Agent Dale Cooper (Kyle MacLachlan, in a dual role that becomes a triple) is driving a truck at night. The headlights illuminate the bends of the road, recalling the opening credits of *Lost Highway*, though here they are accompanied by an overbearing, synth-like track in a minor key that is instantly unsettling. He is accompanied by his son, the criminal Richard Horne (Eamon Farren), though the pair don't speak until they reach a large rock in a remote field that matches a set of coordinates Cooper's double has acquired. At his father's instruction, Richard climbs the rock, then, seemingly betrayed, receives a violent electrical shock. For nearly 30 seconds, Richard spasms and screams and smokes, electric sparks flying from his writhing body, before he finally explodes, with a satisfying pop, and disintegrates into thin air. Evil Cooper sends a text message and gets back into his truck.

Here, Hurley talks us through how some of the soundscape accompanying this scene was achieved.

DEAN HURLEY: I picked this scene because it contains a lot to chat about; there's variety, and there are ideas at play that continue to shape my approach to sound today. It's a fairly subdued scene, but it touches on some broader aspects of the role that postproduction sound has in filmmaking.

The piece of music that opens the scene and reprises later, "Night Electricity Theme," operates as a sort of thematic prelude. It might sound like just a synth track, but it's actually a sampler patch that was made from a recording of transformer hum. So it's the literal sound of electricity mapped onto two octaves of a keyboard, and replayed as a series of notes. I'd wanted a bit more to the instrument than just the one sample, so there is a layered string element in there as well, with the attack delayed quite a bit. That way, triggering a note, you get the initial flavor of the sample, and then the string sample swells up so there's a little more character and evolution to the sound.

The track itself was actually made years before *Twin Peaks: The Return* even came about... I would often build custom sampler patches like this for David and me to mess around and experiment with. The idea was to load in a bunch of themed sound effects into a sampler, map them out, program velocity and behavior, and make, like, a little random garden to discover something in. We'd record long improvisations using things like these and then David would mine the recordings and implement bits as score in scenes. This one in particular—I had remembered it from the library of past experiments and just threw it in an Avid music bin along with a bunch of other material. Duwayne Dunham, the picture editor, first laid it in this scene, and as soon as I heard it being used here, I thought, "That is thematically kind of perfect." It's such a fitting usage given what it was made from and its employment. When stuff like that happens, it can interlock and fuse in a way that is far more truthful or pure than someone just sitting down—maestro at a keyboard—and thinking, "I'm going to write music to what I am looking at."

A few years back, preparing a live show, I went back and hunted down the original sample. It's just a couple of seconds. Like *wrrrr*. But harmonically, it's all there. I love how with samplers you can take this tiny sonic fingerprint and tease out and expand it into a much broader compositional idea. It's the same with the thematic overtones. I think of it as the "DNA of an idea." If you have the seedling of a really good concept—like *Twin Peaks* was for David and Mark Frost—it can contain an incredible amount of information. The original source code can possess every permutation that could unfold and ripple out forever. It's kind of like that documentary *Powers of 10* (1977) by Charles and Ray Eames: you can zoom out or zoom in endlessly... Sometimes the world contained within an idea is as complex and expansive as the universe outside. David always talked about the fact that *Twin Peaks* was a "continuing story." It's like nature: it keeps growing, and it's got this program in it that tells the small seed how to become a giant oak with a multitude of branches, leaves, everything. Overtones of this were happening throughout the entire production, but Duwayne's usage of this piece of music is a good example.

The experience that *really* crystalized this concept for me was when we were doing remote sessions with Angelo [Badalamenti]. He was in New Jersey; David was in his studio in LA. We were using Source-Connect, an ISDN alternative that can broadcast 320 kbps audio over the internet, so David could hear Angelo's synthesizer coming through in full-quality audio. He also had Angelo on a video call, so they could communicate and see each other react, just like in the early days of their partnership. They did a few sessions where they were just trying to generate material. David would throw out buzzwords and descriptions, and Angelo would respond by improvising on a keyboard. One day, they wanted to get a few versions of "Laura Palmer's Theme" down with a couple of new sounds for it, just to have, and Angelo played it through like three times in a row. We were recording both audio and MIDI.[1] Later, as I was going through the session, I saw that when he'd been playing "Laura Palmer's Theme," the MIDI was zigzagging up and down and making a visible pattern. I thought, "That really looks like a mountain range." Then I zoomed in on a single iteration of "Laura Palmer's Theme," and the MIDI formed two peaks. That song—it's used throughout the original series again and again, underscoring so many moments. It really is the core composition for the show—seeing what it visually represented and reflected was like a deep revelation. I went to show David, and asked him, "What does this look like to you?" He said, "It's

1. MIDI (Musical Instrument Digital Interface) is a technical standard that allows electronic musical instruments and other devices to communicate and interact with each other. Instead of recording sound waves, MIDI records musical data, describing and transmitting information such as timing, pitch, and velocity.

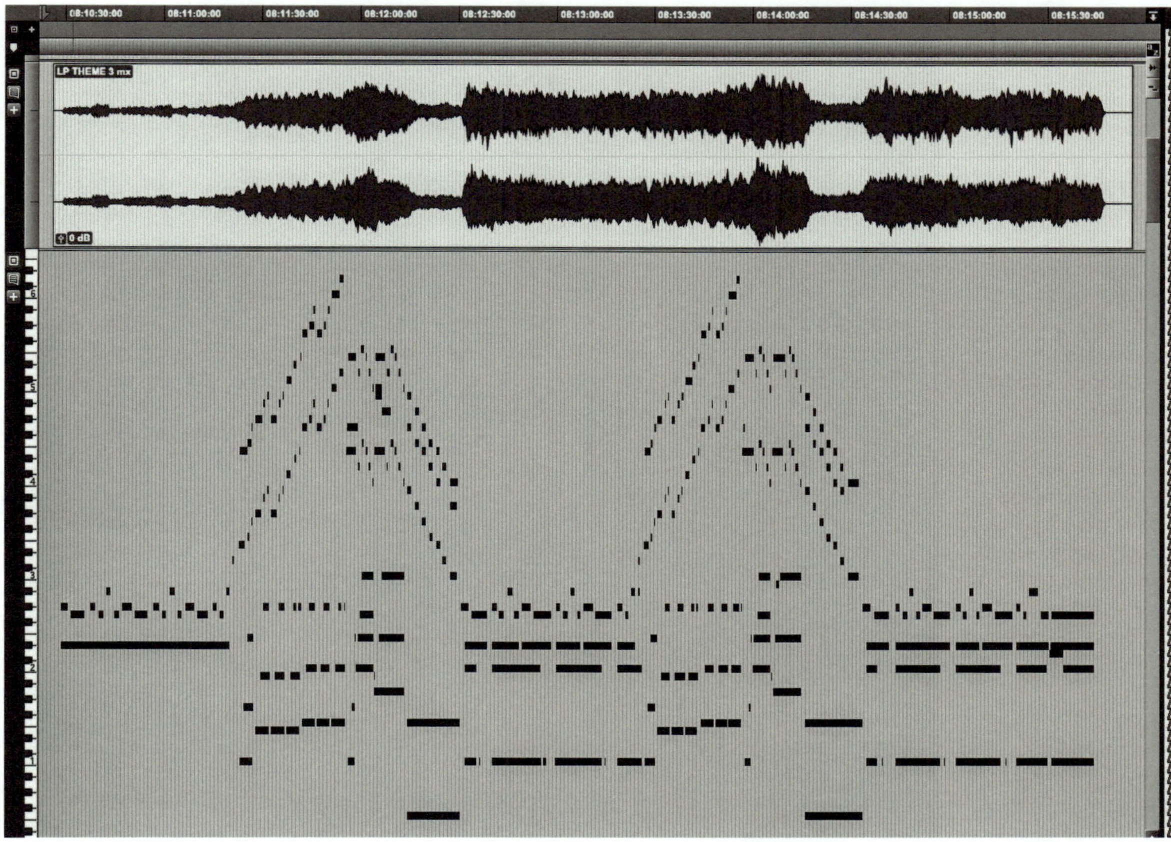

The MIDI notation of "Laura Palmer's Theme"—an instrumental song composed by Angelo Badalementi for the original ABC series *Twin Peaks* that ran from 1990-1991—which resembles the two peaked mountains that appear on the fictional Washington State town's welcome sign.

Twin Peaks, what about it?" I told him where it came from, and he just started shouting, "It's cosmic, it's cosmic!" Seeing that really confirmed this notion of idea DNA.

When things are in harmony… It makes perfect sense to me why "Night Electricity Theme" just effortlessly fell into use for this scene, because it has that same DNA of concept. That's when you get these weird synchronicities. It doesn't always happen. Sometimes you struggle and claw. But when the architecture of what an idea holds is strong, things can feel effortless. You hear songwriters talk about how certain songs seem to write themselves. I think it's true. And it has a lot to do with that original seed. If the DNA is strong, it can magnetically attract other harmonious elements that yield rich fruit.

TO PREPARE FOR *Twin Peaks,* I read the script front to back in a day and a half—I had to read one of only a few full scripts printed, then return it as soon as I was done. David includes a fair amount of sound cues in his writing—things like "the air is filled with an uneasy electric buzz" or "a hairy electrical hum emanates." You get it on an instinctual level. It's got a personality. As you read, you can see the blueprint—the instructions are there. Sound isn't being used to describe every scene, but whenever something is important and has a distinct quality. That's the way David wrote, which I loved. It reaches out and grabs you. And I feel like—word to all the aspiring filmmakers out there—sound actually has a place in the script. One of the most incredible examples of how sound can infuse the written word is "The Old Pond," a haiku by the 17th-century poet Bashō: "Ancient pond / A frog jumps in / Splash! Silence again." Right there you have, in the most economical way possible, the essential building blocks of drama. A setting, an action, rhythm, and a sound effect used to evoke. When I'm reading, it always jumps out at me when people take a moment to describe a sound with a poetic turn of phrase. It can really light a fire in the reader's mind.

You realize a writer can be the primary sound designer of any film. You can lay a soundtrack into a script, and David would often. He was such an instinctual artist that he just did this stuff. He was a master at that, without even consciously trying. Sentences like "a strange sound builds until it fills the air; like fear mixed with a low-pitched jet engine" become little recipes for a scene's sound. When I look back, I can see that he was always pulling on a multitude of tools to emphatically get across the vibe, the mood, the statement of what he was doing. And nothing was off limits.

THE ELECTRICAL EXPLOSION in this scene was written into the script. I don't remember exactly how it was described, but I'm sure it was something evocative. There are a lot of steamy, searing kinds of

An eclectic stack of musical inspirations found in David Lynch's LA studio, including releases by girl group The Paris Sisters (whose 1961 single "I Love How You Love Me" features in Part Five of *Twin Peaks: A Limited Event Series*), the Everly Brothers–inspired alt-country act The Cactus Blossoms (who appear in Part Three, performing at the Roadhouse), and Houston rockers ZZ Top (whose song "Sharp Dressed Man" plays in Part 15 during a Roadhouse bar fight).

sounds here, which I use because they contain great dramatic movement. That was something I learned early on. You want sound effects with movement in them. The electrical explosion is a good example. It has energy, there are perspective shifts, and everything adds a degree of dynamic energy to juice what is happening visually.

I had done an early version of the explosion, but what we hear in the final includes a lot of additional intricacies that my friend Luke Gibleon cut—little nuanced layers that kicked it up from a level four to a level seven. There's also a lot of stuff going on at the end of the explosion. Sparks that fall, for example. But when you are designing a supernatural event like that, you can't just throw welding sparks in there. It's not right. The scale of something small like that just doesn't track.

We were looking for something similar, though, something larger. It had to be an exaggerated version of electricity in real life. What ended up working here were giant tree splits—the sound of a tree trunk splitting. It's brief, but I'd like to think it subliminally informs the audience's sense of scale. A lot of the time, finding the right sound is like casting a role—I mean, sound effects are really like little actors. They're indicative or evocative of real-world events, but sometimes need to be larger than life for an emotional result. A movie sound effect can be almost a caricature of a real-life sound.

For example, the truck. There is an animalistic quality to the roar of a truck's V8 engine. And the door slam that you hear when they get out. Again, you're casting the sound. Not all production vehicles sound how they look; that is part of the job of the sound supervisor, to cast the right truck sounds. And then David, like certain other directors (I believe Christopher Nolan is also one), always tries to use production dialogue as much as humanly possible, the sincere in-the-moment performance. So the production sound recordist's objective is to capture the best possible dialogue, which means that when some of these scenes come in, they're very dry and absent of surrounding environmental sounds. There's little ambience, and that has to be addressed during the edit.

THESE EPISODES WERE mixed fairly quickly. Each episode, top to bottom, took about four days to mix. To paint the picture for you, Ron Eng handled dialogue and foley, because those two elements usually live in the same world, and I handled sound effects and music. This way, we could collectively handle more across the console faders at once. We would spend a day pre-dubbing individually, meaning we'd go through our separate sessions, set our levels and EQ; the following day, we'd combine our work and balance the whole. We'd get the mix to a point where David could come in fresh and a lot of the minutiae wouldn't bog him down. He could directly watch something that was already relatively cohesive and react broadly: "Let's try a piece of music here," or, "Let's add another element to shift it here." It takes hearing the whole soundtrack with all the elements balanced to be able to start determining how to fine-tune and get things really singing.

A mix session is typically organized by "food groups," starting with dialogue. Qualms are common, and were especially with David: "Can we get any more clarity out of that line?" If this came up, then Ron could do his thing. Sometimes he'd find an alternate take: if a character says the word "emphatically" but it sounds like they're saying "em-PAT-ically," he'd scan the different takes, find a version that has the phonetic hard F, and swap that syllable in.

Next up is foley material: footsteps, prop-oriented items handled by the actors onscreen. For example, giving a police officer what we call "cop jingle," the movement of metallic handcuffs that might hang off an officer's belt. They might be walking without necessarily making any noise; you add that cop jingle, and it can really come to life and evoke a personality. And "leather creak" is fantastic as well—squeezing a wallet or folded piece of leather. There's none in this scene, but it's used in others: you add that leather creak, and if you emphasize it, it can provide an intimidating element to a character, underscore a dirty cop or a bad guy. I mean, it's the sound of a dead animal's skin creaking. People don't think about it so much, but we have a guttural physiological reaction to what certain sounds represent.

Then there are hard effects—door slams, cars, gunshots, etc.—and backgrounds, which are atmospheric tonal environments. A background array can consist of two to 10 tracks—perhaps there are detailed crickets, then a distant city wash, the kind where you walk outside and from the presence of white noise you know there's a highway a mile away, which tells you that you're not far from civilization. Whereas if you're looking to make something feel more remote, you might not want that there. Think about a medieval period piece: the suggestion of a plane or car or distant traffic would not only kill the mood, it would immediately kill the illusion of the world you're trying to build. Sometimes the array consists of mono-channel material along with multichannel material... things that are going to be maybe a little nondescript for the surrounds, versus things that are going to be pinpointed background details. Maybe there's an individual car in the distance that provides a nice airy cascade of a sound, which helps bridge a cut to make it feel less abrasive. As an audience member, the cuts start to disappear when sounds straddle across them, blending and hiding the break in time. There are all kinds of subtle tools like that in a sound editor's belt.

I PARTICULARLY LOVE the foley team who worked on this, Dan O'Connell and Richard Duarte. They are really top shelf. We didn't have a ton of money, so we had to be judicious with what we utilized them for. I ended up doing a lot of the simpler foley elements myself. When it came to the really nuanced footsteps—multi-terrain, like dirt to gravel to grass, things like that—that's where Dan and Richard excel. An incredible amount of attention goes into making every little moment reinforce the overall narrative of what's going on. It can expand the world outside of the visible frame.

That stuff is a lot of fun to do, and it's additive in a subliminal way. Many people have seen the quintessential image of the foley artist watching playback on a screen and mimicking the actors' movements in an acoustically controlled studio environment. When you achieve the illusion, when it syncs up, you know instantly; the phrase that's used is "I'll buy that." Your brain connects the separate picture and sound and they fuse together as one.

David could be a bit lukewarm about foley. Ron and I mixed *INLAND EMPIRE*, and early in the process, David was like, "Is that foley? Throw it out. That's bullshit. I don't want to hear foley, mute it all." So it was a big concern going into *Twin Peaks*. One of the early scenes we mixed involved a character watching a black glass box to monitor the portal. There's *zero* exposition, no dialogue, and there were beautiful opportunities for ambient shifts and subtle foley movement to describe that environment. At one point David asked, "Is that foley?" A little nervous, Ron and I were like, "Yes..." He said, "Okay, cool." And we never had the conversation again.

OVER THE YEARS, one of the things David and I often talked about were radio plays. He loved the concept of them. Quite a few films even begin with sounds in darkness, playing over the credits, and in a way, you're basically listening to a radio play. You're hearing indicators of what is happening and the environment where it is happening, and your brain is actively trying to assimilate information, piece together aural clues. It's so powerful. And especially when you then start to dial in other elements. You're maybe getting some slivers of information visually, but it's not much, and it allows the sonic component to occupy more of the stage. That push and pull between sound and picture, that's where the magic can happen—the dance, with one withholding some information that the other partially provides. It really activates the brain and its thirst for understanding. I mean, the whole thing is mimicking how we go through life. It's experiential. We're using multiple senses, sometimes even a sixth sense. That's the hologram illusion of cinema. You're tapped into another's experience, sometimes seeing worlds that you never would have been able to. But it's the whole enchilada of the sonic environments, the photography and lensing, the wardrobe, the set decoration, the pacing, everything. When that illusion works, you buy it, you're transported... It's incredible what cinema can do.

4

MARTINI SHOTS

Contents

THE SHOT THAT MADE ME GAY

Nadja Spiegelman: But I'm a Cheerleader

To my father's disappointment, when I was 13 all I ever wanted to watch were rom-coms and teen movies. My father—thanks in large part to his close friend and my godfather, the experimental filmmaker Ken Jacobs—owned stacks and stacks of bootlegged VHS tapes, mostly black-and-white films, which were recorded and re-recorded over each cassette so often that the tape wore thin and the image became a blur of gray static. "This is really good stuff," my father would say, slapping his copy of *Piccadilly* (1929) for emphasis, trying to cajole me into watching it with him. I could sense his dismay as I read Francesca Lia Block instead of Hemingway, or watched *10 Things I Hate About You* (1999) instead of *Pickup on South Street* (1953). He fretted about my cultural consumption the way another parent might worry over their child's habit of pulling the wings off flies.

When we went together to Kim's, he would leave me in the front room of the video store with its meager selection of Hollywood hits while he prowled the shelves of pulpy noirs. He'd emerge, and I would hand him the box for something like *Can't Hardly Wait* (1998). To his credit, he was always curious about my interests, even when they horrified him. "Tomorrow's the future. Tonight's the party," he would read aloud off the box. My dad's sighs were heavy, like he could not believe we shared genetic material.

One dimly lit corner of Kim's housed the erotic movies, the foreign French films too racy for American audiences, and, on the very bottom shelf, the gay and lesbian section. I wasn't allowed in that part of the store, I knew that without being told. But that bottom shelf kept calling to me. While my dad was elsewhere, I crouched down low, trying to look nonchalant. The shelf was small and held barely any tapes with women on the cover. Then—*But I'm a Cheerleader* (1999) leapt into my hand. I was mesmerized by the image of Natasha Lyonne, in her bubblegum-pink spaghetti strap dress, emblazoned on the VHS case. It was a forbidden film, from the forbidden shelf, but to my father, it looked like all the other junk I rented. I tucked it under my arm, then whirl-winded back through the rom-coms, pulling every stupid cheerleading-themed movie I could find as a further disguise. When my dad was ready to leave, I handed him the towering pile. "You can't rent all these!" he said. I grabbed them back. "Oh, fine. Just this one, I guess." He brought the tape to the counter. My adrenaline surged. It was rare, as a 13-year-old, that I wanted anything this badly. And yet I couldn't articulate to myself why I wanted it so much.

That night, I stayed up for hours, watching the movie once, twice, then three times in a row. My ears were half-cocked to the door, ready to slam the pause button if I heard footsteps. I had never seen anything like Clea DuVall's bad girl college student Graham. Louche, cynical, sensual. The way her dark hair fell into her eyes and her sideways grin. The way her long slim fingers held a cigarette. I was entranced by the angles of her slouch, the tilts of her head, the rebellious boyishness that defied the pink dresses she was forced to wear at the conversion therapy camp. Her eyes slid over to look at you too long, dark pools of desire. Everything about the way she moved said she had already fucked a hundred girls. My toes curled. Of course, what I remember most is the sex scene. Lyonne (incomprehensibly not actually gay) and DuVall (who wouldn't come out publicly till nearly two decades later) steal a night together on pink satin sheets. Cello music swells, fingers graze a belly button, a silk robe is pushed up a thigh, mouths lock

in silhouette. Every gesture is languorous. There is no end goal, only catches of breath and more kissing. The lyrics to "Glass Vase Cello Case," by the short-lived grrrl pop band Tattle Tale, gasp "Are you? Still breathing? Are you still breathing?" I wasn't. I watched that sex scene over and over, rewinding, trying to memorize every detail, to follow every hand to where it trailed offscreen. My own hands strayed as I watched. Didn't everyone want this? Didn't everyone want Clea DuVall? Didn't everyone want the softness of a sleepover to lead to such gasps? That must be why they hid the tapes at the back of the store. Who, when confronted with this as a possibility, could resist?

"Everyone looks at other girls all the time," Lyonne's character says early in the movie. "I thought everybody had those thoughts." It took me a long time to connect my desires to the word "gay." Why should who I want define who I was? It would take cruelty and losing friends and feeling unsafe holding hands in the streets for me to understand about discrimination, and then identity, and then community, and then pride. Even when, at 16, I burst into my dad's room to tell him, excitedly, that I had my first girlfriend, I didn't understand that I was coming out. My dad didn't seem to think I was either. He was reading *The New York Times* in bed. He looked at me over the top of the paper and said, "How modern of you." It was, my parents agreed, a phase that would pass. I did grow out of teen movies, did learn to appreciate Tolstoy and Nabokov, did eventually learn that black-and-white films could be spectacular when the image was sharp. But my attraction to watching DuVall in the dark? That wasn't a phase at all. I'd found the forbidden shelf of treasures, and I wasn't giving them back.

Paul McAdory: Final Destination 2

Have you ever eyed a healthy rack on a topless biker broad and thought, "I am going to die"? Further down the road, have you seen a chain buckle and snap on a flatbed, its cargo of multi-ton tree trunks bundle into traffic and tomato-splat a policeman? Have you squinted at the opaque windscreens of thanatotic trucks as they crush wounded motorists against their grilles? Have you, in

Illustrations by
Grant Schaffer

The first tingle of sexual awakening elicited by the movies.

sum, watched the premonitory highway massacre in *Final Destination 2* (2003) and questioned why your preteen dick isn't like an unleashed log or a raging semi driven berserk by the spectacle of pink nipple?

By age 10 I had long since lost sleep to *Halloween* (1978), *The Shining* (1980), *Deep Blue Sea* (1999), and myriad other horrors, which I rented from Blockbuster to watch with my indulgent mother. After some movie nights, it was her who I imagined entering my room brandishing a rictus grin and butcher knife, a victim of sudden-onset cinematic psychosis. But that scene from *Final Destination 2*, clips of which continue to circulate regularly on social media, confronted me with a real nightmare: my lack of heterosexual desire.

The *Final Destination* movies make Death an invisible bogeyman. Think of him as the viewer's bloodlust hypostatized in the camera's gaze. He feints and fools and then complexly trisects, beheads, and roasts a fresh batch of survivors, who, thanks to the protagonist's paranormal foresight, have dodged a catastrophic plane crash or an interstate apocalypse or a freakish roller coaster malfunction but who cannot void the prerogatives of the genre and so must watch as their names are subtracted one by one from Death's ledger through ever more outlandish, violent means. To the paranoiac closet case, homosexuality hangs in the air like an analogous force, an omnipresent threat that must be guarded against always lest it annihilate you. You flee it forever uselessly; flight becomes your life.

Or you might try locking yourself in a padded room at a psychiatric institution like the first film's lone survivor, one Clear Rivers, who has escaped Death by not living. She explains to the sequel's final girl, Kimberly Corman, that Death scatters hints about his plans. "Have you ever seen anything creepy or ominous—an in-your-face irony sort of thing?"

During the interstate scene, these unsubtle omens include drunk driving, drugs and tobacco, homelessness, AC/DC's "Highway to Hell," jocks in a school bus chanting the word "pileup," and, for what I experienced as three bone-chilling seconds, a suggestively open-mouthed blonde on the back of a motorbike inexplicably flashing her breasts at the Tahoe driven by Corman. Regressive, absurd, eternally obvious: say what you will, but these fugitive seconds of flesh nearly killed me. I failed to launch. I did not feel the ritual awkwardness of excitement washing over me in the presence of a parent. Said parent, seated in a recliner

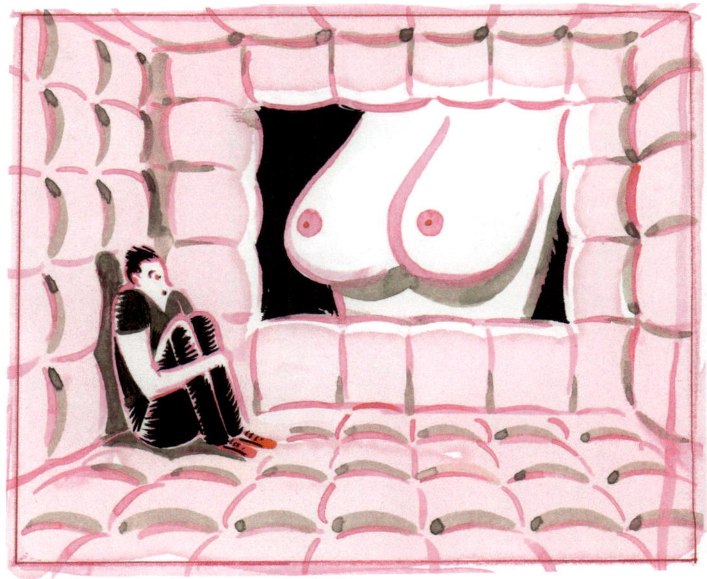

across the living room, did not observe me squirming in discomfort amidst the clash of un-cancelable want and filial proximity. The scene shredded my veil of denial. My attempts to masturbate to images of women had resembled the film's kills: soft meat pulverized. But I'd believed I could change, would change, because I had to, because of who I was: a straight dude. Now that dream was crippled. My mother didn't know any of this, but as the awooga-cues accelerated out of frame I knew that she could, that one day she would. The image of her wielding a butcher knife and rictus grin recurred to me, with a difference: might she use them to cut me from her life?

Corman eventually discovers that to conquer Death she must create life. She drowns herself. A doctor resuscitates her. She is free, or freer. Coming out is a comparable act, one that kills the old self, inaugurates a new one, and vitalizes the spirit for a time, even as it fashions you into a target for fresh forms of violence. It delivers unto you drive, high drama, purpose, clarity (illusory and real), and the thrill of an unfolding revolution of the self, of the monad remaking itself, of agency claimed. Answer "I am going to die" with "Okay." Become your own killer. The afterlife isn't heaven, but it's electric.

L

Metrograph A–Z
L is for Stan Laurel

Words by
Vladimir Nabokov

The names of Sternberg and Lang never meant anything to me. In Europe I went to the corner cinema about once in a fortnight and the only kind of picture I liked, and still like, was and is comedy of the Laurel and Hardy type. I enjoyed tremendously American comedy: Buster Keaton, Harold Lloyd, and Chaplin. My favorites by Chaplin are *The Gold Rush* (1925), *The Circus* (1928), and *The Great Dictator* (1940)—especially the parachute inventor who jumps out of the window—and ends in a messy fall which we only see in the expression on the dictator's face. However, today's Little Man appeal has somewhat spoiled Chaplin's attraction for me... Laurel and Hardy are always funny; there are subtle, artistic touches in even their most mediocre films. Laurel is so wonderfully inept, yet so very kind. There is a film in which they are at Oxford [*A Chump at Oxford*, 1940]. In one scene the two of them are sitting on a park bench in a labyrinthine garden and the subsequent happenings conform to the labyrinth. A casual villain puts his hand through the back of the bench and Laurel, who is clasping his hands in an idiotic reverie, mistakes the stranger's hand for one of his own hands, with all kinds of complications because his own hand is also there. He has to choose. The choice of a hand. [I last watched it] 30 or 40 years ago... I am an ardent memoirist with a rotten memory; a drowsy king's absent-minded remembrancer. With absolute lucidity I recall landscapes, gestures, intonations, a million sensuous details, but names and numbers topple into oblivion with absurd abandon like little blind men in file.

RIDICULISTS: THE ARTISTS WHO TOILED ON POVERTY ROW

No money? No stars? No problem! Seven filmmakers who honed a personal style on the fringes on Hollywood.

Written by
Will Sloan

Illustrations by
Marc J Palm

Film has always been an uneasy blend of art and business, and these two spheres are not always a strict binary. Though the most celebrated directors of Hollywood's Golden Age—your John Fords, Howard Hawkses, and Alfred Hitchcocks—had to struggle to make personal movies within an assembly-line system, these conditions also offered certain advantages. MGM, Warner Bros., 20th Century Fox, and the other major studios held monopolies on national theater chains, strong-arming owners into booking their entire annual slates and taking a hefty percentage of the box office. This plainly corrupt, artistically compromised system nevertheless fostered decades of a smoothly functioning, creatively inspired American cinema, setting a standard for the world.

Elsewhere in Hollywood, an assortment of smaller studios worked with smaller theaters in much the same way, generating B-movies for underserved rural, suburban, and inner-city venues. "Poverty Row," as it came to be known, encompassed a suite of companies like Republic Pictures, Monogram Pictures, and Producers Releasing Corporation (PRC). They didn't actually share a street, but they did have a common business model: selling their product inexpensively on a flat-fee rental basis. This meant that no matter how much a film earned for the theaters, the studios' earnings remained the same. The upside to this system was that films were in profit even before cameras rolled. The downside was that the companies had little incentive to make the movies good. Indeed, why rock the boat? Why risk alienating theater owners with something too artsy or ambitious? Were critics really going to notice if the next comedy starring the Bowery Boys (Monogram's tenured purveyors of lowbrow slapstick) was a little better than the last?

In 1948, the case of United States v. Paramount Pictures, Inc. brought a celebrated Supreme Court ruling that outlawed the studios' stranglehold on theaters. This created opportunities for independent producers and distributors—good news for Samuel Z. Arkoff and James H. Nicholson, whose American International Pictures (1957's *I Was a Teenage Werewolf*, 1965's *Beach Blanket Bingo*, etc.) would define the next generation of exploitation film... but bad news for the existing Poverty Row studios, whose profit margins were already precariously thin. PRC had already folded in 1947. Republic adapted by refocusing its attention on television. Monogram was forced to up its game and rebrand as "Allied Artists," improbably winning Oscars for *Cabaret* (1972) before finally closing in 1979.

Today, the financial and artistic ethos of Poverty Row lives on in new forms: made-for-cable Christmas movies, "geezer teaser" action flotsam with aging stars like Bruce Willis and Sylvester Stallone, Tubi Originals, and "mockbusters" (e.g., 2022's *Top Gunner: Danger Zone*, 2024's *Road Wars: Max Fury*). Like this contemporary schlock, most Poverty Row productions were assembled in a week or two by journeyman directors just trying to make their days. Casts and crews comprised industry lifers who had aged out of the studio system alongside those who never quite made it. A few stars, like John Wayne and Ava Gardner, rose from this primordial ooze; others, like Bela Lugosi and Harry Langdon, set up shop on Poverty Row after their mainstream fame had crested. None of them thought they were doing much more than biding time and cashing checks. Colloquially, PRC was known as "Pretty Rotten Crap."

But these films were still made by human beings, and humans are built to want more. Against all odds, amid the pressure of tight deadlines and miniscule budgets, several distinctive authorial voices emerged. Herein we celebrate seven of the heroic artisans who made silk purses out of sows' ears, or at the very least found ways to put lipstick on their pigs.

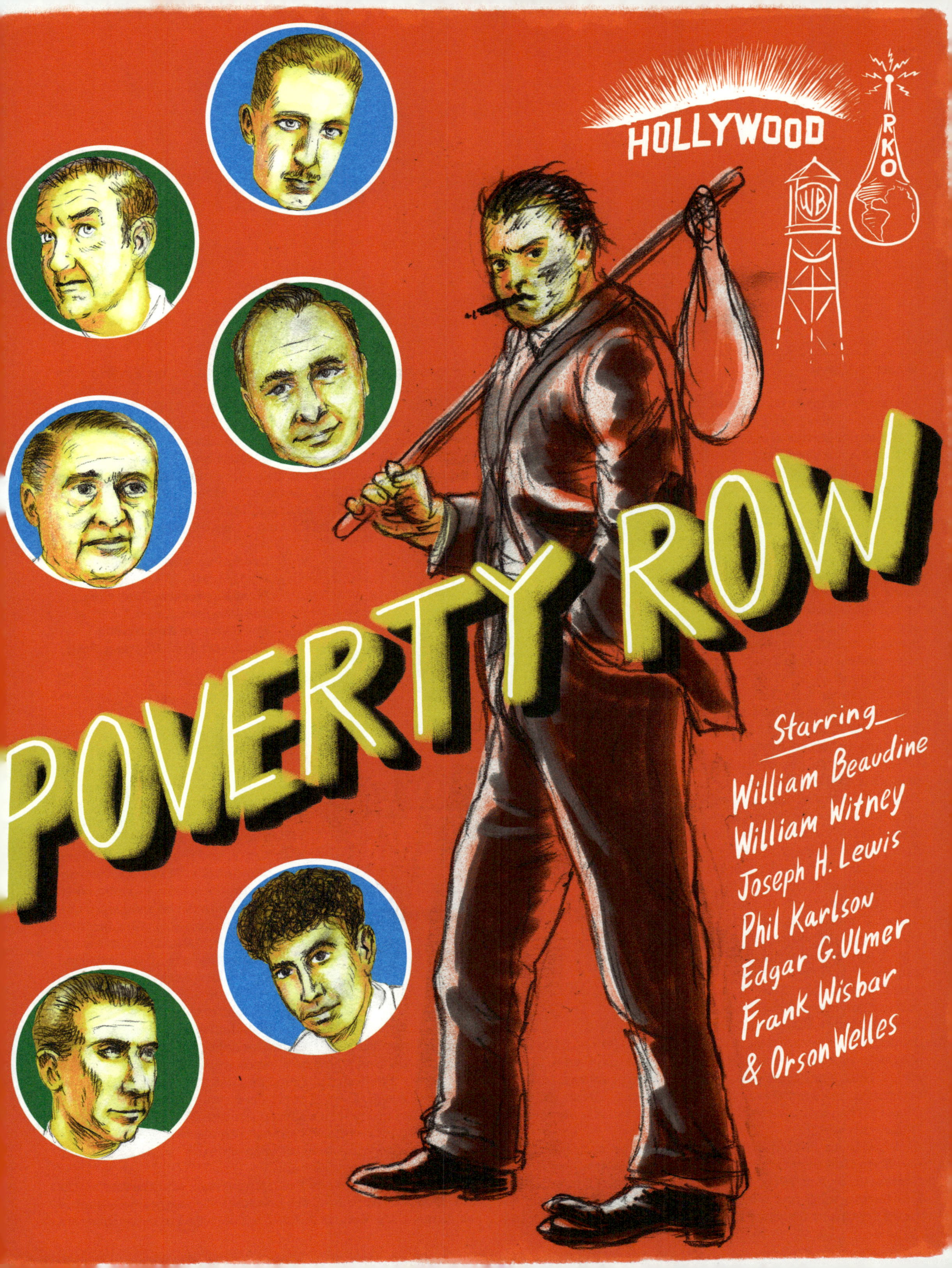

HOLLYWOOD
WB
RKO
POVERTY ROW
Starring
William Beaudine
William Witney
Joseph H. Lewis
Phil Karlson
Edgar G. Ulmer
Frank Wisbar
& Orson Welles

Edgar G. Ulmer

"Nobody ever made good films faster or for less money than Edgar Ulmer," declared the filmmaker Peter Bogdanovich. "One of the minor glories of cinema," wrote the critic Andrew Sarris. Ulmer may not have quite the legacy of his onetime boss F.W. Murnau, but he did become cinema's greatest embodiment of a certain important archetype: the artist who prevails under the most adverse of conditions.

Though he shrouded his early career with fabulism, Ulmer can truthfully be said to have intersected with several of the key talents of Weimar Berlin: he served as an assistant on Murnau's *Sunrise* (1927), set designer for Max Reinhardt's theater company, and co-director of *People on Sunday* (1930), whose all-star creative team included Robert Siodmak, Billy Wilder, and Fred Zinnemann. In Hollywood, he brought the influence of Murnau to *The Black Cat* (1934), his Bauhaus-inflected Boris Karloff–Bela Lugosi horror film. It was a hit, and should have been Ulmer's breakthrough; instead, an affair with (and later a marriage to) the fiancée of the producer—who happened to be the nephew of powerful Universal Pictures head Carl Laemmle—led to the director being blacklisted. Ulmer spent the rest of the 1930s ping-ponging around North America, directing meager assignments wherever he found them: a Canadian "quota quickie" mystery (*From Nine to Nine*, 1936), an "all-Black cast" drama (*Moon Over Harlem*, 1939), and movies for the Ukrainian (*Cossacks in Exile*, 1939) and Yiddish-speaking Jewish (*Green Fields*, 1937; *The Singing Blacksmith*, 1938) diasporas. In every assignment, the artist was present: Ulmer's *Goodbye, Mr. Germ* (1940) is the most beautiful National Tuberculosis Association PSA ever made.

Finally he landed at PRC, where he brought whatever neo-Expressionist flair he could to assignments like *Girls in Chains* (1943). For *Detour* (1945), his masterpiece, Ulmer evoked Manhattan with just a streetlamp and some mist. Good reviews for this and other films made him the closest thing to a prestige director for the disreputable studio; his Poverty Row period climaxed with more upscale features, like the "million-dollar production" *Her Sister's Secret* (1946), which actually cost much less, and *Ruthless* (1948), an extraordinary imitation-*Citizen Kane* (1941). The major studios ought to have finally welcomed Ulmer, but that never quite happened, and the '50s found him once again itinerant. The same year that François Truffaut declared Ulmer his favorite American director, Ulmer was pseudonymously directing a nudist camp movie, *The Naked Venus* (1959). And yes, it is the most beautiful nudist camp movie ever made.

Crowning Achievement:
Detour (1945)
Most Expressive Esoterica:
The Man from Planet X (1951)
For Extreme Auteurists:
Beyond the Time Barrier (1960)

Joseph H. Lewis

Watch any film by, for example, Poverty Row workhorse Edward Bernds and you are likely to encounter scenes in which three to five characters stand side by side reciting dialogue to one another. The camera moves only when it has to, and the shots last as long as possible. There were many filmmakers like Bernds, so in this context the modest Lugosi-starring horror film *Invisible Ghost* (1941) stands out: in several scenes, the camera is positioned inside a fireplace, with the flames in the immediate foreground and the actors behind the flickering. Such is the unique visual imagination of Joseph H. Lewis, a director dubbed "Wagon-Wheel Joe" for the Westerns in which he constantly framed his actors behind wagon wheels (for example, 1958's stylish and melancholic *Terror in a Texas Town*). Lewis's roving camera, mastery of light and shadow, and interest in activating multiple planes of the cinematic frame and composition in depth made him arguably the most dynamic visual storyteller to endure a lengthy residency on Poverty Row.

Lewis moved between PRC, Monogram, and the major studios' B-movie units until the breakout success of his Columbia assignment *My Name Is Julia Ross* (1945) led to better budgets and resources. Later collaborations with great cinematographers like Russell Harlan (*Gun Crazy*, 1950) and John Alton (*The Big Combo*, 1955) pushed Lewis to new heights, but he was a fully formed stylist from the beginning. If you watch only one movie featuring the East Side Kids (that gang of comical street toughs who later became The Bowery Boys), you could do a lot worse than Lewis's *Pride of the Bowery* (1940), with its artful shots of Leo Gorcey in nature.

Crowning Achievement: *Gun Crazy* (1950)
Most Expressive Esoterica: *My Name Is Julia Ross* (1945)
For Extreme Auteurists:
Invisible Ghost (1941)

Frank Wisbar

Like many of cinema's most celebrated artisans, Frank Wisbar settled in Hollywood after fleeing the Nazis. Unfortunately, he didn't leave until 1939, after working in the Third Reich much longer than most of his fellow Hollywood émigrés. The former Franz Wysbar began his directing career in 1932, and benefited from the German film industry's purge of Jewish talent following Hitler's rise. In fact, Wisbar's wife was Jewish—just one reason why he is said to have maintained a frosty relationship with Joseph Goebbels—but the critical and festival success of films like *Fährmann Maria* (1936) made him an asset to the regime for most of the decade. Still, all it took was a few flops to halt his career. Fearing the draft as war with Britain loomed, the Wisbars headed west.

The marriage apparently didn't survive far beyond the Atlantic voyage, and Wisbar struggled to gain footing. Finally settling in Hollywood in 1943, he found employment at PRC, where his greatest talent was for atmospherics. He loosely remade *Fährmann Maria* as *Strangler of the Swamp* (1945), a pungent, fog-shrouded mood piece about a bayou haunted by the ghost of a wrongly hanged man. His second most-famous credit, *Devil Bat's Daughter* (1946), is nothing special, but *Lighthouse* (1947) is an appealingly stripped-down love-triangle drama, and I have a soft spot for *The Prairie* (1947), an entirely stage-bound frontier adventure that follows a settler family post-Louisiana Purchase; as they move through fake wheat fields in front of painted cloudscapes, the effect is lightly surreal, and with a certain handmade beauty. Such visual pleasures did little for Wisbar's professional standing. Instead, he enjoyed his greatest success as creator/producer of NBC's *Fireside Theatre*, the first television series shot entirely on film. After that success, he returned in triumph to a resurgent national film industry in Berlin, where he made his last features.

Crowning Achievement:
Fährmann Maria (1936)
Most Expressive Esoterica:
Strangler of the Swamp (1945)
For Extreme Auteurists:
The Prairie (1947)

William Witney

Republic Pictures president Herbert J. Yates established his career as the owner of a film processing lab, and built his empire by acquiring six of the Poverty Row studios that he served during the Depression. Founded in 1935, Republic quickly became the unquestioned financial powerhouse of Poverty Row thanks to punchy, action-packed serials (*Dick Tracy*, 1937; *The Lone Ranger*, 1938) and Westerns that were a cut above their low-budget competitors. Like Roger Corman or Golan and Globus decades later, Yates was a schlock merchant with a yearning for class, which made Republic the only Poverty Row studio to occasionally get into the auteur market. Today, Republic is best remembered for films like Frank Borzage's *Moonrise* (1948), Nicholas Ray's *Johnny Guitar* (1954), and Ford's *The Quiet Man* (1952).

Nevertheless it was action movies that kept the lights on at Republic, and William Witney's were the best. A master of efficiency, Witney delivered elaborate four-hour serials like *Adventures of Captain Marvel* (1941) on shooting schedules of less than a month. He brought a two-fisted energy to the many Westerns he shot with beloved cowboy star Roy Rogers, and, drawing inspiration from the Fred Astaire–Ginger Rogers musicals, he incorporated sophisticated fight and stunt choreography (not just free-for-all brawls) that set a new industry standard for the genre. Superfan Quentin Tarantino, a known connoisseur of onscreen violence, has done much to boost Witney's profile, going so far as to compare him favorably to Ford. The dubious assessment is most defensible in the case of *Stranger at My Door* (1956), an exciting and tender story about a bank robber who takes refuge at the home of a preacher, who makes it his mission to save the wretched criminal. The film is best remembered for a jaw-dropping stunt sequence involving a wild stallion, which also serves as the film's central metaphor: all those around the preacher want to kill the horse, but he is convinced that anyone, man or beast, has a core of goodness that can be made manifest. Undergirding Witney's best action films is a fondness for his human and animal stars—articulated memorably in his charming 1989 biography of Rogers's horse, *Trigger Remembered.*

Crowning Achievement:
Stranger at My Door (1956)
Most Expressive Esoterica:
The Golden Stallion (1949)
For Extreme Auteurists:
Spy Smasher (1942)

Phil Karlson

Some artists are born great. Others, like Phil Karlson, discover greatness slowly. Karlson completionism is a long and only fitfully rewarding journey, with unhappy visits from the stroke-addled Jerome "Curly" Howard of *Swing Parade of 1946* (1946), the leering Dean Martin of *The Wrecking Crew* (1968), and of course the Bowery Boys, whom Karlson directed competently but unspectacularly. But if you're an incurable cinemaniac, don't let me stop you from taking the scenic route and seeing what you find. Karlson's Charlie Chan mystery *Dark Alibi* (1946), for instance, has a little bit of visual panache—if you don't believe me, check Tubi.

Those without endless time and patience should focus on Karlson's crime movies of the 1950s, with their blunt, unfussy style and startling violence: *Kansas City Confidential* (1952), *Scandal Sheet* (1952), *99 River Street* (1953), and *The Brothers Rico* (1957). An itinerent journeyman, Karlson returned to his old home at Monogram (by then known as Allied Artists) to direct his masterpiece, *The Phenix City Story* (1955), a riveting ripped-from-the-headlines thriller about a town overrun by vice. An early scene in which a little girl's corpse is thrown from a moving vehicle signals Karlson as a director without guardrails. After his golden '50s run, he continued to ply his trade wherever he was hired: an Elvis vehicle here, a sword-and-sandal pilot with William Shatner (as Alexander the Great!) there. But when he had the kind of material he believed in—stories of systemic corruption like the 1958 western *Gunman's Walk*—the difference was clear. It's a blessing that he ended his career with a pair of rootin'-tootin' Joe Don Baker action vehicles, *Walking Tall* (1973) and *Framed* (1975). The latter features a bloody, sweaty, and very beefy fistfight between Baker and character actor Lawrence Montaigne, which lets Karlson's flair for grit and brutality flourish in the new permissiveness of the 1970s.

Crowning Achievement:
The Phenix City Story (1955)
Most Expressive Esoterica:
Framed (1975)
For Extreme Auteurists:
Dark Alibi (1946)

Orson Welles

The Great Man took only a brief residency on Poverty Row, but *Macbeth* (1948), his sole production for Republic, raises interesting questions about the stylistic language of "prestige." Smarting from a run of bad luck in film, theater, and radio, Welles was lured by the offer to direct a Shakespeare adaptation of his choosing. Republic's 23-day shooting schedule and $700,000 budget would have been luxurious for Witney but represented a mighty comedown for the director of *Citizen Kane*. He met the challenge with a film that is very much about the idea of filming Macbeth on Poverty Row—"a charcoal sketch of a great play," as he later described it. Welles never allows audiences to forget that they are watching a movie, and an inexpensive one at that, with the flagrantly artificial mise en scène—plastic sets, visible studio floors—emphasized through assaultive camerawork and exaggerated lighting. The film opened in the shadow of Laurence Olivier's *Hamlet* (1948), a tasteful production in a Cinema of Quality tradition. Critics mauled it, and Welles fled for Europe, but his *Macbeth* has survived as one of the most cinematic interpretations of Shakespeare. Its aesthetic foreshadowed the jagged, half-finished energy of Welles's late work, and its production marked a crucial disavowal of Hollywood careerism—a fork in the road that led Welles to become a continent-hopping underground filmmaker and Jess Franco associate.

Crowning Achievement:
Citizen Kane (1941)
Most Expressive Esoterica:
The Other Side of the Wind (2018)
For Extreme Auteurists:
Movie theater sequence from *Don Quixote* (unfinished, 1957)

William Beaudine

A popular, apocryphal story about William Beaudine is that while directing one of his many comedies with the Bowery Boys, a studio boss told him that he was running behind. The director replied, "You mean someone out there is actually waiting to see this?" The story is apocryphal—Beaudine was always on time—but it resonates with his reputation as a director of un-self-consciously abject trash. That movie, whichever it might have been, is one of nearly 400 film and TV credits that Beaudine accumulated across what was once considered the longest directorial career in Hollywood history. To include Beaudine here is a deliberate provocation: a textbook journeyman who shot quickly and with no identifiable personal style, he was all but built in a lab to be compared unfavorably to Ulmer. But like all received wisdom, Beaudine's canonical status as a Bad Director could benefit from a little prodding.

Beaudine's film career spanned virtually the entire first half of the medium. Beginning as a bit-part actor and odd-job man at D.W. Griffith's Biograph studio circa 1909, Beaudine directed his first short comedy in 1915; reached his pinnacle with two of Mary Pickford's best films, *Little Annie Rooney* (1925) and *Sparrows* (1926); and lasted long enough to shepherd Bruce Lee through episodes of *The Green Hornet* (1966-67). A major-studio craftsman in the silent era, Beaudine spent much of the '30s working in Britain, and upon returning to the States found himself forgotten. He swallowed his pride and settled at Monogram, grinding out dozens of movies. Among the most fondly remembered are *The Ape Man* (1943), *Ghosts on the Loose* (1943), and *Voodoo Man* (1944), three Lugosi spookies that suggest a filmmaker without much vanity.

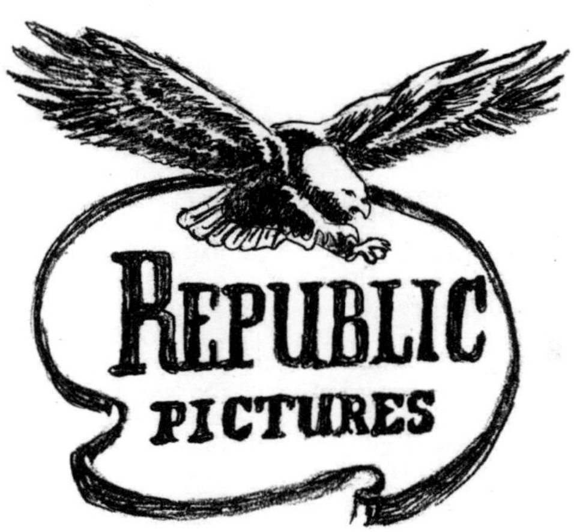

"Long ago I quit thinking that every picture I did was going to be an Academy Award contender," Beaudine once said. "I'm a commercial director. I know how to save money and get something on the screen. I let those artsy guys shoot the scenes through chandeliers or from behind the wine glass." He may well have been taking a shot at Lewis, but, while there may be no *Gun Crazy* in Beaudine's oeuvre, there is something to be said for a director so comfortable in the art (if that is the correct word) of directing: the day-in, day-out nature of running sets, managing technicians, and adapting to circumstance. There is also much to be admired in a filmmaker with the tenacity to endure across decades, from directing Pickford at her peak to the Bowery Boys at their nadir. And in fact, Beaudine's long-suppressed pride was stirred during his last public appearance, weeks before his death in 1970, at a screening of his silent drama *The Canadian* (1926) at the Los Angeles County Museum of Art. Greeted with a standing ovation, he told historian Kevin Brownlow, "Seeing it now, maybe I wasn't such a bad director after all. In fact, I was quite good in spots." Anyone who has welcomed *Bela Lugosi Meets a Brooklyn Gorilla* (1952) into their heart knows this already.

Crowning Achievement: *Sparrows* (1926)
Most Expressive Esoterica: *Billy the Kid Versus Dracula* (1966)
For Extreme Auteurists: *Ghost Chasers* (1951)

Puzzle created by
Anna Shechtman

A METROGRAPH CROSSWORD: "SHHH …."

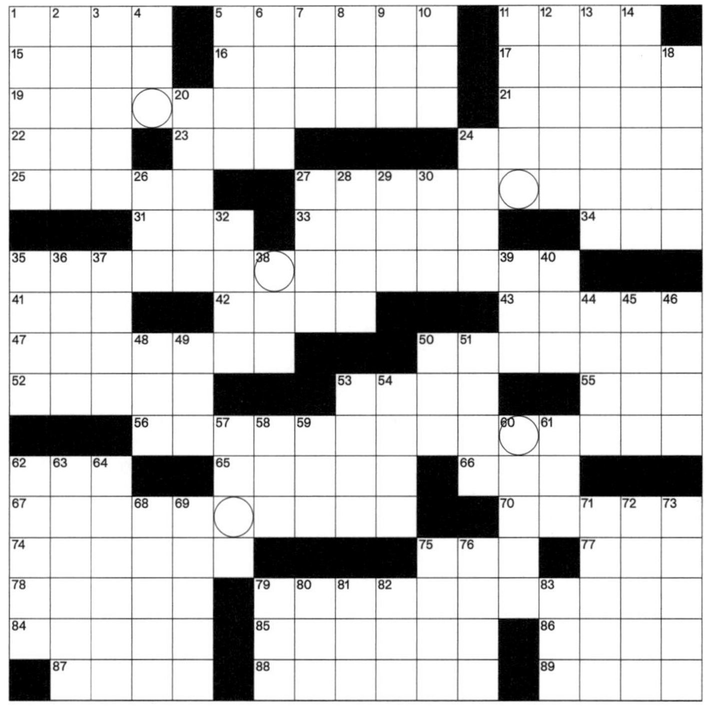

ACROSS

1. *Intolerance* (1916) actress who invented the close up, according to Bette Davis
5. Danish director of *Vampyr* (1932)
11. ___ Rohrwacher, actor sister of director Alice
15. Items worn across the chest of John Rambo and Chewbacca
16. Adler who was the *New York Times*'s chief movie critic in 1968-9
17. Work with a scene partner, in a way
19. 1956 Alfred Hitchcock noir [2008 Oliver Stone biopic … shhh!]
21. Murphy's *48 Hrs.* (1982) costar
22. *The* ___ (1997 Palme d'Or winner)
23. Hirsute co-star in 56-across
24. Mickey Mouse's job in a 1938 Disney short, adapted from a Grimm's fairy tale
25. 2016 M. Night Shyamalan thriller
27. 1935 William K. Howard spy thriller [1969 Costa-Gavras historical drama … shhh!]
31. Quaff featured in many Lifetime Christmas movies
33. First name of blue-eyed Melville favorite who passed away last year
34. ___ Aurand, figure in Berlin's experimental cinema scene since the 1980s
35. 1995 Robert Longo cyberpunk action movie [1931 Fritz Lang mystery thriller … shhh!]
41. Gov. agency featured in Todd Haynes's *Dark Waters* (2019)
42. Emulate King Arthur in a classic fight with The Black Knight in *Monty Python and the Holy Grail* (1975)
43. Like Schwarzenegger's jacket in *Last Action Hero* (1993)
47. Winner of the "Unique and Artistic Picture" Oscar at the first Academy Awards in 1929
50. Fellini called him "a sort of Adam, from whom we are all descended"
52. Expressed disapproval, like the Man in Black to Buttercup in *The Princess Bride* (1987)
53. Set designer for the dream sequence in Hitchcock's *Spellbound* (1945)
55. MGM mascot replaced by a computer-generated version in 2021
56. 1952 Howard Hawks comedy [2015 S. Shankar drama … shhh!]
62. *The Grand Budapest Hotel* (2014) amenity
65. Head to the cinema
66. *Babe* (1995) setting
67. 1963 Luschino Visconti historical epic [2001 Tim Blake Nelson modern Shakespeare adaptation … shhh!]
70. Board used in *The Exorcist* (1973)
74. Hockey team whose 1986-7 season is chronicled in *The Boys on the Bus* (1987)
75. Fictional espionage agency in a Tom Cruise franchise
77. *Platoon* (1986) extras, in brief
78. Match eyelines, according to classical editing norms, say
79. Predecessors to Talkies … or what 7-Across, 21-Across, 41-Across, 67-Across, and 82-Across include in their circled letters?
84. Filming locations
85. Operator of the Black Maria, the first movie production studio
86. The Necronomicon in Sam Raimi's *Evil Dead* (1981), for one
87. Cameo, e.g.
88. Settings in *Female Trouble* (1974) and *Shampoo* (1975)
89. Giants and ___ (Yasuzō Masumura's 1958 satire of postwar consumer culture)

DOWN

1. Oscar Micheaux's response to *Birth of the Nation* (1915), 1920 drama *Within Our* ___
2. "___, Daddy-O. I'm into the Ramones": *Rock 'n' Roll High School*
3. ___-O-Vision
4. Start of film titles starring Marilyn Monroe (1953) and Kate Hudson (2003)
5. ___ *Dead Gorgeous* (1999 camp comedy)
6. Director Clair who Truffaut dismissed, claiming he made "films for old ladies who go to the cinema twice a year"
7. Closed captioning option: Abbr.
8. New ___ Festival & Awards (annual Nollywood celebration)
9. Basque terrorist organization represented in *Blinded* (1997) and *Munich* (2005)
10. Akira Kurosawa's 1985 interpretation of *King Lear*
11. Ball's costar, and real-life husband, in Vincente Minnelli's *The Long, Long Trailer* (1954)
12. He was played by Trevor Howard in the 1972 historical drama *Pope Joan*
13. Cat played by Jane Fonda in 1965
14. Rebel without a cause?
18. Like Clint Eastwood's The Man With No Name, say
20. Emulate Henry Hill vis-à-vis Paulie and Jimmy in *Goodfellas* (1990)
24. Setting for Keaton's *The General* (1926): Abbr.
26. *Holiday* ___ (Bing Crosby-Fred Astaire 1942 musical)
27. __ Lakshmibai, Jhansi revolutionary depicted in Sohrab Modi's *The Tiger and the Flame* (1956), the first Technicolor film made in India
28. Like the school in *School of Rock* (2003), for short
29. *Apocalypse Now* (1979) setting, in brief
30. American-born Black Sabbath frontman who appears in Liam Lynch's *Tenacious D: The Pick of Destiny* (2006)
32. *Million Dollar Baby* (2004) and *Personal Best* (1982) settings
35. *Infinite* ___, eponymous movie in a David Foster Wallace's novel, which is said to be fatally entertaining
36. One of many crafted in Miloš Forman's *Amadeus* (1984)
37. Actor Worden who portrayed a cracked cowpoke in John Ford's *The Searchers* (1956) and a bellhop in *Twin Peaks*
38. Murray who starred in von Stroheim's *The Merry Widow* (1925)
39. Godard's *A Woman* ___ *Woman* (1961)
40. "The ___ of a carpenter," (Indiana Jones's pursuit in his last crusade)
44. Paul Verhoeven 2016 thriller, for which he said no American actresses would take the lead role
45. Bruce Willis famously does this in the opening scene of *The Sixth Sense* (1999)
46. Brothers Brian and Roger featured on the soundtrack of David Lynch's *Dune* (1984)
48. Rock band that wrote the soundtrack to the Andy Kaufman biopic *Man on the Moon* (1999)
49. Some rom-com endings?
50. *The Return of the Living Dead* (1985) star Gulager
51. *Snakes on a Plane* (2006) soundtrack?
53. Film scholar Richard, with the influential books *Stars* and *White*
54. Like Maud, for much of *My Night at Maud's* (1969)
57. Employers of Rachel Weisz's characters in *The Constant Gardener* (2005) and *The Whistleblower* (2010), e.g.
58. Keystone ___, one of a recurring crew in Mack Sennett comedies
59. ___ *Mujer*, 1969 melodrama watched in Almodóvar's *Bad Education* (2004)
60. *Set* ___, 1996 heist movie starring Jada Pinkett, Queen Latifah, Vivica A. Fox, and Kimberly Elise
61. Charlie Kaufman and Kenneth Lonergan's alma mater
62. Classical porticos featured in *Cabiria* (1914) and *Bill and Ted's Excellent Adventure* (1989)
63. First name of composer for *Mishima: Life in Four Chapters* (1985) and *Candyman* (1992)
64. 1924 science fiction movie deemed the first Soviet blockbuster
68. *Ballet Mécanique* (1924) director Fernand
69. Lubitsch who directed *The Patriot* (1928), a part-Talkie
71. Structure featured in *Nanook of the North* (1922)
72. Actor Stewart about whom President Truman said, "If Bess and I had a son, we'd want him to be just like [him]"
73. Balthazar and EO, for two
75. Zoom ___ (get closer to)
76. The "hills" that are alive in *The Sound of Music* (1965): Abbr.
79. "Le cœur a ___ raisons que la raison ne connaît point" (Pascal quote said to inspire Rohmer's *Six Moral Tales* series)
80. Winner of the 2015 Best Foreign Language Oscar (the first winner from Poland)
81. ___ Timmy Tim, high school rap alias for Timothée Chalamet
82. How a 1990 Stephen King adaptation was marketed in Spain
83. *The Addams Family* cousin

No cheating, but visit *metrograph.cowm/crosswordanswers* for the solution to this puzzle.